Polling and the Public

What Every Citizen Should Know

Sixth Edition

Herbert Asher
Ohio State University

CQ PRESS

A Division of Congressional Quarterly Inc.
Washington, D.C.

CQ Press
A Division of Congressional Quarterly Inc.
1255 22nd Street, N.W., Suite 400
Washington, D.C. 20037

202-729-1900; toll-free, 1-866-4CQ-PRESS (1-866-427-7737)

www.cqpress.com

Cover design: TGD Communications, Alexandria, Va.

♾ The paper used in this publication exceeds the requirements of the American
National Standard for Information Sciences—Permanence of Paper for Printed
Library Materials, ANSI Z39.48-1992.

Library of Congress Cataloging-in-Publication Data

Asher, Herbert B.
   Polling and the public : what every citizen should know / Herbert Asher.—
6th ed.
      p. cm.
   Includes bibliographical references and index.
   ISBN 1-56802-833-4 (pbk.: alk. paper)
   1. Public opinion polls.   2. Public opinion—United States.   I. Title.

HM1236 .A75 2004
303.3'8'0973—dc22

                                                        2003026244

To the memory of my parents,
Joseph and Betty Asher

Contents

Preface   ix

1 Polling and the Public   1

The Importance of Polls   2
The Pervasiveness of Polls   3
Commissioned Polls   5
The Citizen as a Consumer of Polls   14
Citizens' Views of Polls   15
Polling and Democracy   20
Exercises   27

2 The Problem of Nonattitudes   28

An Example of Nonattitudes   31
The Use of Screening Questions   32
Nonattitudes and the Middle Position in Survey Questions   37
Response Instability and Nonattitudes   41
Implications for Democracy and Public Policy   44
Conclusion   47
Exercises   49

3 Wording and Context of Questions   50

Question Wording   52
Question Order and Context   61
Conclusion   67
Exercises   68

4 Sampling Techniques   69

Sampling Designs   70
Sample Size and Sampling Error   77
Total versus Actual Sample Size   80
Response Rates   82
Weighting the Sample   85
Conclusion   87
Exercises   87

5 Interviewing and Data Collection Procedures   89

Methods of Collecting Polling Information   90
Interviewer Effects in Public Opinion Polling   94
Internet Polling   98
Conclusion   102
Exercises   103

6 The Media and the Polls   104

Standards for Reporting Results   105
Substantive Interpretation of Polls   112
Media, Polls, and the News Reporting Emphasis   117
Conclusion   121
Exercises   123

7 Polls and Elections   125

Sponsors of Election Polls   125
Types of Election Polls   126
Uses of Polls by Candidates   141
Polls in the Presidential Selection Process   142
When and Why Election Predictions Are Wrong   147
How Preelection Polls Affect Voters   155
Conclusion   157
Exercises   157

8 Analyzing and Interpreting Polls   159

Choosing Items to Analyze   160
Examining Trends with Polling Data   172
Examining Subsets of Respondents   174
Interpreting Poll Results   180
When Polls Conflict: A Concluding Example   185
Exercises   187

9 Polling and Democracy   189

How to Evaluate Polls: A Summary   190
Polls and Their Effect on the Political System   193
Conclusion   200
Exercise   201

Web Sites   202

References   205

Index   223

Preface

Since the last edition of this book was published, the prominence and pervasiveness of public opinion polling in the United States and in nations throughout the world have grown. After the terrorist attacks on September 11, 2001, Americans were regularly queried about their sense of personal safety, their perceptions of how the war on terrorism was going, and their views on the trade-offs between civil liberties and heightened national security measures. With the economic downturn in 2001 and 2002 and the slow recovery, polls routinely asked Americans about their feelings of economic security; their perceptions of how the country was faring; and their beliefs about the merits of tax cuts, spending initiatives, and budget deficits. And with the crisis in Iraq, Americans were frequently surveyed about their support for the war before, during, and after the conflict. While terrorism, the war, and the economy were the three major challenges facing the United States between 2001 and 2004, pollsters also sought to plumb people's views on many other issues, such as abortion, gay marriage, health care, a prescription drug provision for Medicare, the environment, and on and on.

Not only could Americans learn from the polls what their fellow citizens thought about various things, but they could also learn what citizens of other nations thought about the United States and American policies in the Middle East and elsewhere. As the United States prepared to go to war with Iraq, Americans learned that citizens in countries such as France and Germany—traditional allies—were strongly opposed to American policies. Indeed, the democratization of many previously authoritarian nations and the internationalization of public opinion polling have meant that citizens throughout the world now can express their views through polls and learn what the citizens of other nations are thinking.

In the last few years, the methodology of polling has faced new challenges. Traditional telephone polling has become more difficult with the growth in the use of cell phones and call screening devices. The huge growth of the Internet has resulted in a dramatic increase in Web surveys, some done with care and sensitivity to good polling standards and others simply modern versions of the pseudopolls that magazines and radio and television stations conduct, in which respondents select themselves to participate. Thus, we are witnessing important developments in polling with respect to the substantive topics amenable to polling, the geographical reach of the polling enterprise, and the methodological challenges facing pollsters.

Despite their prominence, polls are still not well understood. My central objective when I first wrote this book was to help citizens become wiser consumers of public opinion polls. In revising the book for a fifth time, I still have that same objective. The prevalence of public opinion polls and their frequent misuse make it imperative that citizens be able to evaluate critically the various assertions that people make on the basis of the polls. Candidates for public office, officeholders, and many different public and private groups sponsor public opinion surveys to advance their own objectives. As polling data become more central to political and civic discourse, it is more important that citizens understand the factors that can influence poll results.

Chapter 1 explains the types of polls, their importance, and Americans' varying attitudes toward public opinion research. Chapters 2–5 address the methodological aspects of polling, such as nonattitude assessment, the wording and ordering of questions, sampling techniques, and interviewing procedures. These topics are treated in a nontechnical fashion with numerous examples that illustrate the major points. Chapters 6–8 are more analytical, focusing on how the news media cover polls, the role of polls in campaigns and elections, and the interpretation of polls. The last chapter considers the place of polls in a democratic polity. A new feature of this edition is a series of exercises at the end of each chapter designed to help the reader become a more skillful judge of public opinion polls.

This book should be readily understandable to a diverse audience— college students taking courses in American politics, public opinion, communications, and journalism, as well as practitioners in the fields of journalism and campaign management. In addition, the general public should find it a helpful guide to evaluating the methods and merits of public opinion polls. As with earlier editions, no statistical expertise is assumed or required.

Michael Hissam was a superb student research assistant in the preparation of this sixth edition. And I am grateful to Gary F. Moncrief, Boise State University; Brian S. Vargus, Indiana University–Purdue University

Indianapolis; and a third, anonymous reviewer who offered helpful revision suggestions as I planned this new edition. The staff of CQ Press did its usual fine job of editing and getting the book into print in a timely fashion. In particular, I am very grateful for the many insightful suggestions and contributions made by Michael Kerns and for his patience throughout the revision process. I appreciate the copyediting and production expertise of Nancy Geltman in her work on this edition. Finally, I express my deep appreciation to the various polling organizations and newspapers that are so generous in sharing their surveys with the broader public. They provided many of the substantive examples I used here. In particular, the CBS News/*New York Times* polls, the ABC News/*Washington Post* surveys, the Gallup Organization, and the Program on International Policy Attitudes (PIPA) at the University of Maryland have been invaluable resources in the preparation of this edition.

—Herb Asher

☑ 1 Polling and the Public

Americans today are inundated with the results of public opinion polls sponsored by the news media, candidates for public office, incumbent officeholders, and many public, private, and nonprofit organizations. Some of the polling is on matters of immediate national importance, such as the war on terrorism, the health of the American economy, or the war with Iraq. But polls are conducted on almost any conceivable topic, be it a genuine public policy issue such as abortion, education policy, health care, the environment, or gay rights, or something more frivolous such as the guilt or innocence of a celebrity accused of a crime. As a result, Americans are learning more and more about the attitudes of their fellow citizens.

And as public opinion polling has spread throughout the world, with the demise of the Soviet Union and its empire as well as of totalitarian regimes in other parts of the world, Americans have been able to learn about the attitudes of people in other nations, including what they think about American popular culture and foreign policy. In 2002 and 2003, during the lead-up to the war in Iraq, many Americans were surprised by the widespread hostility that polls in other countries revealed and by street demonstrations by citizens of traditional allies such as Germany and France against the proposed U.S. action. The internationalization of polling is also evidenced by the growing use of polls (and American-style campaign techniques in general) in national elections throughout the world. For example, in the 1999 Israeli elections the victorious Barak campaign employed the services of various Democratic Party operatives from the United States. One was polling practitioner Stanley Greenberg, who had served as President Bill Clinton's pollster in the 1992 presidential election and in the early years of his administration (Nagourney 2000).

In the United States, polls are increasingly being used not only to inform, but also to convince and even manipulate Americans in ways advantageous to the polls' sponsors. The aim of this book is to help citizens become more astute judges of polls, so that they will not be misled by assertions made on the basis of polling data. I will accomplish this objective by explaining in nontechnical language the factors that can affect poll results—such as question wording, sampling techniques, and interviewing procedures—and by critiquing various types and uses of polls.

The Importance of Polls

Why should citizens become more astute consumers of polls? One reason is simply to avoid being manipulated by those who use polls inappropriately to promote their own ends. Other reasons are more positive. Some people make major economic and career decisions on the basis of public opinion polling. For example, the businessperson who commissions a survey on customer preferences or the television station manager who underwrites a survey on audience demographics will use the information obtained to make important business decisions. Potential candidates for public office may commission a poll to assess their electoral prospects before deciding whether to run. In these cases a commercial polling organization is likely to conduct the polling. But the more knowledgeable the businessperson and the would-be candidate are about polls, the better able they are to communicate their objectives and requirements to the survey organization and to apply the results of the survey to their own decision making.

Polls also are important for the average citizen. Through the substantial coverage the news media give to polls, citizens can compare their own beliefs with their compatriots'. As citizens use the polls in this manner, they need to be aware of the factors that affect the poll results so that they do not accept or reject them too quickly or uncritically.

Polling plays an integral role in political events at the national, state, and local levels. In any major event or decision, poll results are sure to be a part of the news media's coverage and the decision makers' deliberations. How should an international crisis, such as North Korea's nuclear threat, be resolved? How should the United States respond to events in Afghanistan or the Middle East or Liberia? Should the governor of California be recalled from office? What is the best location for a new library in the community? Should state taxes be raised? Because polls may influence how politicians respond to such public issues, citizens need to understand the essentials of public opinion polling.

Finally, public opinion polls are playing an ever-larger role in political discourse in the United States because of the improved technology of polling, the introduction of courses in polling methodology in journalism curricula, the widespread assumption (challenged by Benjamin Ginsberg—see chapter 9) that polls are the best way to measure public opinion, and the belief that public opinion polls are instruments of democracy because they allow everyone's views to be represented. More worrisome is the huge growth in the use of pseudopolls—nonscientific and often biased polls conducted by private and public groups through a variety of mechanisms, including the print and electronic media and the Internet, and often confused with legitimate public opinion polling. All of these factors ensure that even greater reliance on the polls will characterize future political debate. To participate in that debate in an informed and analytical fashion, Americans will have to come to grips with public opinion polls—a useful tool of government and a valuable source of information to citizens and leaders alike.

The Pervasiveness of Polls

That public opinion polling is a growth industry in the United States is undeniable. The polls most familiar to Americans are those conducted for and reported by the major communications media. For example, each of the three major television networks sponsors polls in collaboration with a print news organization: CBS News with the *New York Times,* ABC News with the *Washington Post,* and NBC News with the *Wall Street Journal.* The major newsmagazines often commission polls on national issues. Thus *Newsweek* regularly employs Princeton Survey Research Associates, *Time* (often in conjunction with CNN) has used Yankelovich Partners Inc. and more recently Harris Interactive, and *U.S. News and World Report* has often employed the Tarrance Group and Lake Sosin Snell and Associates.

Polls are omnipresent in major news stories. An examination of the stories featured on the covers of the three leading U.S. newsmagazines—*Time, Newsweek,* and *U.S. News and World Report*—between 1995 and mid-2003 reveals that about 30 percent of them cited public opinion polls. Other stories incorporated polling data. Readers of these magazines, then, will be more astute judges of the reporting if they are knowledgeable about the strengths and weaknesses of public opinion polls.

The proliferation of polls also is evident in newspaper and television news coverage. Typically, the polls the stories cite have surveyed citizens about their views on political issues, candidates, and incumbents (especially the president); their preferences about possible courses of government action; their general attitudes toward politics and the political process; and countless other political and nonpolitical matters. Since late 2001 polls have frequently queried Americans about terrorism and national security matters, and in 2002 and 2003 the war in Iraq, economic and tax policy, and health care were high on the polling agenda.

Sometimes survey questions seem to violate standards of good taste. After President Ronald Reagan's surgery for what turned out to be colon cancer, a survey commissioned by *Time* asked respondents how serious they thought the president's health problems were, and both *Time* and an ABC News/*Washington Post* poll asked Americans whether they thought the president was likely to complete his term. A *Newsweek* poll inquired whether citizens were concerned that the president might not "be able to meet the demands of a second term." Many citizens undoubtedly had questions in their own minds about the president's health, and therefore the media thought their readers and viewers would be interested in reading about public opinions on the matter. Ghoulish speculation was the result.

When an issue or event becomes visible and especially controversial, the public is usually surveyed to assess its reaction. For example, in 2003 the U.S. Supreme Court in the case of *Lawrence v. Texas* struck down the Texas antisodomy law and affirmed the privacy rights of adult gay citizens engaged in consensual sex. Some reporters wrote exaggerated stories about what the Court decision meant for gay rights and gay marriage, and very quickly the pollsters were asking Americans their opinions about various aspects of gay life.

Almost any topic seems amenable to polling. For example, the January 31, 2000, issue of *U.S. News and World Report* featured a story on "Hell" that described a public opinion poll in which a sample of Americans was asked whether there was a Hell (64 percent said yes) and what they thought it was like. As the final episode of the television show *Cheers* neared in 1993, the *Times Mirror* Center for the People and the Press queried Americans about such weighty topics as whether Sam should have stayed single, married Diane, or married Rebecca. That survey also asked Americans who their favorite *Cheers* character was and which character they would like to see continue in his or her own series (Mills 1993). Clearly, polling is everywhere.

The prominent national polls are complemented by the visible and reputable state and local polls that focus on state and local matters as well as national affairs. For example, the New York *Daily News* and the television program *Eyewitness News* (produced by the ABC affiliate in New York City) have polled people in the city over the years on their views of the New York police, New York mayors, the likelihood of the Yankees and Mets baseball teams' making the World Series, and other matters of local concern. Likewise, the *New York Times,* in conjunction with WCBS-TV, has conducted extensive studies of race relations in New York City. Many states have first-rate polling organizations, often affiliated with a university or a major news organization. For example, the Eagleton Institute at Rutgers University, working with the *Newark Star-Ledger,* surveys New Jersey residents about their state government and about New Jersey as a place to live. Publications such as *Public Opinion Quarterly* and *Public Perspective* have provided summaries of state and local (as well as national) poll results.

The polls I have mentioned thus far are the most prominent and probably the most credible to the American public. Their prominence stems from the often substantial media coverage their results receive; their credibility derives from the public's perception that they are conducted scientifically and that the news organizations and other entities that sponsor them are themselves legitimate and objective. The most critical factor in making these polls scientific (and thus valid) is a carefully selected sample of respondents (most often 1,000 to 1,500 persons); after all, no polling organization can interview the entire adult American population of more than 200 million. From such a sample, the public and the media can generalize (within certain limits to be discussed later) to the larger population from which the sample was drawn.

Commissioned Polls

Although polls by the big news organizations seem the most prominent, they are only a tiny fraction of the public opinion polling done in the United States. Many other organizations commission polls for purposes other than informing citizens. For example, companies may hire a polling firm to gauge the public response to their products, and academic investigators may use surveys in their research. The results of those polls may not attract much public notice, but they still can affect the lives of citizens. An excellent example of a commissioned poll was the one that the Internal Revenue Service (IRS) paid for in 1984 to study the problem of tax cheating. Among the items in the survey were these statements, with which the respondent was supposed to agree or disagree:

> It's not so wrong to hold back a little bit on taxes since the government spends too much anyway.

> The present tax system benefits the rich and is unfair to the ordinary working man or woman.

> Since a lot of rich people pay no taxes at all, if someone like me underpays a little, it's no big deal. (Sussman 1984b)

Of the survey respondents 19 percent admitted cheating on their returns; young, upwardly mobile professionals were the most likely to cheat. The IRS study also investigated ways to reduce cheating and found that Americans strongly rejected the use of paid informants to catch cheaters

(Sussman 1985c). Although the honesty of tax cheaters' responses to questions about tax cheating is questionable, the IRS probably gained some useful insights into the magnitude of the cheating problem and the feasibility of alternative solutions.

The IRS study is typical of thousands that public and private bodies commission to address specific concerns. Some of the surveys are based on national samples; others, on specialized samples that are more appropriate to the research questions being addressed. Commissioned surveys of this type are likely to be high-quality enterprises mainly because the sponsors have a genuine need for accurate information to address some organizational goal or problem. To that end the sponsors employ a reputable firm to design and conduct the survey and perhaps to analyze the data and interpret the results. Many other groups, however, conduct surveys for a different reason—not to address a public concern scientifically and objectively but to promote a certain position and to convince the public of the rightness of that stand. The sponsors design these surveys to yield the desired results, most often through highly loaded questions, although subtler methods also are used. Sometimes in such surveys the people interviewed are chosen to ensure a predetermined outcome. In many cases, the poll itself is secondary to the real aim of the group: to raise money to support its objectives.

With the advent of computerized mailings, many organizations have entered the business of raising funds and conducting polls through direct mail. The polling then becomes a device to generate donations—that is, the sponsoring organization encourages recipients of the mailings to make their views known *and* to contribute to a good cause. Many of these appeals come from political groups, ranging from the Democratic and Republican Parties to the Wilderness Society, the Union of Concerned Scientists, the National Right to Work Committee, the Religious Coalition for Abortion Rights, and many others. For example, in 2002 the Republican National Committee mailed a "State of the Nation Public Opinion Research Survey" to thousands of potential contributors on the GOP's mailing lists. The survey included thirty questions as well as a direct appeal for funds (see page 7).

Until the early 1990s, the Democrats lagged behind the GOP in the use of computerized mailings. But the "2003 Democratic Leadership Survey" that the Democratic Congressional Campaign Committee sponsored demonstrated that they too had learned the advantages of attaching a poll to a fund-raising effort (see page 8). The American Association for Public Opinion Research, the major professional association of public opinion researchers, part of whose mission is to protect the integrity and reputation of the polling enterprise, has condemned the practice of "FRUGing"—

2002 STATE OF THE NATION
Public Opinion Research Survey

Republican National Committee
310 First Street, Southeast
Washington, DC 20003
www.RNC.org

COMMISSIONED BY THE LEADERSHIP OF THE
REPUBLICAN NATIONAL COMMITTEE

PERSONAL REGISTRATION INFORMATION

Survey Participant:

Registered Survey #:   N2P-J04

Date Due: May 6, 2002

INSTRUCTIONS: Please complete the Survey Registration section and then proceed to answer the questions. Your participation in this effort is greatly appreciated. Please return your contribution and completed 2002 State of the Nation Survey to RNC headquarters in the postage-paid envelope enclosed.

SURVEY REGISTRATION

Dear Chairman Racicot,

I am pleased to join with thousands of grassroots Americans in reaffirming my faith in President Bush's leadership and assisting the RNC in determining how the American people truly feel about many of the core issues confronting our nation.

To help finance this grassroots effort to gather the opinions of millions of Americans and ensure that the Republican Party emerges victorious in the 2002 election campaigns so that they can successfully advance President Bush's reform agenda, I am pleased to enclose my most generous contribution of:

☐ $500   ☐ $250   ☐ $100
☐ $50   ☐ $25   ☐ $_____ Other

☐ I cannot join as a full participant in this campaign to help solve America's problems. However, I am enclosing $15 to help pay for the tabulation and distribution of my Survey answers.

Signature: _____ Date: _____

Please make checks payable to: **Republican National Committee**

Contributions to the Republican National Committee are not deductible as charitable contributions for federal income tax purposes.

Please visit our website at www.rnc.org

2003 DEMOCRATIC LEADERSHIP SURVEY

Registered To:

★ DEMOCRATIC
★ CONGRESSIONAL
★ CAMPAIGN COMMITTEE

Survey No: P3EP006   305005617231

Tabulation Deadline: September 5, 2003

YES, I WILL STAND UP FOR DEMOCRATIC VALUES!

To keep Congress focused on helping working families, and counter the influence of big-money special interests, I am taking the following actions steps:

☐ **PROVIDING MY INSIGHTS** on the critical issues Congress needs to address in this session. Please share my survey answers below with the Democratic Leadership Team.

☐ **JOINING THE DEMOCRATIC CONGRESSIONAL CAMPAIGN COMMITTEE (DCCC)** to restore a Democratic majority in the House. My membership contribution is enclosed for:

   ☐ $25   ☐ $35 ✳   ☐ $50
   ☐ $100   ☐ Other $____

✳ *Gifts at this level are urgently needed!*

My email address is: _____

I want to make my contribution by credit card:
☐ MC   ☐ VISA   ☐ AMEX   ☐ DISCOVER

Credit Card #: _____   Exp. Date _____

Name: _____

Signature: _____   Date Signed _____

Contributions to the DCCC are not tax-deductible. Please make your check payable to the DCCC and return it along with your completed survey in the enclosed postage-paid envelope to P.O. Box 96039, Washington, DC 20077-7243.

The DCCC cannot accept funds from corporations, labor unions, or non-federal PACs. If your check is drawn on your business account, is it:
       ☐ *sole proprietor*   ☐ *partnership*

Signature _____

Federal law requires us to use our best efforts to collect and report the name, mailing address, occupation and name of employer for each individual whose contributions exceed $200 in a calendar year.

Occupation _____

Employer _____

fund-raising under the guise of surveying. Nevertheless, the practice continues and citizens should be wary of it.

Indeed, many groups involved in fund-raising, and/or generating survey responses that support their own agendas, mail extremely biased literature and then ask respondents for their opinions. Consider these examples: The Committee Against Government Waste has asked, "Before you received this letter, were you aware of the gross mismanagement and waste of funds in the U.S. Department of Defense's purchase of parts?" The American Farmland Trust has asked, "Were you aware of the gravity of the problem of our vanishing farmland before receiving this mailing?" In case the literature accompanying the poll does not convince respondents of the correctness of the group's position, a carefully constructed question or statement may achieve the same end, as illustrated by the following questionnaire items and their sponsoring organizations:

> Are you in favor of allowing construction union czars the power to shut down an entire construction site because of a dispute with a single contractor, thus forcing even more workers to knuckle under to union agents?   *National Right to Work Committee*

> Our nation is still blessed with millions of acres of public lands, including roadless wilderness areas, forests and range lands. Land developers, loggers, and mining and oil companies want to increase their operations on these public lands. Do you think these remaining pristine areas of your public lands should be protected from such exploitation?   *Sierra Club*

> Do you feel that all of the TV networks are in serious danger of losing the public's confidence and trust because they hire so many liberal Democratic activists as top corporate executives who formerly worked for Ted Kennedy, Walter Mondale, Gary Hart, George McGovern, Mario Cuomo, Jimmy Carter and the National Democratic Party?
> *Fairness in Media*

> Chief lobbyist for the NRA, Tanya Metaksa, announced recently, "We have the assurance of the Speaker [Newt Gingrich] that there will be repeal" of the assault weapons ban. Do you agree that concern for public safety and the will of the people should matter more to Congress than the dangerous agenda of the National Rifle Association?
> *Handgun Control*

> Do you believe that gun owners should be required to submit to "safety training" by government bureaucrats before they're allowed to exercise their Second Amendment Right to Keep and Bear Arms?
> *National Rifle Association*

Although tobacco is estimated to kill at least 418,000 people each year, and to cost you and me and every American taxpayer more than $100 billion, our federal government continues to spend millions to encourage the growing of tobacco and to subsidize the tobacco industry. Therefore, do you think the government should: immediately discontinue all aid to tobacco, phase out all aid for tobacco over a longer period of time, or continue to aid tobacco growers and the tobacco industry at present levels?   *Action on Smoking and Health*

All of the preceding items were carefully constructed to generate responses sympathetic to the sponsors' objectives. In fact, for several reasons these enterprises should not be called "polling": First, in most cases the sample is not scientifically selected; instead, the surveys and fund-raising requests are mailed out to lists of citizens who are thought to be likely supporters. Whether the people who actually respond are at all representative of a larger population is of little concern. Second, the questions are often poorly formulated and fundamentally flawed (deliberately so). Third, if the survey data collected are tabulated at all (and many times they are not), little analysis can be conducted because the original survey was very short and omitted key questions about the demographic and political characteristics of the respondents. In other words, collecting opinions is not necessarily polling.

Orton (1982) has identified similar examples of what he calls *pseudopolls*. For example, the print and electronic media often encourage members of their audiences to write or phone to express their views. But even with hundreds or thousands of replies, these "straw polls" are usually not representative simply because the people who volunteer to participate are likely to differ in important ways from the overall population. They may be more interested, informed, and concerned about the topic at hand and thus hold views different from those of the overall population.

In 1992, shortly after President George Bush's State of the Union address, the CBS television program *America on the Line* featured telephone call-in surveys. At the same time, CBS conducted a scientific poll that included questions identical to those on the call-in survey. The results of the two surveys differed. For example, in response to the question of whether they were better or worse off than they were four years ago, 54 percent of the callers in the phone-in poll said they were worse off, compared with only 32 percent of the respondents in the scientific survey (Morin 1992a).

Radio talk shows and call-in polls became more prominent in the 1990s. A 1993 *Times Mirror* poll revealed that citizens who listened to and called radio talk shows were not representative of the overall citizenry; instead, they tended to be more Republican, more conservative, more

male, and slightly more wealthy and educated (Kohut 1993). It is thus not surprising that radio phone-in polls often generate results more conservative and pro-Republican than the outcomes obtained through scientific polling.

Other examples of pseudopolls are the questionnaires that members of Congress send to households in their congressional districts. Typically, these are addressed to "Postal Customer," and there is no sure way of knowing just who in the household actually completed the survey. Although thousands of these questionnaires may be returned to a congressional office, it is difficult to ascertain whether the respondents' demographic characteristics and opinions are truly representative of the broader constituency. In some instances the questions are loaded to guarantee responses compatible with a legislator's predispositions and record. This is not to say that completed questionnaires are ignored or discarded; in most cases the results are tabulated and later reported to the constituency in a newsletter. But, as Sussman (1985g) argues, these questionnaires are mainly "a public relations gimmick, aimed at convincing voters that officeholders care about the folks back home." And as Morin (1987) observes, "Too many of these polls reek from a kind of self-serving flatulence that insults the average voter while exposing the unctuous pomposity of the elected official."

Other examples of pseudopolls are the highly publicized surveys on marital relations once conducted by feminist author Shere Hite and by newspaper columnist Abigail Van Buren, otherwise known as "Dear Abby" (Squires and Morin 1987; Smith 1988). Hite distributed 100,000 extensive, open-ended questionnaires to women's groups and to individual women who requested one. She received about 4,500 replies, a response rate of only 4.5 percent. In one of her columns, Abby wrote, "Readers, I need your cooperation for an important survey. Questions: Have you ever cheated on your mate? How long have you been together? You need not sign your name, but please state your age and indicate whether you are male or female." She received more than 200,000 responses (Smith 1988).

In both the Hite and "Dear Abby" surveys, the sampling method and the questions generated unrepresentative and misleading results, despite the large number of respondents to Abby's poll. (Reputable, scientific national polls typically have a sample of about 1,500 respondents.) Hite found that 70 percent of women married five or more years were having extramarital affairs; 15 percent of Abby's married female respondents claimed to have been unfaithful. As Smith (1988) argues, both surveys could not be correct, and indeed both were overwhelmingly likely to be wrong because of the shortcomings in the sample selection and the actual questionnaires. Allowing citizens to select themselves into a survey guarantees biased results because of the motivations that lead people to participate in such surveys in the first place.

Since the 1970s magazines have regularly published the results of sex surveys of their readers. Typically they conduct the surveys by including the questionnaire in the magazine and encouraging readers to complete it and mail it back. *Redbook* and *Cosmopolitan* in the 1970s, *Playboy* in the 1980s, and *The Advocate* in the 1990s are among the magazines that have sponsored such surveys. In some cases the response rate was low, but the number of completed questionnaires very large, simply because of the size of the magazine's readership. For example, the *Playboy* response rate was about 2 percent, but this translated into 100,000 replies. By contrast *The Advocate* response rate was 18 percent with almost 13,000 questionnaires returned (Lever 1994, 18). Despite the large number of replies to a typical magazine survey, one must be very careful when generalizing the results to any broader population, whether it be to straight males based on the *Playboy* survey or to gay males based on the *Advocate* poll. The reason: self-selection presents a double problem. First, the readers and subscribers to a particular magazine may not be representative of the broader population of which they are members. Second, the people who actually complete the questionnaires may not be representative of the magazine's total readers and subscribers. Nevertheless, the results of these surveys typically receive a lot of news media coverage (that probably enhances magazine sales).

The latest development in pseudopolls is the online survey on the Internet. Many businesses, media outlets, and other organizations invite visitors to their Web sites to participate in online surveys. Like other pseudopolls, the online survey may generate many thousands of responses, but it is not a valid survey because respondents selected themselves to participate rather than being part of a scientifically selected sample. Such respondents are unlikely to be a representative sample, because only those people who are sufficiently interested in the topic are likely to participate. Moreover, many citizens do not have access to the Internet in the first place. For example, AOL users on August 7, 2003, could participate in a two-part survey about mortgage refinancing: "Were you a refi junkie? What did you do with the money you saved by refinancing?" Citizens who went to the CNN Web site that day could respond to the item, "Should Al Gore change his mind and seek the Democratic nomination in 2004?" (Two-thirds voted no.) Even though thousands of people responded to these questions, there is no guarantee that they are representative of any larger group of people. Fortunately, both AOL and CNN cautioned their users on this point, although AOL users had to go the link "Note on Poll Results." If they did, they were told, "Poll results are not scientific and reflect the opinions of only those users who chose to participate." The CNN users were provided a more detailed cautionary note right below the actual results; it read: "This QuickVote is not scientific and reflects the opinions of only those Internet users who have chosen to participate. The results cannot be assumed to represent the opinions of Internet users in general, nor the public as a whole. The QuickVote sponsor is not responsible for content, functionality or the opinions expressed therein." Online surveys and conditions under which they might provide useful information are discussed in greater detail in chapter 5.

The key point, of course, is that pseudopolls are highly flawed and may give misleading portraits of public opinion because of loaded and unfair question wording, self-selection bias in the respondents, outright efforts to stack the results, or other deficiencies. Despite their deficiencies, however, these unscientific enterprises have a place here under the rubric of polling because they are becoming more prevalent in the United States. At times, Americans hear the results of a pseudopoll and pass them along to colleagues as if they were legitimate public opinion research findings, thereby giving the pseudopoll greater credibility and dissemination than it merits. Indeed, there is some evidence that a substantial number of Americans give credence to various kinds of pseudopolls. Brodie et al. (2001, 13) report that 26 percent of Americans believe that a survey in which readers fill out a questionnaire printed in a magazine almost always or most of the time accurately reflects what the public thinks. Twenty seven percent believe that Internet surveys almost always reflect what the public thinks, and 35 percent give high marks to surveys in which people are mailed a questionnaire and asked to complete it. According to Brodie and her colleagues fewer than 40 percent of Americans realize that selecting survey respondents at random produces a better, more accurate result than relying on self-selected samples such as radio call-in or magazine write-in polls.

These findings suggest that bad polling practices and results can mislead many Americans. Citizens are subjected to many different kinds of polls, all of which may later affect them in some way through the decisions that are based on poll results. That is why it is important that citizens be aware of the gamut of polls and be able to evaluate them. If they are able to recognize unscientific polls and their associated deficiencies (as well as the shortcomings of scientific polls), then people are less likely to be misled by the results of such surveys. This leads to the central concern of this book—the citizen as a potential consumer of public opinion polls.

The Citizen as a Consumer of Polls

Whatever the quality of the polls, they can affect the attitudes and behavior of citizens. Even media-sponsored polls designed simply to report citizens' attitudes (and perhaps to keep up with the competition and improve ratings) also may help to *shape* preferences, particularly during a presidential primary season. At such times polling is frequent, and the links among a candidate's poll standing, news media coverage, and primary election fate are pronounced. (The role of polls in elections is considered in chapter 7.)

Americans are major consumers of public opinion research on a wide variety of topics. But are they smart consumers? Americans should be aware of the problems and limitations of polls before they "buy" anything from them. Often someone is actively promoting the poll results to generate support for his or her objectives. It might be the president, citing polls to argue that the American people support administration policies. It might be a local builder, waving the results of a neighborhood poll purporting to show local support for a rezoning ordinance to permit his commercial construction project to go through. It might be a regional transportation commission, citing poll results to justify the establishment of bus lanes on freeways. Or it might be a friend or neighbor, selectively using poll results to win an argument.

Citizens need not become experts at drawing samples, constructing questionnaires, or analyzing data to be better consumers of public opinion research. Instead, they can become aware of the steps involved in conducting a survey, and the possible consequences of the steps, so that they are better able to reject bad "merchandise" and appreciate good buys.

Readers should not construe this book as a condemnation of public opinion research; most of the highly publicized polls, as well as many private polls, reflect high standards of polling. In fact, public opinion polling has improved dramatically over the past sixty years in areas such as sample design, question wording and format, interviewing techniques, and methods of data analysis. Interested readers may consult the fiftieth anniversary issue of *Public Opinion Quarterly* (1987) for discussions of how polling practices have changed over time. And of course they have changed even more since that was published. An appreciation of the art of conducting and analyzing surveys will leave citizens less susceptible to the intellectual tyranny that can occur when a public opinion poll is deemed by its sponsor to be scientific and its results therefore beyond question or challenge.

Citizens' Views of Polls

Historically, ordinary citizens' reactions to public opinion polling have often been positive, although their views of pollsters themselves are much more skeptical. One study rated the credibility of forty-four different professional groups that speak out on public issues; pollsters finished thirty-forth in the ranking (Morin 1999b). But 25 percent of the respondents in a 1996 Gallup survey said they regularly followed the results of a public opinion poll in a newspaper or magazine, and an additional 16 percent said they did so occasionally (Morin 1996b). Fifty-nine percent of the respondents said they did not follow a poll regularly in a print medium; of course, they might sporadically read about polls, or they might be aware of the polls through the electronic media. The Gallup poll and others like it have indicated that Americans held fairly positive views about the accuracy of polls. More than two-thirds of the Gallup sample said the polls were right most of the time. Eighty-seven percent supported polls as "a good thing."

In 2001 the Henry J. Kaiser Family Foundation, in conjunction with *Public Perspective* magazine, conducted an extensive survey on the role of polling in a democracy and on the views of the public, policy leaders, and the media toward polling (Brodie et al. 2001; Witt 2001). The opinions of the public were mixed. Twenty-eight percent of the respondents said that conducting a public opinion poll was a very good way to learn what a majority of people in our country think, and an additional 56 percent said it was a somewhat good way. But when they were asked to choose among town hall meetings, polling, talking to people on the street and at shopping malls, or talking to people who call, write, or e-mail public officials as the best way for officials to learn what the public is thinking, 43 percent opted for town hall meetings and only 25 percent for polling.

The same study also asked how useful people thought polls are for enabling officials in Washington to understand how the public feels on issues. Twenty-two percent of the respondents said that polls were very useful; 54 percent said somewhat useful; 13 percent, not too useful; and 8 percent, not useful at all. The 75 percent (54 + 13 + 8) who rated polls as somewhat useful or lower were then presented the following question:

> For each of the following statements, please tell me if you think it is a major reason polls are only somewhat useful or not useful for officials to understand how the public feels about important issues, a minor reason, or not a reason:

Statement	Percentage rating it a major reason
Polls don't accurately reflect what the public wants.	43%
Polls don't ask for the public's opinion on the right issues.	39%
The results of polls can be twisted to say whatever you want them to say.	58%

In the same survey, only 50 percent of the respondents strongly agreed or somewhat agreed that "public opinion polling is based on sound scientific principles," whereas 80 percent strongly or somewhat agreed that "the questions asked in polls often don't give people the opportunity to say what they really think about an issue" (Brodie et al. 2001, 22–23). All of these results suggest that Americans have some genuine reservations about the polling enterprise itself and about politicians' use of polls

Other, anecdotal evidence also supports that finding. Most teachers and practitioners of public opinion polling have encountered citizens who have expressed utter distrust of polling. Some complain that they have never been interviewed and don't know anyone who has, and they therefore wonder just how representative samples can be. Koch (1985) finds that people who have never participated in a poll are dubious about the accuracy of survey results.

Others base their doubts on the size of the samples. In talking about polling with diverse audiences, I repeatedly hear people ask how a sample of 1,500 respondents can possibly represent 200 million adult Americans. And despite my brilliant answer by analogy—a doctor takes only a sample of a person's blood (fortunately), and a chef need taste only a spoonful of

DON'T FORGET THAT ELECTION YEAR IS
ALSO LIE-TO-THE-POLLSTERS YEAR.

Reprinted by permission of the *Detroit Free Press*

soup (assuming the soup is stirred properly) to test its seasoning—much
skepticism about polls remains. Indeed, a 1985 Roper survey produced an
estimate that only 28 percent of Americans believed that national polls
with sample sizes of 1,500–2,000 could be accurate, while 56 percent
said they could not be (Sussman 1985e). The 1996 Gallup survey obtained
similar results. Another study found that citizens who questioned the accuracy of polls attributed their skepticism to characteristics of the respondents as well as aspects of the polling enterprise itself (Dran and Hildreth
1995). Skeptics worried whether pollsters talked to the right people, as
well as whether sample sizes were adequate. (I will discuss sampling and

what makes a poll scientific in chapter 4.) Other concerns focused on poll-ster manipulation of surveys and media misuse of polls.

Polls have received much criticism pertaining to their growing role in elections and in election coverage by the news media. The argument is of-ten made that polls have contributed to the packaging of candidates: as-piring leaders are accused of first consulting the polls and then staking out their positions, thereby abdicating their leadership responsibilities on vital public issues. Polls are seen as encouraging a horse-race mentality among the news media, which concentrate on who's ahead and who's behind, who's gaining and who's falling back, as measured by the polls, instead of focusing on issues and the candidates' qualifications. Candidates them-selves have complained about the role of polls. For example, former Ten-nessee governor and now U.S. senator Lamar Alexander, an unsuccessful candidate for the GOP presidential nomination in 1996 and 2000, wor-ries that the polls have too much influence on media coverage of candi-dates and on campaign contributions in the early stages of the presidential selection process. Alexander asserts that "if the polls are combined with the $1,000 limit on contributions [since increased to $2,000], or other fac-tors, to weed out people based on these premature [surveys], then that's unfortunate for the process because it deprives voters of having the widest range of choices" (Rivlin 1999).

Exit polls—interviews with citizens just after they have voted—en-able the television networks to project election outcomes even before the voting is finished. This practice has angered many citizens and political elites. Newspaper columnist Mike Royko encouraged voters to lie to exit pollsters, and others (such as Munro and Gans 1988) have simply en-couraged a public boycott of exit polls. Congress has conducted hearings in an effort to get the networks to alter voluntarily the ways they report exit polls and election projections. The election night debacle in Florida in 2000 was a major black eye for exit polls, pollsters, and the broadcast me-dia. When television networks prematurely called Florida for Gore early on election night and later, again prematurely, called it for Bush, the excesses and frailties of media election coverage, with its reliance on exit polls, were fully exposed.

Other observers have condemned the impact of polls on American politics, none more harshly than Daniel Greenberg, who wrote:

> Given the devastation that opinion surveys have brought to the Ameri-can political process, we shouldn't be asking how polls can be sharpened but rather why they are endured and how they can be banished.
>
> Polls are the life-support system for the finger-to-the-wind, quick-change politics of our time and, as such, are the indispensable tools for

the ideologically hollow men who work politics like a soap-marketing campaign. . . .

The effect of this—on campaigns, as well as on administrations between campaigns—is an obsession with salesmanship rather than with governance. (1980)

The nation's political cartoonists, many of whom are syndicated in newspapers that themselves conduct polls, have had a field day attacking the polls, particularly their frequency, duration, and intrusiveness in the presidential selection process. Smith (1987, 209) found that polls were treated negatively in 61 percent of the comics and cartoons he analyzed and worried how this would affect citizens' reactions to polls. More recently, political commentator and writer Arianna Huffington has established a Web site called "Partnership for a Poll-Free America." Huffington has been particularly critical of the polling enterprise because of low response rates (a topic discussed in chapter 4).

Various practitioners of polling and survey research have become concerned about what they see as increased skepticism, cynicism, lack of interest, and even hostility toward polls. Prominent pollsters such as Harry O'Neill, of the Roper organization, and Kathy Frankovic, director of polling at CBS News, have called on their industry colleagues to be more reflective about their enterprise and more sensitive to its shortcomings (O'Neill 1997; Morin 1998a). Black (1991) advocates greater sensitivity to the needs of respondents by (1) making the interview itself a more interesting and rewarding experience for respondents; (2) keeping promises made to respondents in such areas as the length of the interview and the provision of final reports if requested; and (3) maintaining high quality throughout the polling enterprise. Lang and Lang (1984) worry that some of the more recent entrants into the polling business may have weaker ties to the profession and a lesser commitment to the high standards that should characterize public opinion polling (Morin 1992c). They urge careful self-policing by the polling industry to protect the profession and its reputation among the public. Others (such as Tanur 1994) recommend better education of citizens as consumers of polls (which is indeed the main purpose of this book). The point is that there is growing unease among many practitioners of polling because the lofty status that public opinion assessment has enjoyed may be in some jeopardy.

The American Association for Public Opinion Research (AAPOR) in May 1997 issued a publication detailing the "best practices" that should characterize public opinion research. The last recommendation called for the disclosure of "all methods of the survey to permit evaluation and replication" and presented a comprehensive list of items that exceeded the standards for minimum disclosure laid out in the AAPOR code (see chapter 6 for a fuller discussion of disclosure standards). AAPOR also condemned a number of survey practices, such as presenting the results of any self-selected poll as if they were the product of genuine scientific survey research. The AAPOR also sharply criticized "push polling"—an election campaign tactic disguised as legitimate polling. In a push poll, a campaign contacts voters, presents some negative information about another candidate, and then asks some questions about that candidate. The aim of push polls is not to acquire legitimate information about the election contest but to push potential voters away from a particular candidate. (Push polling is discussed in greater detail in chapter 7.)

The Luntz case illustrates how politicians or a political party may use polls to promote an agenda. In April 1997 the executive council of AAPOR formally chastised pollster Frank Luntz for violating AAPOR's Code of Professional Ethics and Practices. Prior to the 1994 congressional elections, Luntz claimed that his research showed that sizable majorities of Americans supported all parts of the GOP's "Contract with America." But when asked to make public the wording of his poll and other information, Luntz refused. AAPOR rebuked him for failing to meet the standards of disclosure (AAPOR 1997a). Later it turned out that Luntz's evidence of support for the Contract with America was highly suspect and misleading. Nevertheless, the House Republican leadership used the alleged poll results to build legislative support for the items in the program. In general, political leaders who use the polls to "prove" that the public supports their positions have an advantage in the public discussion of issues.

Although they are sometimes angry or skeptical about poll results, Americans often think polls are accurate and fair. They often resent the intrusiveness and presumed power of the polls, but they eagerly consume the latest public opinion findings about myriad topics. This love-hate relationship is probably inevitable in the U.S. political system. Americans want their voices to be heard, and therefore they attack the polls when they think such devices are undermining genuine citizen involvement and influence. Yet in a large and heterogeneous nation such as the United States, the polls may be the best mechanism for reflecting the diversity of public opinion. The simple fact that polls generally count all respondents equally bestows on polls a democratic character that enhances their appeal in a democratic society.

Polling and Democracy

Different theories and opinions contend concerning the role of polling in a democratic society. Advocates of polls emphasize that polling is an opportunity for citizens to participate in democracy and that it permits quick and repeated assessments of public opinion. Polling is particularly valued by those who prefer a democracy in which the people govern directly rather than through elected representatives. Some advocate polling citizens on their policy preferences and enacting those preferences, thereby circumventing the "middleman"—the elected representative—although such as system would ignore many important features of the governing process, such as dialogue, bargaining, and compromise. Many in this group are fascinated with the possibility that technological innovations might facilitate direct governance by the citizenry. The huge advances in communications in recent years have rendered the virtues and feasibility of direct democracy through technology even more tantalizing.

Some proponents of the more traditional theory of representative democracy also welcome public opinion polls because they provide systematic information on the preferences of the citizenry. They argue that citizens' opinions should influence the behavior of their elected representatives and that any mechanism that can provide information on citizens' opinions is bound to foster democracy. But the empirical evidence is mixed on the extent to which popular preferences are actually translated into public policy. On the one hand, examples of the government's seeming unresponsiveness to public opinion are numerous. For example, polls regularly showed an overwhelming majority of Americans favoring some form of gun control, such as handgun registration or waiting periods, for years before Congress finally passed the so-called Brady law in 1993. That measure had first been introduced in 1987. Moreover, the Brady law was the first major federal gun control legislation since 1968. On the other hand, some empirical studies have found substantial congruence between the attitudes of the public and the actions of government on certain issues (Erikson 1976; Page and Shapiro 1983, 1992). Although these studies are careful not to hastily attribute government decisions to popular preferences, they do suggest conditions under which citizen influence is likely to be significant.

Another benefit of polls, according to polling proponents, is the opportunity for citizens to learn about their compatriots and to dispel myths and stereotypes that might otherwise mislead public discourse. For example, Morin reported poll results that challenged the stereotype of evangelical and fundamentalist Christians as monolithic, homogeneous supporters of the religious right (Morin 1993a, 1993c). A *USA Today*/CNN/Gallup poll conducted in December 1993 showed that stereotypes of the opponents in the gun control debate were misleading. For example, the attitudes of gun owners on various aspects of gun control did not differ substantially from the attitudes of nonowners, particularly

DOONESBURY © (2002) G. B. Trudeau. Reprinted with permission of UNIVERSAL PRESS SYNDICATE. All rights reserved.

concerning less-sweeping forms of gun regulation. Other public opinion polls have provided insights, sometimes surprising ones, on race and prejudice in the United States. A Louis Harris poll conducted in 1993 showed that the traditional victims of bigotry—blacks, Asians, and Latinos—

often expressed intolerant views of other minority groups. And a study by Sniderman et al. (1993) debunked the simplistic notion that conservatives were prejudiced toward blacks and liberals were not. Although on many items conservatives were less tolerant than liberals toward blacks, the key point for Sniderman and his colleagues was that the differences were often very small.

In contrast to the favorable arguments of proponents, many critics of polling worry about the harmful consequences of polls for a democratic political system. They agree that citizen influence is a key component of a democracy and that public opinion, properly measured, can be useful in governing. But they argue that polls give a misleading impression of how a democracy actually operates. Public opinion is not synonymous with the results of public opinion polls, yet today the two are treated as though they were identical. A focus solely on poll results ignores the dynamics of how opinions are formed and how they change and often overlooks factors that may shape (and manipulate) public opinion, such as the behavior of leaders and interest groups. Polls may present an overall picture of the distribution of opinion, but the reporting and use of polls often ignore important differences in preferences among subgroups. The result is a misleading picture of similar attitudes across different segments of the American population. Margolis (1984) claims that polls may not be the optimal way to measure public opinion on politically and socially sensitive topics. He argues that in some instances actual behavior provides a more valid expression of public opinion than verbal responses to survey questions.

A more radical criticism of polls is that they are simply a sop to the citizenry, that they give people a false sense of being influential when in reality political power is held and exercised by elites who may or may not act in the public interest. Social scientist Johan Galtung (1969) makes the point most effectively when he argues that surveys are too democratic: they generally count all respondents equally, whereas people are tremendously disparate in the resources and skills they bring to bear on political decisions. To the extent that a survey is seen as a quasi referendum on an issue, it is misleading because the participants in the referendum have different degrees of opportunity to shape government outcomes.

Weissberg (2001) argues that polls should not shape public policies and that policymakers should ignore the polls. He provides an elaborate rationale for this position but essentially argues that poll respondents do not and cannot incorporate all the factors that policymakers have to consider when adopting specific policies. Weissberg claims that although polls measure what citizens want, those wishes do not in most instances take into account the costs or risks of the stated preference. That is, it is easy for respondents in a poll to say that they prefer more spending on education or health care, but such responses do not reflect the costs or the potential problems associated with that increased spending. Only the policymaker has that information, and it is the policymaker who must make the ultimate decision based on much more than citizen preferences.

A related criticism of polls concerns their consequences for leadership in the United States. The simplistic version of this argument says that officeholders blindly follow the polls rather than work to educate and persuade the public. This argument is exemplified by an editorial in the *Akron Beacon Journal* (May 8, 1994) entitled "Foreign Poll-icy." It begins by asserting, "The name of Stanley Greenberg may not be familiar to most Americans. It should be. He is Bill Clinton's pollster, and for all intents and purposes, he conducts the country's foreign policy." Other observers, such as Barnes (1993), have also described the critical role Greenberg played in the Clinton administration, just as he did in the presidential campaign itself. Likewise, polling results in 1998 and 1999 on health care, patients' rights, and prescription drugs showed that Americans cared about these issues, prompting the GOP congressional leadership to offer its own health care proposals to head off any political backlash from its opposition to the Clinton administration's proposals (Alvarez 1998).

Other critics of polling argue that the widespread awareness of public preferences that polls generate has limited the ability of leaders to make unpopular choices. Still others complain that leaders can easily manipulate the polls—for example, by giving a major, televised address that can influence opinions in polls taken right afterward, thereby generating poll results that paint an inaccurate picture of the extent of support for their policies. Some make the fundamental point that polls (and the news media) have altered the style and substance of governance by emphasizing the consequences of politicians' actions for the next election. The result is a shortsighted approach to problem solving. Compare this with poll proponents' defense of the impact of polls on leadership, which argues that officials should have information about citizens' attitudes before they make major decisions and that the polls, whatever their limitations, are the best way to acquire that information.

The cartoon on page 22 is a jab at the Bush administration and the president himself for his reliance on public opinion polling. In the 2000 presidential election, candidate George Bush criticized the Clinton/Gore administration for slavishly following the polls and claimed that in a Bush administration decisions would be made on the bases of principles and values and not because of polls. In hindsight, there are striking similarities between the Clinton and Bush administrations, and one marked difference, when it comes to polling and political research in general (Harris 2001a, 2001b). The similarities are simply that both administrations used polls, focus groups, and the like extensively to ascertain what Americans were thinking, how citizens would respond to various policy alternatives, and what were the best ways to package those alternatives. The major difference between the two was that Clinton himself was actively involved in reviewing the poll results in weekly meetings with key members of his administration (Harris 2001a), whereas Bush relied more on recommendations from his chief political operative, Karl Rove. Harris discussed how polling results affected Clinton administration policies. For example, a needle exchange program for drug addicts, to combat the spread of AIDS, was dropped when polls indicated substantial public opposition. In another example, when the Clinton administration enjoyed a federal budget surplus, it did not want the Republican Congress to spend that surplus on a tax cut. Public opinion polling helped the Clinton administration learn that the public overwhelmingly preferred devoting the surplus to Social Security rather than to tax cuts. Thus the President challenged the Congress to "save Social Security first," a theme that put the Republicans on the defensive on tax cuts until George Bush became president.

These two examples raise important points. Surely the Clinton administration was using polls for political purposes to build support (on how to use the surplus) and avoid voter anger and opposition (on the needle exchange proposal). Yet it was also the case that the polls were telling the administration what popular preferences were, and the administration then followed those preferences. Obviously the question for leadership is, To what extent does one follow the polls and public opinion, and to what extent does one lead and try to change citizens' opinions? Any presidential administration does both. Harris points out that the Clinton administration took major actions on trade policy, military intervention in the Balkans, and other matters that went against the grain of American public opinion at the time. Murray and Howard (2002) found that the Reagan and Clinton administrations polled extensively from their first days in office, whereas the Carter and first Bush administrations polled only sporadically in their first three years but became very active in polling in their fourth year. They conclude that the public opinion polling operation has become institutionalized in the White House but that there are differences in how each administration uses polls and political research in general. The evidence from the second Bush presidency suggests that polling, focus group, and political research activities are as central as they were during the Clinton administration despite claims to the contrary (Harris 2001b; Tenpas 2003).

What, then, is the verdict on opinion polls in the United States? They are now an integral part of the political and social landscape, and they are likely to become more prominent in the future, even as the technology of polling changes. Polls can provide citizens and leaders with useful information; they also can be highly misleading and inaccurate. Polls may enhance the opportunities for citizen influence; they also can serve to manipulate the public. In 1965 George Gallup wrote optimistically about the future of the polls:

> As students, scholars, and the general public gain a better understanding of polls, they will have a greater appreciation of the service polls can perform in a democracy. In my opinion, modern polls are the chief hope of lifting government to a higher level, by showing that the public supports the reforms that will make this possible, by providing a *modus operandi* for testing new ideas. . . . Polls can help make government more efficient and responsive; they can improve the quality of candidates for public office; they can make this a truer democracy. (Gallup 1965–1966, 549)

Almost four decades have passed since Gallup made those claims, and discourse about the polls has become much more critical. Nevertheless, as citizens become wiser consumers of polls, Gallup's lofty aspirations are more likely to be realized.

The chapters that follow consider polls in detail and raise some methodological points, often in the context of important substantive examples. Chapter 2 addresses the problem of "nonattitudes"—they are what polltakers measure when citizens do not have genuine opinions on a topic and yet answer the poll questions anyway. Despite pollsters' best efforts, citizens often respond to questions on which they have no real opinions, so that the poll yields misleading results.

Chapter 3 discusses the wording of questions and their order and context. Examples of poorly worded questions likely to produce skewed results have already been cited, but the wording of a question is not the only important consideration. A survey is, after all, a series of questions, whose placement and context can greatly affect the results.

Chapter 4 focuses on various sampling techniques and their advantages and disadvantages. It also deals with sample size and error. Chapter 5 explains in detail how different interviewing procedures can affect results.

Chapter 6 examines how the news media report the polls, and chapter 7 analyzes the role of polls in elections. Because Americans learn about polls primarily through the mass media, how they cover polls greatly influences public opinion. This influence is particularly interesting in the case of high-visibility national polls because the organization that reports the polls also is responsible for conducting them. Chapter 7 argues that the polls have come to play an intrusive role in elections and that their use by candidates and their reporting by the media often ill serve citizens and the electoral process. Elections are the most visible opportunity for citizens to influence their government, and to the extent that polls affect elections, citizens should be sensitive and wary.

Chapter 8 explains that the analysis of poll results is more an art than a science—and one that affords many opportunities for manipulative interpretation and dissemination of poll results to sway public opinion. Chapter 9 ties together the various themes, offers suggestions about better ways to use polls, and discusses the effects of polls on the American polity.

Exercises

1. Keep a one-week log of the public opinion poll results that appear in your local daily newspaper. Note the topic of the poll and the source. Also note how much information was provided about how the poll was conducted. What conclusions can you make based on these findings? Do you think adequate information was provided about how the poll was conducted?

2. Pick one of the national newsmagazines (*Time, Newsweek,* or *U.S. News & World Report*) and examine how it used and reported polls during one calendar month. Keep a record of the topics of the polls and how much information was provided about how they were conducted. Also note how the poll results were used. Were they incorporated into and discussed in the story, or did they appear as a sidebar?

3. For one week, go to AOL and to the CNN Web site each day and record the daily poll questions that they ask their users. Also record the results of the poll questions. Then try to find genuine public opinion polls that have asked similar questions around the same time. Compare the results of the Internet and the scientific polls on similar topics. How similar or dissimilar are the results of the two? How would you explain this?

4. On pages 9 and 10 in this chapter are a number of survey items that the author claimed were biased. Do you agree that these are biased questions? If so, what do you think makes them biased? Be specific in your critique of the items.

2 The Problem of Nonattitudes

To produce an informative and accurate public opinion poll, a researcher must perform several tasks successfully. They include constructing a questionnaire with properly worded and ordered questions, selecting a representative sample, correctly interviewing the respondents in that sample, analyzing the data appropriately, and finally, drawing the correct conclusions. But before any of these tasks can be performed, a researcher must ask a fundamental question: Is the proposed topic of the poll one on which citizens have genuine opinions? If it is, then the topic is suitable for a public opinion survey. But if the topic is so remote from citizens' concerns that they do not hold real views on it, then any poll on the topic will measure *nonattitudes* rather than attitudes. Any information obtained will be suspect—even if the questions are properly worded, the sample is scientifically selected, and the data are appropriately analyzed.

The presence of nonattitudes is one of the simplest yet most perplexing problems in public opinion polling. Too often in a survey context, people respond to questions about which they have no genuine attitudes or opinions.[1] Even worse, the analyst or the poll sponsor or the news media treat the nonattitude responses as if they represented actual public opinions. Under these circumstances, a misleading portrait of public opinion can emerge because no distinction is made between people with real

---

1. The terms *attitude* and *opinion* are used interchangeably. Many social scientists differentiate between attitudes and opinions by treating opinions as more transitory, as verbal manifestations of some underlying attitude, words elicited by the public opinion survey. For the purposes of this chapter, this distinction is by no means critical, although the reader should recognize that public opinion data at times may simply be verbal responses (opinions) that pollsters hope accurately reflect some underlying attitudes.

views on an issue and those whose responses simply reflect their desire to appear in an interview as informed citizens. Unfortunately, pollsters often find it difficult to differentiate between genuine attitude holders and persons merely expressing nonattitudes.

It is tempting to assume that citizens are interested in and informed about the issues that public officials and the media are widely discussing. Researchers often take for granted that citizens know the basic facts about their government and political system. But sometimes those assumptions lead pollsters to include questions on topics that people know very little about even though the topics are prominent. For example, an obvious topic for public opinion polling is the state of the economy. Although citizens can certainly express valid opinions about their own and the nation's economic situation, an extended inquiry might be hindered by citizens' ignorance about key facts of economics. Morin (1993b) cites studies demonstrating the public's deficiencies in economic knowledge. In those studies only one in five respondents came reasonably close to knowing the national unemployment rate, and only about half could identify the correct definition of the federal budget deficit among four choices presented to them. The public also has major gaps in its knowledge of the American political system. A study that compared citizens' levels of knowledge in the 1940s and 1950s with contemporary ones found that, after controlling for educational levels, Americans today at each level of education are less informed about many aspects of politics than were their counterparts in the earlier decades (Delli Carpini and Keeter 1991). The study speculated that today people are simply less interested in politics. Because respondents with low interest are more likely to express nonattitudes, these results suggest that pollsters must exercise great care to avoid measuring nonattitudes.

The presence of nonattitudes in survey responses has been well documented (Converse 1970; Taylor 1983; Norpoth and Lodge 1985). A particularly intriguing study by Bishop, Oldendick, and Tuchfarber (1980) included a fictitious item in surveys conducted in the greater Cincinnati area. Respondents were presented with the following statement and question about a nonexistent Public Affairs Act: "Some people say that the 1975 Public Affairs Act should be repealed. Do you agree or disagree with this idea?" One-third of the respondents offered an opinion. After an effort to filter out nonattitude responses on this fictitious question, researchers found that 10 percent of the sample still offered an opinion. When the *Washington Post* included a question on the nonexistent Public Affairs Act in a 1995 national survey, 43 percent of respondents offered an opinion: 24 percent supported repeal of the act and 19 percent were opposed (Morin 1995a). The *Post* also administered slightly modified versions of the question to two other samples of respondents. One sample was asked,

"President Clinton said that the 1975 Public Affairs Act should be repealed. Do you agree or disagree?" The other sample was asked: "The Republicans in Congress said that the 1975 Public Affairs Act should be repealed. Do you agree or disagree?" The responses changed when references to Clinton and the Republicans were included; 53 percent of respondents now offered an opinion. And, as expected, the Clinton version of the question found Democrats more favorable than Republicans to repeal of the act by a 36 percent to 18 percent margin. But in the Republican version of the question the results were reversed, with 36 percent of the Republicans favoring repeal compared with only 19 percent of the Democrats. Clearly, respondents were seeking cues and guidance from the wording of the question itself, something more likely to happen when people are confronted with topics that they have no meaningful attitudes about.

The existence of nonattitudes is not surprising; after all, an interview is a social situation in which a respondent interacts, in person or by telephone, with an interviewer the respondent does not know. Few people in such circumstances want to admit that they are uninformed, particularly on a popular or timely issue. So most people answer the questions, and the interviewer duly records their responses.

But ascertaining the cause and extent of nonattitudes is a much more complicated task than simply blaming citizens for their low level of information and scant regard for public affairs. For example, one potential sign of nonattitudes is response instability. That is, if the same citizens give different responses to identical survey questions asked at different times, it suggests that their responses are not deeply rooted in any underlying belief and instead reflect nonattitudes. An alternative explanation is that genuine attitude change may have occurred during the multiple administrations of the survey. Perhaps societal conditions were in flux; perhaps the news media or the actions and statements of political leaders have influenced citizens' responses. Or perhaps there were changes in the survey, such as slight modifications in question wording or different placement of survey items within the overall questionnaire (see chapter 3 for a discussion of the importance of question order and question context).

With all these possible influences at work, it would be difficult to assess how much of the response instability is due to nonattitudes rather than other factors. The problem is made more difficult when a survey measures a complex issue or phenomenon with only one or two items. At this point, an illustration of how a public opinion survey based on nonattitudes can go astray and mislead the public might be useful.

An Example of Nonattitudes

Some years ago I was part of a sample of Ohioans queried about their views on land use problems. The interview took place over the phone, and the sample was probably picked from the telephone book. (I surmised this because the interviewer knew my name.) After the interviewer identified herself and the sponsor of the poll, she asked, "Tell me, Mr. Asher, what comes to your mind when you hear the term *land use?*" As a social scientist familiar with public opinion polling, I recognized this as a screening question aimed at determining whether it was worthwhile for the interviewer to proceed with the interview. Surely, if I did not have the vaguest idea what *land use* meant, there would be little point in continuing the interview. In any event I responded, "Hmmm. Land use. How you use the land!" This response must have been sufficiently brilliant for the interviewer to continue with the survey, for she then asked me, "Mr. Asher, what do you think is the most important land use problem facing Ohio?" I mentally squirmed and silently gave thanks that the telephone interviewer could not see my difficulty in thinking up a land use problem. After a delay of about ten seconds, I responded with something like "Planned growth and development." She then asked, "Which level of government—state, county, or local—do you think should have primary responsibility for addressing the problem of planned growth?" I responded, although to this day I cannot recall which level of government I mentioned.

The interview continued, and about three minutes later the interviewer asked me, "Mr. Asher, what do you think is the second most important land use problem facing Ohio?" This time I really had to struggle for an answer. Finally I uttered triumphantly, "Sufficient parks and green space." And, of course, the interviewer then asked me which level of government—state, county, or local—should have primary responsibility for rectifying this problem. I gave an answer (which I cannot recall) and said to myself that if the interviewer asked me about the third most important land use problem facing Ohio, I was going to blast her and the entire research project on the grounds that it was measuring nonattitudes. Fortunately for the interviewer, she never asked that question, and the interview was concluded.

Some months later, a government report based on this survey described which land use problems Ohioans ranked as most important and which levels of government Ohioans wanted to take the lead in addressing them. The report also contained policy recommendations and cited scientific evidence to support its conclusions. As I read the report I grew angrier and angrier; it used survey results derived from what I assume were nonattitudes, opinions from respondents like me who gave answers in response to the questions but had little information about or interest in land use.

As sponsors of public opinion polls should recognize, not every issue of central importance to them will be an appropriate topic of inquiry for the citizenry at large. Different people have different concerns, and those who conduct public opinion polls must incorporate that fact into their plans and proceed accordingly.

The Use of Screening Questions

Researchers can take steps in opinion polls to minimize the number of responses that are superficial reactions to the interview stimulus. The simplest strategy is to make it socially acceptable for respondents to say that they are unfamiliar with the topic of a question. This response would result in that question's being skipped. Another strategy is to employ screening or filter questions to separate likely attitude holders from nonattitude respondents. The study by Bishop and his colleagues (1980) on the fictitious Public Affairs Act employed a variety of screening questions to reduce the frequency of nonattitudes, for example, "Do you have an opinion on this or not?" "Have you thought much about this issue?" Respondents who could not pass the screening questions were not asked about the Public Affairs Act.

The 2000 American National Election Study, conducted by the Center for Political Studies at the University of Michigan, also used a variety of means to lessen the problem of nonattitudes. One item on that survey asked respondents whether they thought the federal government had become too powerful. The exact wording of the question was, "Some people are afraid the government in Washington is getting too powerful for the good of the country and the individual person. Others feel that the government in Washington is not getting too strong. Do you have an opinion on this or not?"

Of the 1,543 citizens in the sample who responded, 960 (62 percent) said yes and 583 (38 percent) said no. The sizable number with no opinion may surprise readers who are aware that an enduring controversy of American politics is the appropriate size and power of the federal government. This example suggests that topics hotly discussed by political elites may not be of great importance to the average citizen. In this example, asking people whether or not they had an opinion was an effective screening question that eliminated nearly two-fifths of the respondents. But how many of the respondents eliminated would have answered the question if they simply had been asked whether they thought the government was becoming too powerful or not? As it was, among the 960 citizens with an opinion on the issue, 622 (65 percent) thought government had grown too powerful, 293 (31 percent) thought it had not, and the rest said that it depended or that they did not know (even though they had stated in response to the screening question that they had an opinion on the issue).

Another screening question used in the same 2000 election study allowed respondents to say that they had not thought much about the issue. Those who chose that response were not asked their opinions, thereby reducing the measurement of nonattitudes. The item read as follows:

> Some people think the government should provide fewer services, even in areas such as health and education, in order to reduce spending. Suppose these people are at one end of a scale, at point number 1. Other people feel it is important for the government to provide many more services even if it means an increase in spending. Suppose these people are at the other end, at point 7. And, of course, some other people have opinions somewhere in between, at points 2, 3, 4, 5, or 6. Where would you place yourself on this scale or haven't you thought much about this?

Of the 1,005 persons who were asked this question, 142 (about 14 percent) said they had not thought much about the matter. This does not mean, however, that the other 85 percent had thought a lot about it and had genuine opinions. The following pattern of their responses to this item raises questions about their answers ($N = 863$):

Response	Number who chose it
1. Provide many fewer services; reduce spending a lot.	46
2.	60
3.	102
4.	251
5.	184
6.	115
7. Provide many more services; increase spending a lot.	98
Don't know.	7

Note that the largest number of responses ($n = 251$) fell in the middle, in category 4. This distribution may reflect large numbers of citizens who are satisfied with the status quo or who genuinely take a neutral position on the issue. Or it may reflect the tendency of some citizens with genuine, nonneutral preferences on the issue to hide their preferences by opting for the safe middle category. Many such responses can be moved out of the middle category by using a branching format question, in which citizens who opt for the middle category are then asked whether they favor one side or the other more (Aldrich et al. 1982).

It is also possible that the presence of a large number of people in the middle category may signal problems of nonattitudes in the measurement. Perhaps some proportion of people in the middle category place themselves there because they do not want to admit to the interviewer that they have not thought much about the issue or are unable to place themselves along the scale. For them, the middle category may appear to be a safe position that makes them seem informed without having to take sides on the issue. If so, then some of the category 4 responses may be nonattitudes rather than genuinely neutral opinions, and the portrait of American public opinion on this issue may be misleading.

The 2000 American National Election Study used so-called thermometer questions to assess citizens' feelings toward various political figures. But before the respondents answered, they were given the option of skipping over names that they did not recognize, to lessen the measurement of nonattitudes. This measurement tool is based on the ability of people to relate points on a thermometer to figurative degrees of warmth and coldness toward objects. Survey respondents were given the following instructions:

> I'd like to get your feelings toward some of our political leaders and other people who are in the news these days. I'll read the name of a person and I'd like you to rate that person using something we call the feeling thermometer. Ratings between 50 degrees and 100 degrees mean that you feel favorable and warm toward that person. Ratings between 0 degrees and 50 degrees mean that you don't feel favorable toward the person and that you don't care too much for that person. You would rate the person at the 50 degree mark if you don't feel particularly warm or cold toward the person. If we come to a person whose name you don't recognize, you don't need to rate that person. Just tell me and we'll move on to the next one.

Ideally, respondents who do not recognize a name or who feel they are unable to evaluate the person named would indicate that to the interviewer. However, the instructions may encourage some respondents to place the subjects of the survey at the 50-degree mark, including those whose names they do not recognize.

Table 2-1 indicates how the respondents rated various political figures. Keep in mind that Republican George W. Bush and Democrat Al Gore were the major party candidates for president in 2000, and Ralph Nader and Pat Buchanan represented minor parties, although both had been on the national scene for a long time.

The percentage of respondents who did not recognize Al Gore or George W. Bush, or who could not evaluate them, was very small; the comparable percentages for Pat Buchanan and Ralph Nader were much higher at 18 percent (7 + 11) and 27 percent (14 + 13) respectively. It appears, then, that the screening questions worked well because many of the

Table 2-1 Thermometer Ratings of Four Political Figures (in percentages)

	Evaluation				
Candidate	Rating other than 50	Rating of 50	Does not recognize	Cannot evaluate	Rating (N)
Bush	82	17	0	2	100 (1,804)
Gore	84	14	0	2	100 (1,805)
Buchanan	57	25	7	11	100 (1,804)
Nader	51	22	14	13	100 (1,805)

Source: 2000 American National Election Study conducted by the Center for Political Studies, Institute for Social Research, University of Michigan.
Note: Table entries are the percentage of respondents ranking each political figure in each category.

respondents did not rate the less well-known minor party candidates. However, it is disquieting that among the citizens who did assign a thermometer score to these political leaders, more gave a rating of 50 to Buchanan and Nader than to Bush and Gore. Of those citizens evaluating Gore on the thermometer, only 14.3 percent (14 / (84 + 14)) gave him a score of 50; the comparable percentage for Bush was 17.2 percent (17 / (82 + 17)). But the proportions of citizens using the thermometer who placed Buchanan and Nader at the midpoint were 30.5 percent (25 / (57 + 25)) and 30 percent (22 / (51 + 22)) respectively.

Since Buchanan and Nader were not as well known as Gore and Bush, it is not surprising that more respondents rated them at 50 on the thermometer scale. But the problem of measuring nonattitudes may also be at work here. Perhaps the higher proportion of 50 ratings for Buchanan and Nader indicates that the screening questions did not eliminate all those persons who had no genuine attitudes about the two candidates. Perhaps some respondents assigned a score of 50 to Buchanan and Nader as a safe answer when they had little knowledge and weak-to-nonexistent attitudes about them.

An indirect test of this notion appears in Tables 2-2 and 2-3, which show how educational levels and degree of interest in the campaign were related to assigning political figures a thermometer score of 50. One might expect citizens with higher levels of education to make more discriminating evaluations and therefore to be less likely to assign thermometer scores of 50. As Table 2-2 indicates, this expectation holds up reasonably well; about twice as many respondents in the lowest education category gave a rating of 50 as respondents in the highest education category.

Table 2-3 relates the frequency of ratings of 50 to the respondents' levels of interest in the campaign. As expected, the more interested the respondents, the less likely they were to assign a score of 50 because of their greater awareness of and involvement in the campaign. This pattern holds for all four political leaders. But note that 28 percent of the low-interest respondents rated Gore at 50, while 43 percent placed Buchanan at that midpoint. These numbers may suggest that little information went into the evaluation of Buchanan and raise the question of what a score of 50 represents: Was it a genuinely neutral point or simply a convenient and safe home for the expression of nonattitudes that were not filtered out by the screening questions? The latter interpretation is given greater credibility by Pat Buchanan's candidacy and issue stances. Buchanan, as a strong conservative and an articulate and passionate advocate for his positions, is not likely to generate a lot of neutral responses—unless the respondent really knows little about Buchanan's politics.

A study by Benson (2001) provides a striking example of the consequences of including a screening question. In a study of citizens' attitudes about school vouchers and charter schools, half the respondents were simply asked whether they favored or opposed these initiatives, with no screening question or "undecided" category. The other half of the sample

Table 2-2   Frequency of Ratings of 50 for Four Political Figures by Respondents' Education (in percentages)

Candidate	Grade school	High school	Some college	College graduate	Post-college
Bush	24	21	19	12	10
Gore	22	18	15	10	12
Buchanan	36	38	32	26	17
Nader	31	35	30	29	21

Source: 2000 American National Election Study conducted by the Center for Political Studies, Institute for Social Research, University of Michigan.

Note: Table entries are the percentage of respondents assigning a thermometer score who gave the candidate in question a score of 50. For example, the 38 in the "high school/Buchanan" category means that 38 percent of respondents with a high school education gave Buchanan a score of 50; the other 62 percent of high school respondents assigned Buchanan a numerical score other than 50.

Table 2-3 Frequency of Ratings of 50 for Four Political Figures by Respondents' Interest in the Campaign (in percentages)

Candidate	Very much interested	Somewhat interested	Not very interested
Bush	11	16	30
Gore	10	12	28
Buchanan	23	32	43
Nader	23	33	36

Source: 2000 American National Election Study conducted by the Center for Political Studies, Institute for Social Research, University of Michigan.

Note: Table entries are the percentage of respondents assigning a thermometer score who gave the candidate in question a score of 50. For example, the 43 in the "Buchanan/not very interested" category means that 43 percent of the not very interested respondents who were able to rate Buchanan gave him a 50, while the other 57 percent gave him a score other than 50.

was asked the same questions with the added phrase, "or haven't you heard enough about that to have an opinion?" For the voucher question asked without the screening question, only 4 percent of the respondents volunteered "don't know" responses. But when provided the "haven't heard enough" option, 33 percent chose it. The charter school differences were even greater. Only 9 percent volunteered "don't know" in the first form of the question, but fully 63 percent said that they had not heard enough to have an opinion in the second form of the item. As Benson (2001, 40) noted, the percentage of respondents favoring charter schools plummeted from 62 percent to 25 percent because of the addition of the screening question. The level of popular support for charter schools looks very different depending on which form of the question one examines.

Nonattitudes and the Middle Position in Survey Questions

The preceding examples illustrate how difficult it is to assess the magnitude of the nonattitude problem. They also raise another problem in attitude and opinion measurement: What does it mean when a person replies to a survey question, "I don't know" or "I can't decide" or "It depends"? Do these responses represent a genuinely neutral stance or something else? Should the responses of holders of nonattitudes be included at the neutral or middle point? Or should they be at a distinct point off the measurement scale, so as not to create a misleading image of large numbers of citizens' thoughtfully adopting the middle position?

The response alternatives included in an item affect the extent of nonattitudes. For example, a CBS News/*New York Times* poll conducted in November 1985 asked a national sample of Americans, "Who should have the most say about what cuts should be made to balance the budget—the President or Congress?" Note that the question did not give respondents the option of stating that the president and Congress should have an equal say. About 4 percent of the sample volunteered that response, but what percentage of Americans would have opted for this alternative had it been explicitly presented? In marked contrast is the following question in a November 1985 ABC News/*Washington Post* poll: "As things presently stand, who do you think is ahead in military power, the United States or the Soviet Union, or do you think they are about the same in military strength?" Twenty-four percent said the United States was ahead, 26 percent said the Soviets were, 4 percent had no opinion, and 46 percent said that both nations were about the same in military strength. In fact, in the eight times that ABC News/*Washington Post* pollsters asked samples of Americans this question between 1979 and 1991, the percentage of respondents saying "the same" ranged from 34 to 55, with an average of 44. One can only speculate what the responses would have looked like if the middle choice had not been provided.

Research on the effects of including a middle choice in the response alternatives shows that such an option typically generates about 25 percent more noncommittal responses (Schuman and Presser 1977; Bishop, Oldendick, and Tuchfarber 1980; Presser and Schuman 1980). This finding suggests that the omission of such a choice will result in many substantive responses that are not very meaningful from citizens who have weak or nonexistent attitudes on a subject. In one study, Presser and Schuman (1980) administered survey items in two forms to random subsamples. The only difference between the two forms was that one offered a middle alternative and the other did not. For example, one item asked about the penalties for using marijuana: "In your opinion, should the penalties for using marijuana be more strict, less strict, or about the same as they are now?" The other version read, "In your opinion, should the penalties for using marijuana be more strict or less strict than they are now?" On average, about 23 percent of respondents answered "about the same as they are now" when that choice was included in the question. Only about 8 percent volunteered that response when it was not included.

Research by Bishop (1987) further demonstrates how the presence or absence of a middle response alternative can affect survey responses. Based on a series of experiments, Bishop's work confirmed earlier research in finding that citizens are much more likely to choose the middle alternative when it is included in the question than when it is omitted.

Moreover, simply mentioning the middle category in the preface to a survey question will encourage respondents to select that option even when it is not listed among the response alternatives. More important, Bishop presents evidence that suggests that "people who select a middle alternative when it is offered would not necessarily answer the question in the same way as other respondents if forced to choose between the polar alternatives" when the middle option is not provided (227).

The interpretation of a "don't know" response can be especially problematic, because "don't know" can mean many different things (Coombs and Coombs 1976–1977; Faulkenberry and Mason 1978). For some people, "don't know" simply reflects the absence of a real attitude on the topic, but for others it may represent an inability to choose among contending positions. Smith (1984, 229) points out other ways in which "don't know" responses might arise. Respondents may be too insecure to take a stance, or they may decline to state their opinions out of a strong sense of privacy or because they do not want to offend anybody. Some respondents may want to hasten the completion of the interview by saying "don't know," thereby avoiding follow-up questions. Finally, just as respondents' nonattitudes may be disguised as attitudes, so too their middle responses (including "don't know") may mask genuine attitudes. Gilljam and Granberg (1993) found that poll respondents who were induced to respond to a survey item after they had initially given a "don't know" response to it expressed attitudes that were predictive of behavior. They concluded that, indeed, some poll respondents who had genuine attitudes kept them concealed by opting for the "don't know" response.

Converse (1976–1977) investigated the characteristics of respondents as well as the properties of survey questions that might affect the frequency of "no opinion" and "don't know" answers. She found, as expected, that the higher the level of education of respondents, the less likely they were to give "no opinion" replies. For question characteristics, she found that the most important feature was the content of the item. As the subject matter of the question became remoter from the concerns and interests of citizens, the frequency of "don't know" responses increased.

Other research sheds further light on how response alternatives and their ordering affect survey responses. Krosnick and Alwin (1987) found that respondents with less cognitive sophistication—less formal education and limited vocabularies—were more likely to be influenced by the order in which the responses were stated. Bishop (1990) also found that the effects on responses of using or not using a middle alternative are most pronounced among citizens who are less involved with the particular topic of the survey question. In general, the implications of the Converse, Bishop, and Krosnick and Alwin studies are that the consequences of response

"I'm undecided, but that doesn't mean I'm apathetic or uninformed."

alternatives and their ordering are genuine but complex. Therefore pollsters must be sensitive to the potential distortion, and even manipulation of responses, that might occur because of how the response choices are presented.

Is it a good idea to force responses into polar categories and minimize middle or neutral answers? Or is it better to encourage people to choose the middle position? The answer, of course, is that it depends. If people have genuine attitudes, then the public opinion researcher wants those attitudes clearly expressed. The inclusion of a middle category in such a situation might result in cautious citizens' opting for the middle position, particularly on controversial issues about which they might not want to reveal their true opinions to the interviewer. Yet the omission of a middle category might lead people with weak or nonexistent opinions on an issue to choose one of the genuine response options, thereby creating false impressions of genuine attitudes. A similar dilemma occurs with screening questions. The researcher wants to screen out nonattitudes but does not want to make it too easy for people to avoid answering questions on which they have real views, or too difficult for them to answer questions when they have real, although weak, attitudes.

This is a problem without a simple solution. The public opinion pollster and the consumer of the research must simply be sensitive to whether and in what form screening questions are used on a survey. They must also be aware of the response alternatives provided to the respondents. Finally, the appropriateness of particular substantive questions to particular samples of citizens should always be a central concern of the political analyst and the public opinion consumer. In the political realm, issues of great concern to political elites may be of little interest to the rank and file.

Response Instability and Nonattitudes

If a survey is measuring genuine attitudes, the responses should show some degree of stability over time. Yet often survey responses fluctuate radically over a relatively short period. This type of fluctuation raises questions about how real the measured opinions were in the first place. Instability of responses to identical polling questions asked over time may be an indicator of nonattitudes. Zaller and Feldman (1992), however, offer a different explanation for unstable attitudes. They argue that citizens do not have highly specific, fixed attitudes about many topics; instead, people often have multiple and sometimes conflicting opinions on issues. How people respond to a particular survey question on a topic may be a function of what they happen to have on their minds at the time of the survey. And what is on their minds will be influenced both by their most recent life experiences and by the cues that the survey question provides. It is thus possible for citizens to respond differently on issues over a short period of time without that instability's necessarily indicating nonattitudes: It may be that the real world or the survey context within which people respond to polling questions has changed. Assessment of the magnitude of the nonattitudes problem then becomes even more difficult.

The work of Zaller and Feldman has many implications. First, it serves as a reminder that the responses to survey questions can be affected by characteristics of the survey instrument, including question wording, question order, and response alternatives. Second, it also is a warning that opinions on complex topics should always be assessed using multiple survey items—not just one or two. Unfortunately, in many omnibus public opinion surveys, in which the investigators are trying to cover a wide variety of topics, it may be impossible to include multiple items on a single topic because of time and space considerations. The results one gets are then a function of which particular item was used. (This problem is discussed in greater depth in chapter 8.)

Finally, Zaller and Feldman's notion that the considerations that citizens bring to bear in the survey context affect their responses provides a rationale for giving respondents new information to find out whether their responses then change. For example, suppose one asked a sample of senior citizens about their views on Medicare-provided prescription drug benefits and received overwhelmingly supportive responses. Suppose that a follow-up question asking whether respondents would support such a program if it means higher Medicare premiums then produced much lower support for the program. Is this change in the distribution of opinions an indication of nonattitudes? The answer, of course, is no. The different distribution reflects the different considerations that come into play in the responses to the two questions. The first question evokes a health concern; the second introduces the cost factor and changes how respondents think about the issue. (This example of introducing new information to the respondent should not be confused with the illegitimate push polls discussed in chapter 7. Study of whether respondents' views on an issue change when new information is presented to them is appropriate.)

One strategy that uses multiple items to determine how genuine measured opinions really are is the "mushiness index" developed by the polling firm of Yankelovich, Skelly, and White. It was designed to assess the volatility of the public's views on issues, particularly the ones on which citizens provide answers even though they have little information or understanding about them. The mushiness index has four components in addition to a person's position on a particular issue: how much the issue affects the respondent personally, how well informed the respondent feels he or she is on the issue, how much the respondent discusses the issue with family and friends, and the respondent's own assessment of how likely it is that his or her views on the issue will change (Keene and Sackett 1981). On the basis of these criteria, Yankelovich, Skelly, and White placed issues into three categories, ranging from very volatile, or "mushy," to firm. They found that, in general, attitudes on domestic policy were less mushy than those on foreign policy.

The usefulness of the mushiness index is illustrated by the following example (Keene and Sackett 1981, 51). A sample of Americans was asked, "Do you favor or oppose restricting imports of foreign goods such as Japanese cars, textiles, and steel, which are less expensive than American products?" Fifty-four percent favored restricting imports, 41 percent opposed restrictions, and only 5 percent were unsure. But when the sample was broken down into three groups according to responses to the four mushiness criteria, the patterns of response were quite different. Among the mushiest group, 39 percent favored restrictions, 37 percent opposed them, and 24 percent were unsure; among the firmest group, 62 percent favored restrictions, 37 percent opposed them, and 1 percent were unsure.

How much respondents know about an issue (one component of the mushiness index) clearly affects their attitudes. When expansion of NATO became a prominent political issue in 1997, pollsters began asking questions about it. Because Americans are likely to have low levels of information and substantial nonattitudes about NATO and NATO expansion, a mushiness approach to ascertaining attitudes about the future of NATO would be appropriate. One poll conducted in early 1997 found that about 70 percent of the respondents had heard little about NATO expansion (Morin 1997b). Almost one-fourth incorrectly believed that Russia already was a member of NATO, and about 60 percent were predisposed toward NATO enlargement, a level of support that dropped substantially when NATO expansion was linked to the financial and other costs associated with bringing new members into the alliance. In general, surveys dealing with foreign affairs are more susceptible to the measurement of nonattitudes because such topics tend not to be as salient and interesting to many Americans.

The mushiness index is not used widely in surveys, in part because it is too costly and time consuming to ask all the questions needed to construct it, particularly when the survey covers a number of things. Nevertheless, the concept of mushiness is of interest analytically because it helps to explain a number of apparent anomalies in American public opinion. One puzzle is the rapid swings in public opinion often observed after the president of the United States delivers a speech devoted to a single issue, particularly a foreign policy issue. Public opinion is most volatile on issues that seem (a) distant in terms of their likely effects on people and (b) not especially susceptible to citizen influence. Americans often praise presidents for their ability to move public opinion, not recognizing that on some issues a somewhat mindless "follow the leader" mentality is at work, so that a president would be successful in moving public opinion in any direction, assuming the White House is able to present the issue as beneficial to both the president's and citizens' objectives.

The rationale underlying the mushiness index did not originate with Yankelovich, Skelly, and White. More than fifty years ago George Gallup

(1947) espoused survey designs that measured multiple aspects of a person's opinion. Indeed, Schuman and Presser (1981) and other investigators have emphasized the need to measure the importance of an issue to a person, as well as his or her opinion about it, to better understand the dynamics of attitude change. Yankelovich, Skelly, and White did, however, have the public relations acumen to coin a catchy phrase for their finding, which built on the results of earlier public opinion studies.

One suspects many survey questions of deserving high mushiness scores, but unfortunately those scores will not be calculated because, faced with insufficient time and space on the survey, researchers will not ask the necessary follow-up questions. Thus poll users need to ask themselves whether the topic of a survey is likely to be of concern to respondents or whether they will see it as an abstraction with little immediate and practical relevance. If the former, mushiness and nonattitudes are not likely to be a serious problem. A complicating factor is that the topic of a survey is likely to be of varying importance to different segments of the American population. Unemployed steelworkers and autoworkers are more likely to be concerned about foreign imports and thus to have more stable attitudes about them than, say, college students. Senior citizens are more likely to have well-developed views on Social Security and Medicare than a youthful population group. American public opinion on a particular issue includes the rather divergent views of various subgroups of the population, some of whom have genuine attitudes on the issue while others do not. Moreover, for those seeking to relate public opinion to the processes and decisions of government, the whole of public opinion may be less important than the opinion of a particular subset of people. On certain issues the views of a few people with genuine attitudes may have the greatest impact on government policy and policymakers.

Implications for Democracy and Public Policy

There is growing debate about how serious the problem of nonattitudes is in public opinion polling. Although there is widespread agreement that the American populace (or substantial portions of it) is poorly informed on many aspects of politics and public life (Delli Carpini and Keeter, 1991, 1996; Alvarez and Brehm, 2002), there are differing conclusions about what that ignorance about particular topics means for public opinion polling and for the functioning of a democracy. Some blame citizens for their disengagement and low information levels and wonder whether poll results can really tell us anything meaningful about citizens' policy preferences on some matters. Others say that part of the blame must be shared by the methods of polling, which do not provide citizens a full opportunity to elaborate on their preferences and opinions. Other scholars try to resolve this by partitioning the citizenry into separate groups defined by differing levels of political knowledge and then determining what impact those varying knowledge levels have on opinion formation and opinion stability. For example, Gilens (2001) distinguishes between general political knowledge and policy-specific information and examines their impact on the policy views of Americans. He observes that ignorance of policy-specific information leads many citizens to hold political views different from what they would profess had they acquired policy-specific knowledge. But he finds that the impact of policy-specific information is greatest for Americans with the highest levels of general knowledge; it is those citizens who are most likely to incorporate new information into their political judgments and perhaps change their views. In this situation, attitude change is not response instability and evidence of nonattitudes but instead is an indicator of "learning" upon receipt and incorporation of new information.

In a related vein, a study of the 1997 Canadian election took advantage of the fact that three of the political party leaders were new to the national scene; there thus appeared the opportunity to study the impact of learning on public attitudes toward them (Blais 2000). In a poll conducted prior to the election, respondents were asked whether they knew a lot, a little, or nothing at all about each of the leaders. In another survey conducted after the election, the same respondents (including those who earlier claimed they knew nothing about the leaders) were asked whether they liked or disliked each leader. One basic finding was that on average 74 percent of the Canadian respondents who indicated they were uninformed about a leader were willing and able to offer an opinion about that person, a reflection of the tendency of people to provide answers even when they have a meager knowledge base. Nevertheless, the expressed likes and dislikes about a leader did have a predictable impact on vote choice, more so for the most knowledgeable respondents but also for the least knowledgeable. The authors concluded that the least informed respondents were not answering randomly and expressing nonattitudes but instead were providing a meaningful rating of the leaders.

My own view (shared by Perlmutter [2002] and many others) is that Americans express opinions on many things, even when they have little information, and that the very act of polling and asking questions often creates opinions that might not otherwise be evident. The seriousness of the nonattitudes problem is partially a function of the purpose for which the polling results are being used. If one is merely describing the distribution of

Americans' responses to some survey item, then the presence of some nonattitude responses in that distribution is not very worrisome. But if the poll results are being used to justify the adoption, continuation, modification, or elimination of some policy or program, then nonattitude responses are a more serious problem. And because descriptive polls are often exploited and distorted in policy arguments, the problem of nonattitudes must remain a concern. When we hear policy advocates cite reputable polls showing that Americans favor peacekeeping in Liberia, expanded free trade agreements, negotiations with North Korea, or greater engagement in various regions throughout the world, we must wonder how careful the investigators were to minimize the problem of nonattitudes during the data collection stage and how sensitive they were to the problem in publicly reporting their results. And lest readers believe that the problem of nonattitudes arises only in the context of foreign policy and international affairs, let me conclude this section with a discussion of a state-level poll. In 2001, a statewide poll was conducted in Ohio about citizens' support for passenger train service (Williams 2001). The two key items in the survey were the following:

Ohio officials have considered promoting the development of passenger-train services. Do you strongly favor, favor, neither favor nor oppose, oppose, or strongly oppose passenger-train services in Ohio?

Strongly favor	30%
Favor	50%
Neither favor nor oppose	11%
Oppose	5%
Strongly oppose	1%
Refused to answer	0%
Don't know	3%

If you were considering a trip to somewhere 75 to 300 miles away from home, and a fast, modern rail system was available in Ohio, how likely is it you would consider traveling by train?

Very likely	47%
Somewhat likely	37%
Somewhat unlikely	6%
Very unlikely	9%
Refused to answer	0%
Don't know	1%

Proponents of passenger rail service trumpeted the poll results. Bill Hutchison, president of the Ohio Association of Railroad Passengers, a sponsor of the study, said,

We had an idea that people were supportive [of rail] but had no way to back up that assertion. Mobility is being threatened by a transportation system that has all the balance of a two-legged stool. A third leg needs to be added, and that leg is rail passenger service. We hope public officials, community leaders and others will pay close attention to the results of this survey. (Williams 2001)

Clearly the advocates of passenger rail wanted to use the poll results to help make the case for their cause. Why might citizens be wary of how the poll was used by advocates of passenger rail?

First, there was no screening question used to try to weed out respondents who really had not thought about the issue. Second, the wording of the first question did not offer a "don't know" alternative but instead pushed respondents into one of the five mentioned categories. Third, the wording of the second question is somewhat suspect inasmuch as it asks respondents how likely it is that they would *consider* traveling by train and not the more direct question of how likely it is that they would travel by train. The question was also a bit leading and argumentative in its reference to a "fast, modern rail system." Fourth, there are probably insufficient items to measure the many aspects of passenger rail service, including how passenger rail would be funded. There was only one question in the survey about funding; it asked respondents which of four revenue sources they preferred: using state general revenue funds such as sales taxes (24 percent), borrowing money through a state bond issue (23 percent), raising the state gasoline tax by a penny per gallon (21 percent), or taking money from highway and transportation funds (19 percent). This is not a bad question, but it makes paying for passenger rail seem fairly easy to accomplish without much burden to the citizenry. The question does not truly tap how willing Ohioans are to spend more for passenger rail service or to take dollars from other programs to pay for it. Overall, the survey makes it easy for Ohioans to endorse passenger rail; after all, who would be against rail service if it could be established so easily? There are likely many nonattitudes in the responses; at minimum, the results seem to be a good candidate for a "mushiness" evaluation. The bottom line is that the poll results are being used to influence the outcome of a public policy debate on passenger rail.

Conclusion

The problem of nonattitudes remains one of the least considered aspects of public opinion polling. Other facets of public opinion research, such as question wording and sampling, receive much more attention, even to the point of being mentioned in television and newspaper reports of public opinion polls. But very few people raise the fundamental questions: Was the topic of the survey of interest to the respondents? Did the poll query people on topics about which they held genuine views? Did the survey questions adequately capture the complexity of the issue being studied?

Assessing the size of the problem of nonattitudes is a difficult task made even more so by the tendency of people to respond to questions not in terms of the questions' actual purpose and content but in terms of the cues that the questions provide and whatever meaning (often idiosyncratic) respondents read into them. For example, a person who is asked whether she favors selling military equipment to Saudi Arabia might answer the question not on the basis of any knowledge about Saudi Arabia but on the basis of a predisposition toward the weapons industry in general (she might be a stockholder in a firm that manufactures weapons). Citizens asked whether they favor joint U.S.-Russian space ventures might respond on the basis of their underlying view of Russia rather than on the basis of opinions about the best way to explore space.

Although nonattitudes can be a polling problem, Americans should not disregard polls, because on many issues the general public has genuine attitudes and is willing and able to express them. Only a small subset of the public may have real opinions on other issues, but even then events may transform such an issue into one that engages the serious attention of the mass public. Sometimes the public may even seem fickle on the issues it cares about and its positions on them. For example, Oreskes (1990) observed that in 1989, 64 percent of Americans said the drug problem was the most important one facing the nation. Yet a year later only 10 percent cited drugs as the most serious problem. Certainly it was not victory in the drug war that led citizens to downgrade the importance of the drug problem. Instead, it was more a matter of media and presidential emphasis. When the media and the president focused on the drug menace, then many Americans saw the issue as the critical one facing the nation. But as new issues arose and media and political attention shifted, Americans' views of which issues were critical also changed.

Nonattitudes are more a problem of the respondent than of the measuring instrument—that is, nonattitudes can arise even when a question is carefully constructed without any loaded words or implied alternatives. Nevertheless, deficiencies in the questions themselves can contribute to the problem of nonattitudes, as well as to many other difficulties encountered in public opinion polling. In the next chapter we take a closer look at how question wording, question order, and question context can affect the results of public opinion polls.

Exercises

1. In the first and second exercises in chapter 1, you were asked to keep a log of newspaper and newsmagazine polls. Now examine the subject matter of those polls and make your own judgment about whether nonattitudes are likely to be a problem. Then examine the actual wording of the questions (where available) to see whether screening questions were used and whether the "don't know" alternative was explicitly included.
2. Design a five-item survey on some aspect of popular culture that you believe would generate genuine attitudes among a sample of college students but would produce many nonattitudes among a sample of the parents of college students.
3. Go to the Web site of any polling organization, such as Gallup, Harris Interactive, or PIPA, and look for a summary report or press release on any poll dealing with foreign policy and international affairs other than Iraq and the war on terrorism. Examine that report or press release and draw your own conclusions about whether nonattitudes are likely to be a problem.

3 Wording and Context of Questions

Of all the pitfalls associated with public opinion polling, question wording is probably the one most familiar to consumers of public opinion research. The use of a loaded word or an inflammatory phrase can affect the pattern of responses to a survey question. For example, for a poll to show weak support for federal assistance to financially beleaguered entities (such as the savings and loan industry in the 1990s), the pollster need only ask Americans whether they favor a federal "bailout" of those entities. Few people favor a bailout, but many more support federal loans with proper safeguards that the moneys will be repaid. A poll likely to indicate scant support for providing foreign aid will ask an argumentative and leading question such as, Do you favor giving foreign aid to other nations when there are children in the United States who are suffering from hunger? To demonstrate support for foreign aid, a pollster could "load" the question differently: Do you favor giving foreign aid to other nations to help them resist terrorism and thereby enhance our own national security?

Individuals and groups with an ax to grind can easily construct questions that will generate the responses they want. The response alternatives they provide the interviewees also can help them achieve the intended result. As noted in chapter 2, if a middle alternative is not listed as one of the choices, fewer citizens will opt for that choice, and that can alter the interpretation of a poll. For example, if a mayor wants a poll to indicate support for a city's spending policies on garbage collection, he or she might ask this question: Do you think the city is spending too much, too little, or about the right amount on garbage collection? Clearly, the response "about the right amount" is an endorsement of the mayor's current policies, and its inclusion as an explicit response alternative will provide a portrait of public opinion more supportive of the mayor's policies.

If an advocacy group wants to demonstrate through public opinion surveys that its issues are at the forefront of citizens' concerns, it might simply commission polls that ask citizens to select from a list of problems the most important one facing the nation, and place that group's issue on the list among a group of relatively minor problems. For example, if an environmental group wanted to demonstrate the importance of the environment, it might ask Americans which of the following is the most important problem facing the nation: environmental quality, excessive telemarketing, traffic congestion, and ticket scalping at entertainment events. Undoubtedly, this survey would discover that environmental quality was the number one issue cited. But what if the environmental group presented the results of this rather silly example without providing the actual question wording and response alternatives? Citizens might mistakenly assume that education, national defense, Social Security, health care, and other prominent issues were on the list and that environmental quality came out on top in competition with all of those other major issues.

Even when the sponsor has no obvious ax to grind, question wording choices greatly influence the results obtained. In many instances highly reputable polling organizations have arrived at divergent conclusions simply because they employed different (although well-constructed) questions on a particular topic.

Less obvious than the impact of question wording is the effect on responses of the order and context in which specific questions are placed. A typical public opinion survey includes many questions, and the placement of a particular question can affect the responses to it. Yet most consumers of public opinion research know little about item order and therefore have little sense of how the context has helped to shape the responses.

Consider the following hypothetical example—a survey assessing popular attitudes toward economic relations with China. The key question measuring support for most-favored-nation trade status for China is preceded by a battery of items about Chinese human rights violations. Obviously, the early questions on Chinese human rights violations will predispose respondents to be more hostile toward granting China favorable trade conditions. Or imagine a survey in which the popularity of the president is measured after a series of questions dealing with administration scandals and difficulties with the economy and Congress. Reactions to the president will be more negative when respondents are first reminded of these problems.

It will become clear that some "question effects" are obvious and therefore less likely to mislead people, whereas others are subtle and more problematic and may indeed manipulate and mislead unsuspecting consumers of public opinion research.

Question Wording

Five decades ago Stanley Payne wrote *The Art of Asking Questions,* a fundamental work on interviewing techniques. In the final chapter he presented a checklist of one hundred considerations, organized around themes such as the topic being studied, the structure of the question and the response alternatives, the treatment of the respondents, the words themselves, sources of bias, and the readability of the questions. Most of what Payne said then still holds true today and demonstrates that constructing good questions is largely a matter of common sense (Payne 1951).

Some problems with the wording of questions are obvious and may even be intentional, particularly in pseudopolls whose sponsors are seeking specific results. Clearly, the use of loaded words will affect the results. For example, referring to labor union officials as union czars or union bosses, rather than union leaders, will certainly affect opinions about union officials. Questions also can be argumentative, pushing respondents in a particular direction. For example, the American Foundation for AIDS Research asked the following question in 1994:

> The AIDS epidemic is a national emergency. It has already claimed over 180,000 lives in the U.S. alone. Over one and a half million Americans now carry the AIDS virus. Do you think the majority of Americans realize how widespread this tragedy has become, and that the worst is still ahead?

Note that this is a compound question. It asks about two topics—the extent of the epidemic and its future—yet the respondent is not allowed to distinguish between the two. Sometimes compound questions are more disguised, so that the duality of the item is not evident until one interprets the responses. Classic examples are such questions as, Do you still beat your spouse? Have you stopped using illegal drugs? Either a yes or a no answer to these questions leaves the impression that at some point respondents beat their spouses and used illegal drugs. Obviously, the solution here is to use two questions: Did you ever use illegal drugs in the past? Are you currently using illegal drugs?

Problems with Wording in Straightforward, Factual Questions

Wording problems can arise on routine topics in legitimate surveys. Seemingly straightforward questions that employ relatively simple language can seem ambiguous to respondents. Even basic questions about the number of persons in a household or the number of children in a fam-

FRANK AND ERNEST ©by Bob Thaves

IT SEEMS TO ME THAT "HOW MANY IN YOUR HOUSEHOLD?" WOULD BE A SIMPLE QUESTION TO ANSWER, DR. JEKYLL.

POLL

© 1985 by NEA INC   THAVES 12-3

FRANK & ERNEST reprinted by permission of Newspaper Enterprise Association, Inc.

ily can present difficulties. For example, in surveys in which the wife and husband were interviewed independently, their responses did not agree perfectly about such factual items as the number of children they had (Asher 1974b). Perhaps errors were made in transcribing their responses. Or perhaps the question was ambiguous. One spouse might have responded in terms of children living at home; the other in terms of the total number. Or one spouse might have included children from a previous marriage, and the other might not have. Martin (1999) found that respondents' reports of who lived in a household are generally accurate except when the household members are not continually present, such as students, or are away periodically, perhaps for work-related reasons. Martin estimated that up to four million people nationally might be overlooked because of problems in reporting household members. Measurement of a respondent's age also has proven surprisingly problematic. Peterson (1984) showed that four different ways of measuring age in a survey yield substantially different refusal rates (that is, percentages of respondents refusing to answer the question), although the age data obtained were very similar across the four formats. Harker (1998) found that two different ways of measuring a person's income do not affect the response rates but do yield different reports of income levels. Finally, the simple way in which older surveys categorized race—white, black, and other—may no longer suffice as the United States becomes more racially and ethnically diverse and more citizens have multiracial backgrounds. The 2000 Census allowed Americans to identify with more than one race. And in 2003 Californians defeated a ballot proposition that would have banned the collection of data on race.

Fowler (1992) argues that survey questions, even apparently straightforward ones, must be adequately pretested before they are included in an actual poll. He discusses seven questions—used in national health surveys—that were subjected to extensive pretesting and found to have a number of ambiguous terms. For example, the very simple question, "Do you exercise or play sports regularly?" was found to be ambiguous because different respondents had different views on what constituted exercise. The question was then modified to read, "Do you do any sports or hobbies involving physical activities, or any exercise, including walking, on a regular basis?"

Imagine the ambiguity that can arise from the simple question, "Have you taken a vacation in the last few years?" Does "last few years" mean one or two years? Or could it mean three, four, or five years to some respondents? And what constitutes a vacation—going somewhere? Or does staying at home by the swimming pool count?

If question wording can affect measurement of objective matters such as a person's age and the number of children in a family, then how much might wording affect more subjective phenomena? The answer is that wording can make a great difference. In 1982 the Advisory Commission on Intergovernmental Relations sponsored three surveys asking Americans which services they would cut if funds were short (Herbers 1982). One question asked, "Suppose the budgets of your state and local governments have to be curtailed, which of these parts would you limit most severely?" About 8 percent of the respondents cited "aid to the needy" when that response was listed as one of the service areas that could be cut. But when the term "public welfare programs" was used in place of "aid to the needy" and the other choices remained the same, many more respondents (39 percent) opted to cut welfare. Obviously, "aid to the needy" is much more popular than "public welfare," and the program label used in the survey strongly influenced the results. In fact, Americans tend to complain about welfare in general but be highly supportive of specific programs that could justifiably be included under the rubric of welfare.

Double Negative Questions

One general rule in constructing survey questions is to avoid double negatives. Yet such a mistake was made in a 1992 poll that the Roper organization conducted for the American Jewish Committee, on the Holocaust. The results of the poll and the subsequent media coverage generated controversy and consternation (Kifner 1994; Ladd 1994; Moore and Newport 1994; Morin 1994c, 1994d). The Roper question asked, "Does it seem possible or does it seem impossible to you that the Nazi extermination of the Jews never happened?" Fully 22 percent of the respondents said that it seemed possible that the Holocaust never occurred, and another 12 percent did not know. When these results became known, many people expressed shock and concern about American ignorance of the Holocaust and fears about the success of anti-Semitic revisionist historians. But it turned out that the convoluted question was largely responsible for these results. The Roper organization itself was so dismayed that such a poorly worded question had seen the light of day that it redid the survey for the American Jewish Committee. This time the question was: "Does it seem possible to you that the Nazi extermination of the Jews never happened, or do you feel certain that it happened?" With this wording, only 1 percent of respondents said it seemed possible that the Holocaust had never occurred. The Gallup Organization also tested the impact of alternative question wording and got results similar to Roper's (Ladd 1994). The pain and confusion caused by the first Roper question emphasize how careful one must be in wording questions.

Argumentative, Leading Questions

My favorite example of an argumentative question purporting to inform respondents comes from the 1982 Democratic primary race for governor in Ohio. Three major candidates were running: the former lieutenant governor, Richard Celeste; the incumbent attorney general, William Brown; and the former mayor of Cincinnati, Jerry Springer. The pollster for the attorney general included the following question in a statewide survey:

> As you may know, in 1974, Jerry Springer, who had gotten married six months earlier, was arrested on a morals charge with three women in a hotel room. He also used a bad check to pay for the women's services, and subsequently resigned as mayor of his city. Does this make you much more likely, somewhat more likely, somewhat less likely, or much less likely to support Jerry Springer for governor this year?

In addition to being factually incorrect on a number of points, this question was a blatant effort by the pollster to feed consumers information that would generate negative responses about a candidate and then use the replies for political purposes (see the discussion of push polling in chapter 7). In the context of the discussion of nonattitudes in chapter 2, this question was an attempt to create attitudes on the basis of the interview situation—something that can be done in a variety of ways. One technique is to present hypothetical situations to citizens and then ask them to react to those situations. More often than not, the information obtained is of dubious use because the hypothetical situations have forced the respondents into a world that has little real meaning for them.

The Impact of Response Alternatives

Sometimes the response alternatives that a question provides can affect survey results. For example, Kagay and Elder (1992) examined attitudes toward Clinton and Bush as measured in two July 1992 polls, one conducted by Gallup and the other by CBS News/New York Times. The Gallup poll asked voters if their opinions of a candidate were favorable or unfavorable; respondents could volunteer that they did not know enough to offer an opinion. By contrast, the CBS News/New York Times poll presented respondents four choices: favorable, not favorable, undecided, or haven't heard enough about a candidate to have an opinion. Needless to say, compared with the Gallup poll, the CBS News/New York Times poll found fewer Americans offering an opinion because it provided two opportunities for respondents to refuse to rate the candidates, and the Gallup poll provided no such opportunity. Thus the CBS News/New York Times poll found 36 percent of Americans favorable to Clinton, 24 percent unfavorable, 31 percent undecided, and 9 percent stating that they had not heard enough. The Gallup poll, by contrast, found 63 percent favorable toward Clinton, 25 percent unfavorable, and only 12 percent volunteering "don't know."

Morin (1993d) has shown that slight modifications in the choices presented in the standard presidential approval question can alter the results. The standard question reads, "Do you approve or disapprove of the job _____ is doing as president?" Respondents are next asked whether they strongly or somewhat approve or disapprove. Another way of asking the question is to combine opinion and intensity in one item: "Do you strongly approve, somewhat approve, somewhat disapprove or strongly disapprove of the job _____ is doing as president?" In Morin's study, conducted during the Clinton administration, the half of the sample that received the first wording gave Clinton a 53 percent approval rating and a 38 percent disapproval rating. But the other half of the sample, responding to the second version of the question, gave Clinton a 62 percent approval rating (the two approval responses combined) and a 32 percent disapproval rating (the two disapproval responses combined). A Time/CNN poll conducted in August 1994 asked Americans, "Who is more responsible for today's gridlock in government?" Respondents were offered only two choices—"Clinton" or "Republicans in Congress." "Democrats in Congress" was not an option, yet it was a logical possibility. In the results 48 percent of respondents blamed the Republicans, 32 percent blamed Clinton, and 12 percent volunteered that both were equally at fault. Democrats in Congress might have been tempted to trumpet these results, but it was clear that the results were partially a product of the choices provided to respondents.

Jeff MacNelly © 2001, Tribune Media Services, Inc. Reprinted with permission.

As the political parties jockeyed in 2000 and 2001 for political advantage in allocating the (now vanished) federal budget surplus, poll results again indicated that Americans' preferences looked different depending on how the alternatives were presented. For example, Stevenson (2000) asked citizens what they preferred "the leaders in Washington . . . do with the remainder of the surplus." Two alternatives were presented:

Should the money be used for a tax cut, or should it be used to fund new government programs?

Should the money be used for a tax cut, or should it be spent on programs for education, the environment, health care, crime-fighting and military defense?

For the first alternative, 60 percent of Americans favored a tax cut and 25 percent preferred spending on new programs. But for the second alternative, only 22 percent favored a tax cut and 69 percent supported spending for the listed programs. There is nothing necessarily inconsistent about these patterns of response because Americans may have felt that the "new programs" mentioned in the first alternative would be frivolous and not include the important, current programs mentioned in the second alternative. Whatever the case, the wording of the alternatives makes a major difference; support for tax cuts drops when the alternative is additional spending for specific programs and policies that Americans like. This pattern continued throughout 2002 and 2003, particularly when tax cuts were to be weighed against such programs as Social Security and Medicare or against such priorities as paying for the war in Iraq and the fight against terrorism.

Not only will the response alternatives explicitly offered to respondents affect the results of a poll, so too will the alternatives that are not offered. If respondents have to volunteer their preferred response because it was not explicitly included in the question, that will affect the pattern of responses, as shown earlier in our discussion of the presence or absence of a middle category or a "don't know" option. But it is also possible that the omitted alternative might be a much more substantive option. Solop and Kagen (2002) were critical of the polls conducted immediately after the September 11 terrorist attack on the United States, mainly because all of the options presented to Americans about how to respond were military in nature and did not include diplomatic, economic, or other countermeasures. They argued that a more complete portrait of American public opinion would have included those other possibilities.

Small Wording Changes Can Make a Big Difference

As the Republican Congress and President Clinton waged their budget battles in 1995 and 1996, both sides tried to spin poll results to their advantage, and both complained about how the media were reporting the polls. For example, in late 1995 the *New York Times* published poll results showing that Americans, by 67 percent to 27 percent, preferred not to cut Medicare in order to balance the budget, a result described as a setback for the GOP budget plan (Budiansky 1995). The Republicans cried foul, claiming that the polling question was unfair and inaccurate and that their plan did not cut Medicare but simply slowed its growth. A subsequent *Newsweek* poll that talked about "limits" on Medicare rather than "cuts"— and incorporated the GOP tax cut plan—found less opposition to the Republican budget plan; respondents opposed it by only 51 percent to 41 percent. Americans were swayed, then, by whether the focus was on cuts to Medicare or limits to Medicare.

Two other surveys tapping opinions about Medicare found the same thing (Morin 1995c). One survey asked Americans, "Would you favor or oppose major reductions in the rate of increase in Medicare spending to balance the federal budget?" Forty-four percent of respondents supported such reductions in Medicare to achieve a balanced budget. But in another national survey conducted a week later, only 22 percent of respondents agreed with the notion of "cutting Medicare benefits to reduce the budget deficit." It is no wonder that throughout the budget debate the GOP spin doctors were encouraging Republican members of Congress to talk about reducing the rate of growth in Medicare, while their Democratic counterparts were telling Democrats to talk loudly and often about cuts in Medicare (Kolbert 1995).

Another example of the impact of question wording appeared in the furor over the impeachment of President Clinton, presumably a topic about which Americans were informed and felt strongly (whatever their preferences), and therefore one on which question wording was likely to have fewer effects. But even here the wording effects were dramatic, as summarized by Morin (1999a), who reviewed several polls. A *Washington Post*/ABC News poll asked half of a sample of Americans whether Clinton should resign if he were impeached or whether he should "fight the charges in the Senate." The other half of the sample was asked whether Clinton should resign if impeached or whether he should "remain in office and face trial in the Senate." Fifty-nine percent said Clinton should resign rather than fight the charges, but only 43 percent said he should resign rather than face a Senate trial. Morin speculates that the key factor here is the word "fight" in the first alternative; Americans do not like political combat. The second alternative—face trial—is less threatening. An even more surprising result occurred when Americans were asked the following two, very similar questions in a *New York Times*/CBS News poll:

> If the full House votes to send impeachment articles to the Senate for a trial, then do you think it would be better for the country if Bill Clinton resigned from office, or not?

> If the full House votes to impeach Bill Clinton, then do you think it would be better for the country if Bill Clinton resigned from office, or not?

In response to the first question, 43 percent of the sample favored a presidential resignation; in response to the second, more than 60 percent favored resignation. Morin speculates that because the second question did not mention a trial, respondents may have thought that impeachment was equivalent to being found guilty, and thus that the president should resign. But the first question explicitly mentions a trial, which suggested that the process was not yet complete.

Branching and Labeling Effects

Branching and labeling can have a big effect on the apparent stability of attitudes (Krosnick and Berent 1993). *Branching* refers to the follow-up questions asked after an initial query is presented to respondents. For example, political scientists typically measure political party identification by a series of questions. The first simply ascertains whether a person is a Democrat, a Republican, or an independent. If respondents say "Democrat" or "Republican," they are then asked whether they are strong or not very strong Democrats or Republicans. If respondents say they are independents, they are then asked whether they lean toward the Democrats or the Republicans. Note that at each stage of the questioning, the response alternatives are *labeled*—that is, each response option is specified in words. *Unlabeled* options are said to be used when, for example, respondents are asked to place themselves on a scale that ranges from one to seven, where only the endpoints are labeled with words; this type of scale is often used to measure citizens' policy attitudes and positions. Social scientists have shown that political party loyalties seem to be more stable than citizens' policy attitudes. But Krosnick and Berent (1993) argue that that finding may simply stem from polls' measuring party identification by a labeled branching technique and assessing policy attitudes by an unlabeled procedure.

The Use of Multiple Items and Indexes

Often no single questionnaire item can adequately measure the multifaceted construct that a public opinion analyst is studying. The researcher therefore may ask a series of questions and combine the results into an index. For example, *political efficacy* is a concept that has long been of great interest to political scientists (Asher 1974a). It refers to a citizen's feelings of effectiveness in dealing with government. Early measures (since modified) of political efficacy generally relied on four statements:

1. I don't think public officials care much what people like me think.
2. Voting is the only way that people like me can have any say about how the government runs things.
3. Sometimes politics and government seem so complicated that a person like me can't really understand what's going on.
4. People like me don't have any say about what the government does.

These items usually appear in surveys in an agree/disagree format, with a "disagree" response representing the efficacious position on all four items. A researcher could construct an efficacy index by simply counting the number of items to which the respondent gave an efficacious answer. For the four statements just listed, three or four efficacious responses might be classified as high in efficacy, two efficacious answers as medium, and one or zero as low.

Doonesbury   BY GARRY TRUDEAU

DOONESBURY © (2001) G. B. Trudeau. Reprinted with permission of UNIVERSAL
PRESS SYNDICATE. All rights reserved.

The use of an index is justified on both substantive and methodological grounds (Asher 1974c). Substantively, the index does a better job of
representing the complexity of the concept being studied than any single
item could. Methodologically, the use of a multiple-item index can lessen
the harmful effects of the random measurement error that is present in survey data: Whenever a researcher measures opinions, the very process of
measurement may yield results that are not perfectly accurate. If the measurement error is random, the obtained results are just as likely to be above
or below the true value. Thus combining a number of items in an index will
tend to cancel out some of the random measurement error. However, consumers of public opinion polls are often not provided sufficient information
about the components of an index, including the actual wording of the
questions. Moreover, consumers are not informed about the ways in which
separate items relate to each other and how they are combined into an index; they often must accept on faith that the index has been constructed
properly, from individual items that themselves were appropriately
worded. Chapter 8 presents some substantive examples of situations in
which multiple items on a topic were available for analysis.

Question Order and Context

Question order can dramatically affect responses to survey items by al-
tering the framework and context within which a question is answered. An
excellent example of the effect of question order occurred in 1980 when
the Harris organization employed a "double vote" question to measure citizens' candidate preferences in the presidential primaries. Respondents
were asked at the beginning of the interview whether they intended to vote

for President Jimmy Carter or Sen. Edward Kennedy in the hotly contested Democratic nomination battle. Next followed questions about domestic and foreign policy, including items about inflation and the economy, American hostages in Iran, and the Soviet invasion of Afghanistan. Toward the end of the interview, the respondents were again asked how they intended to vote. Surprisingly, over the course of the interview support for President Carter declined sharply. The only explanation for this drop was that as respondents thought about Carter's record, their views of him became more negative.

A similar phenomenon occurred in an ABC News/*Washington Post* study of the placement of a presidential popularity question in a survey (Sussman 1984a). In November 1983 a sample of Americans was asked about presidential popularity twice, once at the beginning of the interview and again at the end, with a variety of issue questions in between. Unlike the preceding example of Kennedy versus Carter, there was very little difference in the overall distribution of the responses at the two time points. Initially, 59 percent approved of the president's performance, 37 percent disapproved, and 4 percent had no opinion. Later, 59 percent approved, 39 percent disapproved, and 2 percent had no opinion. Not obvious from these figures, however, is that more than 15 percent of those sampled changed their opinion about the president over the course of the twenty-minute interview; 8 percent moved from approval to disapproval and 7 percent moved the opposite way.

A national poll conducted in 2002 further demonstrated the impact of question order (Morin 2002). Among the questions in the survey were two standard ones: whether Americans thought the country was headed in the right or wrong direction and whether they approved or disapproved of the job that George W. Bush was doing as president. For half the sample, the Bush performance question was asked first; for the other half the "direction of the country" item was asked prior to the Bush approval question. It turned out that asking the Bush approval question first (the president's poll ratings were very high) increased the percentage of Americans who thought the country was headed in the right direction from 34 percent to 42 percent. But when citizens were first asked about the state of the country (they were not that positive) and then asked about Bush, his job approval rating fell by about 6 percent. Clearly, the response to the first question conditioned the response to the second.

Many researchers have studied the effects of question order and context. Schuman and Presser (1981) demonstrated that effects of question order are important—particularly when the questions are general, somewhat amorphous, and have little direct relevance to respondents—and they recommend that anyone examining the distribution of responses to identical questions asked at different times take into account whether the contexts in which the questions were asked also were identical. The significance of this point is supported by the work of Bishop, Oldendick, and Tuchfarber (1982). They argue that the decline in Americans' level of political interest that a 1978 survey uncovered was partly attributable to changes in the context and order in which questions were asked; the real decline in political interest was not nearly as worrisome as originally thought.

The ability of one question to affect responses to another has been demonstrated by Hyman and Sheatsley (1950), Schuman and Presser (1981), and Schuman, Kalton, and Ludwig (1983). Those studies examined responses to the following two items:

> Do you think the United States should let Communist newspaper reporters from other countries come in here and send back to their papers the news as they see it?

> Do you think a Communist country like Russia should let American newspaper reporters come in and send back to America the news as they see it?

When these two questions were asked in the order just given, support for letting communist reporters come to the United States was much lower than when the questions were asked in the reverse order. The explanation for this pattern seems clear: it was difficult for respondents to deny communist reporters the opportunity to come to the United States if they had already said that American reporters should be allowed to go to the Soviet Union. This effect of context is strong when the questions are contiguous in a survey, but it remains strong even when the items are separated by many other questions.

Another example of context effects is provided by Schuman, Presser, and Ludwig (1981), who studied the consequences of different orderings of a general and a specific question on abortion. Their items read:

> Do you think it should be possible for a pregnant woman to obtain a legal abortion if she is married and does not want any more children? [general]

> Do you think it should be possible for a pregnant woman to obtain a legal abortion if there is a strong chance of serious defect in the baby? [specific]

The authors found that responses to the general item were very much influenced by whether it came first or second—that is, support for abortion in general was much higher when the general item came first. Responses to the specific question were not affected by item order. Their explanation for this finding, although speculative, suggests the kinds of cognitive calculations that may shape a response:

> One plausible explanation for the effect turns on the fact that there are a number of different reasons for supporting legalized abortion. A possible defect in an unborn child is a specific reason that appeals to a large part of the population. When the more general item is asked first, some respondents may say yes but mainly with such a specific reason in mind. When the item on abortion because of a defective child is asked first, however, this indicates to respondents that the general item that follows does not refer to that specific case. Thus respondents who are reluctant to favor abortion except within narrow limits should find it easier to oppose the general rationale after having favored (and "subtracted") the more specific rationale about the defective child. (Schuman, Presser, and Ludwig 1981, 220)

In contrast to the example about communist reporters, in which a particular question order promoted consistency, here a particular ordering generated divergence because some respondents favored abortion in the specific case but opposed it more generally.

Sometimes poll respondents are asked comparative questions: Do you prefer X to Y? or Do you favor A over B? Research indicates that the order in which the alternatives are presented may affect the results—that is, asking respondents whether they prefer X to Y versus asking them whether they prefer Y to X may generate different results (Wanke, Schwarz, and Noelle-Neumann 1995; Wanke 1996). For example, Wanke et al. asked samples the following questions:

> Would you say that traffic contributes more or less to air pollution than industry?

> Would you say the industry contributes more or less to air pollution than traffic?

When traffic was mentioned first, 45 percent of respondents said that "traffic contributes more" and 32 percent said "industry contributes more." But when industry was mentioned first, 57 percent stated that "industry contributes more," compared with 24 percent who cited traffic. Evidently, in these kinds of comparison questions people focus on the first item. In other words, asking people to compare X and Y essentially becomes a judgment on X, with many aspects of Y ignored. If so, the responses to the pollution questions are not that surprising. For the consumer of polls, the order of the items being compared becomes one more consideration in assessing the accuracy of poll results.

A final example of the effects of question order is taken from an analysis by Abramson, Silver, and Anderson (1987). They were puzzled to find that between 1980 and 1984 the percentage of citizens disagreeing with the statement, "If a person doesn't care how an election comes out then that person shouldn't vote in it" dropped from 58.7 percent to 42.8 percent. This statement was one of four items that had traditionally been used to measure feelings of citizen duty. In surveys before 1984 the item had been preceded by two related statements with which Americans typically expressed high levels of disagreement. But in 1984 the item, although identical to earlier versions, was not preceded by the other two questions. Abramson and his colleagues provide convincing evidence that the apparent decline in citizens' feelings of duty between 1980 and 1984 was not real but was instead a consequence of the different questions that preceded this item in the survey. The lesson here is that before the users of polls conclude on the basis of survey data that an attitude change has occurred over time, they must be able to rule out other explanations for change, such as differences in question wording and question order.

Order and Context Effects in Self-Administered Surveys

Assessments of the effects of question order and context are more problematic for self-administered mail and Internet surveys than for telephone and personal surveys. In telephone and personal surveys, the interviewer controls the order in which respondents are given the questions, and the order is consistent across respondents. But for self-administered mail questionnaires and many self-administered Internet surveys, respondents can answer the questions sequentially, they can read the entire questionnaire first, they can jump around and answer questions out of order, and they can go back and change answers after responding to other questions. It is possible to construct Internet surveys so that the questions are presented to respondents in a well-defined order, but many Internet surveys, especially the Internet pseudopolls, do not do this. There is evidence that in some instances question order is less consequential in self-administered mail surveys because respondents are likely to read all the questions before responding or respondents can change answers after reading later questions (Schwarz and Hippler 1995). Thus perhaps in the earlier example about American and Russian reporters the order of the two questions would be less important in a mail survey because respondents may have read both questions, whatever their order, before answering the questions. Or respondents could have changed their responses when they realized they were being inconsistent by supporting freedom for American reporters in Russia but opposing freedom for Russian reporters in the United States.

Other Meanings of Context

Although the ordering of specific survey items among other questions is considered context, "context" also refers to the substantive framework within which questions appear. Pollsters can choose the framework within which they ask questions, and the choice can be very consequential. A survey about the U.S. military buildup posed in the context of the successful military campaign in Iraq would probably elicit more supportive attitudes toward defense spending than a similar survey framed in the context of the huge national debt. In their work on white Americans' attitudes toward affirmative action, Kinder and Sanders (1986) found clear differences in the factors that affect opinion depending on whether the questions were presented in the context of reverse discrimination (affirmative action discriminates against whites) or in the context of undeserved advantage (affirmative action gives blacks advantages they have not earned). For example, whites' opinions were more racially motivated when affirmative action was placed in the context of undeserved advantage.

"Context" can also refer to the broader environment in which an interview is occurring. Personal circumstances, recent societal events, and the content of media coverage can alter the meaning of a survey question for respondents. An identically worded question can mean dramatically different things to respondents depending on the frame of reference they bring to the interview situation, and that includes the broader social and political context at the time of the interview. For example, in their review of surveys on sexual behavior Michaels and Giami (1999) found major changes in how sexual activity and sexual relationships have been conceptualized and studied over time. Whereas surveys prior to the 1970s often linked heterosexual intercourse to marriage, more recently questions on sexual behavior accommodate other kinds of relationships and other sexual behaviors, as societal mores and practices have changed.

One dramatic example of the impact of societal context on poll responses occurred in mid-2003 after the U.S. Supreme Court decision striking down the Texas antisodomy law and affirming the privacy rights of gay adults. The decision was a victory for gay rights, but speculation about what it meant for a whole host of issues, such as gay marriage and gay adoption, went well beyond anything that could reasonably be construed from the case. There was widespread media coverage of gay marriage, for example. Although the Supreme Court decision was favorable to the gay community, public opinion polls conducted weeks and months after the ruling showed a decline in support for gay rights. For example, a Gallup poll (Newport 2003) conducted in May 2003, prior to the Court's ruling, asked Americans, "Do you think homosexual relations between consenting adults should or should not be legal?" A record high 60 percent thought that such relations should be legal. But when the same question was asked in two separate polls in July 2003 (after the Court decision and all its attendant controversy), the level of support for legal homosexual relations had dropped to 50 percent and 48 percent. Similar changes occurred on other survey items. Whereas 54 percent of the May sample thought that homosexuality should be considered an acceptable alternative lifestyle, only 46 percent of the July sample thought so. Support for a right of homosexual couples to legally form civil unions fell from 49 percent in May to 40 percent in July.

What can explain these changes in opinion? One possibility is chance variations among samples, but the declines are statistically significant, exceeding sampling error. More likely the reason is that the July surveys were asked in a different political and social context than the May survey. In May, gay rights were not a prominent topic in the news, on talk shows, and in public discussion. But after the extensive coverage of the decision and its potential ramifications, gay issues were prominent on the agenda. Perhaps for some Americans it was easier to support gay rights as an abstraction in May than as a real possibility in July. Perhaps the scenarios that opponents of the Court decision presented convinced others to change their views. Whatever the case, surely the political and social context had changed. A parallel situation occurred with respect to attitudes about war with Iraq. It is one thing to query Americans prospectively in the prewar era about what the United States should do; at that stage, American opinions were more scattered, with support for a variety of diplomatic, economic, and military measures. But once war began, support for the military option soared. The prewar period was a very different environment in which to conduct polls than was wartime.

Conclusion

For several reasons, citizens are in a better position to evaluate the effects of question wording than they are to assess the consequences of question order. Indeed, much of what is involved in question wording is common sense; people often recognize easily that a question is worded in a misleading and loaded fashion. News reports of survey results often provide the wording of the survey questions. Newspaper and television reports give consumers no information about the overall structure and content of the survey, however (although the major news organizations are very willing to mail the complete report of a poll to interested citizens who request it). Because information is limited, then, citizens normally do not have any basis to judge whether the responses to a particular item have been affected by its placement within the questionnaire. Moreover, the effects of question order and context are likely to be subtle.

Fortunately, polling organizations are becoming more sensitive to the consequences of question order, and survey research textbooks are at last addressing the problem in more detail. Today reputable pollsters give more attention to effects of context and are more likely to inform the consumers of their polls about the potential consequences of question order. Nevertheless, it remains quite easy for the unscrupulous pollster, intent on generating a preferred response to a particular question, to manipulate the public by embedding that question in a survey in such a way as to yield the desired answer.

Exercises

1. Construct a ten-item poll designed to maximize the popularity of President Bush as measured by the question, "Do you approve or disapprove of the job that George Bush is doing as President?" Accomplish this by your selection and placement of items. Each question must be worded fairly and accurately; there must be no loaded words, inaccurate statements, and the like. You must manipulate the results by your careful choice of topics and how you order them.
2. Repeat exercise 1, but now maximize the unpopularity of the president.
3. Construct a ten-item poll designed to maximize the popularity of President Bush, using the same approval/disapproval question, but this time using loaded, misleading questions.
4. Repeat exercise 3, but now maximize the unpopularity of the president.

✓ 4 Sampling Techniques

Of the many aspects of public opinion polling, sampling arouses the greatest skepticism among Americans. One source of the skepticism is the actual composition of the sample, as reflected in the plaintive question, "How come no one has asked me my opinion on that issue?"

An experience I had in October 1984 exemplifies Americans' suspicion of polls. I was to speak about the upcoming presidential election before a group of about seventy labor union leaders. As he introduced me, the president of the Ohio AFL-CIO, who was obviously disturbed by national polls showing Democratic nominee Walter Mondale badly trailing President Ronald Reagan, conducted his own two-part poll. He first asked the audience how many were for Mondale and how many supported Reagan. Everyone was for Mondale. He next asked how many people in the audience had been interviewed by national pollsters about their presidential preference. None had. He concluded by expressing disdain for the entire enterprise of polling. After that inauspicious introduction, he turned the platform over to me so that I might give my poll-based analysis of the 1984 campaign.

Sampling is the selection of a subset of respondents from a broader population. When the sampling process is conducted properly, the subset will be representative of that broader population. *Probability sampling* is typically cited as the number-one characteristic that makes a poll or survey scientific. Although all steps in the survey research process are critical, including measurement and question wording (chapter 3) and data collection procedures (chapter 5), it is probability sampling and statistical theory that enable one to determine sampling error, confidence levels, and the like, and to generalize from the results of the sample to the broader population from which it was selected. Other factors also come into play in making a survey scientific. One must also select a sample of sufficient size. If the sampling error is too large or the level of confidence too low, it will be difficult to make reasonably precise statements about characteristics of the population of interest to the pollster. A scientific poll will not only have a sufficiently large sample; it will also be sensitive to response rates. Very low response rates will raise questions about how representative and accurate the results are. Are there systematic differences between those who participated in the survey and those who, for whatever reason, did not participate? Sampling methods, sample size, and response rates will all be discussed in this chapter.

Sampling Designs

The aim of a good sampling design is to select a sample that is appropriate for the research topic and within the investigator's budget. Because it is impossible to interview an entire population—whether of the United States, of New York, of all doctors, or of all senior citizens—a researcher selects a sample. Typically the sample is of interest because of what it reveals about the overall population and not because of the actual sample characteristics themselves. Thus researchers try to select samples that accurately reflect the broader population from which they are drawn. The process can be carried out in a variety of ways, depending on the nature of the respondents, the objectives of the research, and the resources available to the investigator.

All of the designs discussed here are examples of *probability sampling,* the dominant and preferred mode of sampling public opinion. Probability samples have several advantages. Foremost, they tend to be more representative than other kinds of samples because they generally avoid the selection biases inherent in nonprobability samples, in which the investigator has discretion over who should be included.

Another advantage of probability samples is that they allow researchers to use statistical theory to ascertain the properties of the survey sample. One such property is the *sampling error*, which enables the investigator to estimate, with a certain level of confidence, how discrepant the sample results are from the true population values. The defining characteristic of a probability sample is that it permits the researcher to determine the probability of any single person's being selected for the sample. Nonprobability sampling does not enable one to determine the sampling error. For example, the television reporter who stands at a street corner and interviews people passing by to assess public opinion on an issue has selected a nonprobability sample. The reporter has no way of telling how representative these interviewees are or how accurate the sample results are. Radio call-in surveys also are based on nonprobability samples because the callers who choose to phone in may or may not be representative of the larger community. The questionnaires mailed by members of the U.S. House of Representatives to households in their districts exemplify a non-probability sampling procedure: Thousands of questionnaires may be returned, but there is no assurance that they constitute an accurate sample of the district. In these examples, selection biases affect who is included in the sample. And a similar situation holds with respect to those Internet surveys in which respondents select themselves to participate.

Simple Random and Systematic Sampling

In one method of probability sampling, simple random sampling, every element in the population has an equal chance of being selected for the sample. Moreover, every configuration of elements has the same chance of composing the sample. The chief requirement for simple random sampling is a list or an enumeration of the persons in the overall population. With such a list, the actual process of sampling is straightforward. The researcher assigns a unique number to each person and then selects a sample of these numbers. A primitive way of selecting the sample would be to put all the numbers in a hat, mix them up, and then draw the sample. A more likely method today is to use a table of computer-generated random numbers to select the sample. Simple random sampling is appropriate when a reasonably complete and current listing of the population is available.

Simple random sampling of individuals is not a feasible way to select a national sample of Americans. For one thing, no complete and up-to-date list of all Americans (not even the Census list) exists. But even if there were a good list, random sampling would not be useful, particularly if a researcher planned to interview respondents personally rather than on the telephone. Sending interviewers all over the country would make the cost of the poll prohibitive (see the discussion later in this chapter of cluster sampling techniques, which do allow the selection of samples from large geographical areas when personal interviewing is to be used).

Systematic sampling is a variant of random sampling: the researcher picks every nth name from the list, after picking the first name at random. For example, to select a sample of 500 students from a student directory of 25,000 names (a 2 percent or one-fiftieth sample), the researcher might first pick at random a number between one and fifty. If that number was twelve, the sample would consist of the twelfth name in the directory, the sixty-second name, and every fiftieth name thereafter.

Systematic sampling is easy to conduct. The only caution is that the list of names should have no cycle or periodicity to it, lest the skip interval coincide with the periodicity. Normally, names listed in alphabetical order present no problems of periodicity, as opposed to, say, a list in which male and female names alternate. In the latter case, if the skip interval was an even number, the sample would be composed entirely of either males or females, thus introducing a bias into the study. A less-obvious example of a periodicity problem might be a list of homes in a major housing development. Anyone picking a sample of homes in order to interview the owners would want to ensure that there was no special pattern in the listing. For example, if every tenth house on the list is on a corner lot, the researcher might inadvertently select a sample that includes only corner homes. That could introduce a serious bias to the study because corner-lot houses tend to be larger and more expensive, and thus owned by wealthier people, than houses on the rest of the block. In systematic sampling, every element in the population has an equal chance of being in the sample, as is the case in random sampling. But unlike random sampling, every configuration of elements does *not* have the same chance of composing the sample.

Stratified Sampling

The key characteristic of stratified sampling is that the population is divided into subsets, or strata, according to characteristics of interest to the investigator. After stratifying the population, researchers may sample randomly or systematically within the strata. For example, to interview a sample of members of the U.S. House of Representatives, one might first stratify the members according to political party affiliation (Democratic versus Republican) and seniority (for simplicity, high versus low), two characteristics of relevance to the research, rather than pick a random sample. This stratification creates four categories: high-seniority Democrats, low-seniority Democrats, high-seniority Republicans, and low-seniority Republicans. One would then sample within each of the strata.

Stratification guarantees that a sample will include a sufficient number of cases with characteristics of interest to the researcher, because he or she can determine the size of the sample within each stratum. The major advantages of stratified sampling are a reduction in sampling error and a guarantee of representativeness with respect to the variables used in stratifying. The reduction in sampling error occurs when the strata differ from each other but internally are relatively homogeneous. For example, a researcher seeking to compare the attitudes of northern and southern Republicans in Congress would find it more efficient to set up these strata and sample within them than to pick a sample from among all Republicans.

Cluster and Multistage Sampling

Cluster sampling entails multiple interviews within the same geographical area, typically a neighborhood. The advantage of cluster sampling is economic. It is expensive to support an interviewer in the field and to send that interviewer to a particular site to conduct an interview. The overall cost of a field survey is lower if the interviewer conducts multiple interviews at one site.

Cluster sampling is often part of a multistage sampling scheme employed by organizations that wish to interview personally a national sample of Americans. The Survey Research Center (SRC) of the University of Michigan is one such organization; it uses multistage sampling in which geographical areas, not individuals, are sampled at all stages except the last. Typically, the SRC's sample design selects a sample of counties; then within the sample of counties a sample of cities, townships, and unincorporated areas; then from the sample of cities, townships, and unincorporated areas a sample of city blocks and land tracts; and then a sample of residential dwellings located on the sampled blocks and land tracts. For example, Cook County, Illinois, might be included in the sample of counties; the city of Chicago might be selected within Cook County; a number of blocks would be selected from within Chicago; some dwelling units would be chosen from the selected blocks.

Note that up to this stage in the example geographical units and not individuals have been sampled. Sampling geographical units is relatively straightforward. It is easy to pick a sample of counties and a sample of localities within the counties because lists of counties and municipalities are readily available. Likewise, it is fairly easy to pick samples of blocks and dwelling units because local governments keep such information for the purpose of tax assessment. At each step in the typical multistage design, the probability of a geographical unit's being included in the sample is proportional to its population. Thus Cook County and Los Angeles County are almost certain to be included in a sample of counties, whereas sparsely populated rural counties will have very little chance of being included. A sample concentrated in the major metropolitan areas of the country helps to control the cost of supporting and transporting interview staff.

In cluster sampling, once interviewers arrive at selected dwelling units they consult the instructions given them to determine whom to interview; it is not left to their discretion. The instructions are usually couched in terms of the age and gender composition of the households in the dwelling unit. For example, an interviewer might be instructed to survey the oldest male or the second-oldest female in a household. Note that this information about the characteristics of individuals within the household does not have to be known to researchers earlier in the sampling process; indeed, this kind of sampling scheme requires no prior knowledge about individuals—information that can be difficult to acquire—but only knowledge about geographical entities, which is easily obtained.

Sampling Techniques for Telephone Interviewing

The sampling designs just described are the classic ones covered in most textbooks on survey research. They do not, however, include the dominant technique used by major polling organizations: telephone interviews. Telephone surveys offer several advantages. The first is speed: Often pollsters want to assess as quickly as possible the public's reaction to a major event, such as the presidential debates in 2000. In such situations, personal interviews and mailed questionnaires take too much time. A second advantage is that telephone interviews are substantially cheaper to conduct than personal interviews, yet they still enable the interviewer to collect detailed and pertinent information from respondents. Although respondents tend to become fatigued more quickly in a telephone interview than in a personal interview, there usually is enough time to collect a reasonably extensive set of responses. Third, in many instances a telephone interview has the virtue of being less threatening and intrusive to private citizens; they do not have to let a stranger into their home to participate in the interview.

At one time telephone-based samples were considered suspect because of class bias: poor families were less likely to have phones. Today, almost all Americans have home phones, and that makes telephone samples more appropriate, even though some class bias still exists. According to the 2000 Census, 97.6 percent of American households have telephone service, up from 94.8 percent in 1990. People without telephones are more likely to be uneducated, poor, in a minority group, of low occupational status, and living in a single-adult household.

In earlier years, telephone directories served as the basis for picking samples. Directories are still used today, particularly for local samples, but several problems are associated with their use. One is that telephone directories are always out of date because of the mobility of the U.S. population. Moreover, picking a national sample from telephone directories is a logistical nightmare—one would have to consult almost 5,000 directories. The most serious problem, however, is the popularity of unlisted telephone numbers. In 1996, an estimated 29.6 percent of American households had unlisted phone numbers, compared with only 21.8 percent in 1984 (Survey Sampling Inc. 1997). In some metropolitan areas, particularly in California, the percentage of households with unlisted phone numbers exceeded 60 percent.

Both Lavrakas (1987) and Piekarski (1989) refute the common assumption that upper-income white households are more likely to have unlisted telephone numbers. Instead, they find that unlisted households are more likely to be younger, unmarried, lower income, minority, less educated, and more mobile. National data confirm these patterns (*Genesys News* 1996). For example, Genesys found in 1996 that households headed by people eighteen to thirty-four years old had an unlisted rate of 51 percent, compared with 18.9 percent for those headed by persons over sixty-five. Black and Hispanic households had unlisted rates of 55.2 percent and 58 percent, respectively, compared with 31.2 percent for whites. Only 29.6 percent of homeowners had unlisted numbers, compared with 54.3 percent of renters. Lavrakas (1987, 33) cites a general rule: The farther from the central city a pollster samples, the more the proportion of households with unlisted phone numbers declines. He cites the Chicago area as an example, noting that within the city about 50 percent of households have unlisted numbers. Inner-ring suburbs have an unlisted number rate of about 20–30 percent, outer-ring suburbs a rate of 10–20 percent, and rural areas a rate of about 5 percent.

Households with unlisted numbers fall into two major categories: those that chose not to be listed and those that are unlisted because a change of residence resulted in a new telephone number unavailable to callers until publication of a new edition of the telephone book (telephone directories typically are published annually). There are differences between citizens who are unlisted through choice and those unlisted because of mobility. The "mobility unlisted" tend to be younger, more urban, lower income, and renters; the "choice unlisted" tend to be better off financially (Survey Sampling Inc. 1997). The third and smaller category of unlisted citizens is made up of subscribers who sporadically lose their telephone service because of financial problems and regain it later when their problems are resolved. In general, mobility increases the percentage of unlisted telephone numbers among all demographic groups (*Genesys News* 1996). For example, among households headed by persons eighteen to thirty-four years old the 51 percent unlisted rate increased to 69.9 percent among households that had moved in the past year. Likewise, the 18.9 percent unlisted rate for households headed by persons over age sixty-five soared to 54.2 percent for households that had moved in the past year.

One way around the problems inherent in the use of telephone directories is random-digit dialing, in which random numbers are generated to produce the telephone numbers to be called. In the simplest form of random-digit dialing, it is critical to know the area codes and exchanges (the first three digits in the seven-digit telephone number) in an area. Once this information has been collected, a computer random-number generator or a table of random numbers can be used to provide the last four digits of telephone numbers to be dialed. This procedure does result in unlisted numbers being reached, as evidenced by the surprised reactions of respondents who ask, "How did you get my number? It's unlisted!" When a residential household is reached through random-digit dialing, the interviewer does not automatically interview whoever answered the phone. Instead, interviewers typically first collect information about the number of adults in the household and the number of males and females. Then the interviewers must follow a set of instructions that tell them, for example, to interview the oldest male in the first household or the youngest female in the second household or the second-oldest male in the third household. The combination of random-digit dialing and the instructions about respondent selection generates a sample highly representative of American households. (For more information about actual telephone sampling designs, see Tucker, Lepkowski, and Piekarski 2002.)

Random-digit dialing has become more complicated with the revolution in communications technology. For example, more area codes are being added because of the proliferation of new telephone numbers. Typically, telephone service providers divide an existing area code region into two new regions, each with its own area code. Thus people may find themselves with a new area code but with the same seven-digit telephone number. Pollsters and samplers then need to update their area codes.

Many of the more than 40,000 phone numbers added daily in the United States are for cellular phones, faxes, pagers, and modems, as well as for the extra phone lines needed to accommodate talkative family members (Survey Sampling Inc. 1997). An increasing number of households in the United States have multiple phone numbers—and a greater chance of being selected for the sample. Today reputable pollsters correct their samples for this problem lest they introduce an affluence bias.

Another development on the horizon that may lessen some of the advantages of random-digit dialing is number portability (*Genesys Q & A* 1997). Currently, the three-digit exchange in a telephone number represents a well-defined geographical area within a community; a circumstance that can be useful to pollsters and other researchers. For example, the geographical information provided by the three-digit exchange may enable researchers to incorporate contextual data—information about the properties of the geographical region—into their analyses. With number portability, citizens will be able to keep their telephone numbers when they move. If number portability becomes commonplace, it will become difficult to use random-digit dialing to contact households in specific geographic areas.

Piekarski, Kaplan, and Prestgaard (1999) argue that random-digit dialing has become a less-efficient method of sampling residential households in recent years because of the huge increase in the volume of telephone numbers. They note that while the estimated number of households with telephones increased about 11 percent from 1988 to 1998, from about 85 million to 95 million, the total volume of telephone numbers soared 89 percent, from 400 million in 1988 to almost 719 million in May 1999. This huge increase stemmed from the proliferation of fax machines, pagers, modems, and cellular phones. Thus, in today's random-digit samples, a smaller proportion of the phone numbers may actually be attached to a residential household.

Cell phone use has grown, as has the tendency to replace regular phones or landlines with cellular service. One recent estimate is that about 7.5 million Americans have given up their regular service and now rely solely on cell phones. The number of landline phones dropped by more than 5 million (3 percent of the total) between 2000 and 2003 (Carroll 2003). The increase in cell phone use is particularly troublesome for telephone sampling for a number of reasons. Typically, commercial organizations that sell telephone number information for sampling purposes do not include cell phone number prefixes; moreover, there are no directories of cell phone numbers. A variety of federal regulations and restrictions also come into play with respect to cell phones. For example, federal regulations limit pollsters and others from calling people on their cell phones because it costs cell phone users to take the call. There are also restrictions on how calls can be made. But even if the pollster does call cell phone users, there may be great problems with response rates, perhaps because cell phones are often shut off, or because it costs the cellular customer to take the call, or because some cell phone users think of their cellular service as a private line that should not be available to telemarketers, pollsters, and the like. Finally, even if a pollster succeeds in contacting a cellular user, the respondent may be engaged in an activity, such as jogging or driving, that makes it difficult to complete an interview.

Sample Size and Sampling Error

Many Americans wonder how a national sample of 1,500 respondents can accurately represent the views of 200 million adult Americans. Contributing to the confusion is that an equally accurate statewide survey requires a sample similar in size, even though any state's population is only a small proportion of the national total. In fact, few respondents are required for a good sample, and a very weak relationship exists between the size of the sample and the size of the population from which it is drawn. Many people who are aware of these apparent anomalies are skeptical of the validity of the entire polling enterprise.

Statistical theory and probability theory explain why such small sample sizes suffice to generate valid results, but those theories are not very enlightening to people who lack an extensive mathematical background. More helpful perhaps is an analogy. To perform a blood test, a medical technician need only draw a drop or two of blood from the patient. This very small sample of the total amount of blood in the patient's body is sufficient to produce accurate results because any one drop has properties identical to those of the remaining blood. Another analogy is that of a chef trying to decide whether to add more spices to a large kettle of soup. The chef can sample the soup's flavor by tasting one spoonful, certainly a very small sample. Now, all spoonfuls of soup may not be comparable unless the chef first carefully stirs the mixture. But if the soup is stirred properly, a spoonful is sufficient to determine whether more spices should be added.

Because the biggest expense in public opinion polling is the cost of interviewing the selected sample, it is critical that the researcher select a sample that suits both the purposes and the budget of the project. There is no particular virtue in large samples. If poorly selected, they provide no guarantees of accurate results. The classic example is the infamous *Literary Digest* poll of 1936, which confidently predicted a sweeping victory for Republican presidential candidate Alf Landon based on a sample of more than two million people. In the election, however, incumbent Democratic president Franklin D. Roosevelt carried forty-six of the forty-eight states. The *Literary Digest* poll failed because of the unrepresentativeness of the respondents, who were selected from telephone directories and automobile registrations, a procedure that skewed the sample to the upper end of the socioeconomic scale. This method of sample selection had worked well for the *Literary Digest* in previous elections, but it failed in the Depression year of 1936. Moreover, additional problems with low response rates and a nonresponse bias were such that those who responded to the poll were more likely to be for Landon than for Roosevelt (Squire 1988).

One determinant of sample size is the amount of *sampling error* that can be tolerated in a poll. Sampling error is simply the difference between the estimates obtained from the sample and the true population value—for example, the percentage of people in the sample who approve of the president's performance versus the percentage in the overall population who do. Investigators often select national samples of sufficient size to generate a sampling error of about 4 percent. This means that if the sample indicates, for example, that 52 percent of respondents approve of the president's performance, the actual value is likely to be in the range of 48–56 percent (52 percent plus or minus 4 percentage points). How likely it is that the actual value will fall within that range is measured by the *confidence level*. In this example a 95 percent confidence level would mean that 95 out of 100 samples that might be selected would generate an estimate of approval within the range of 48–56 percent. One way to reduce the sampling error is to increase the sample size, but larger samples entail higher costs. A 4 percent sampling error is normally considered acceptable.

Several caveats about sampling error should be kept in mind. First, in some instances a 4 percent error will be too large for the predictions that the investigator wants to make. For example, if the sample shows that in an upcoming election 51 percent of voters, with a 4 percent sampling error, are planning to vote Republican, the election outcome cannot be firmly predicted because the Republican vote could be as low as 47 percent or as high as 55 percent. But if the poll indicates that 70 percent plan to vote Republican, then a sampling error of 4 percent or even higher will scarcely affect the conclusions.

Second, although the sampling error of the overall sample may be only 4 percent, the sampling error associated with estimates based on subsets of the sample can be substantially higher, particularly for the smaller groups within the sample. In subgroup analysis the original sample is subdivided into a number of mutually exclusive subsets. For example, a researcher interested in comparing the political attitudes of Protestants, Catholics, and Jews based on a national sample of about 1,500 respondents would subdivide the sample into these three religious groups. The sampling error associated with estimates for the Jewish subgroup would be much higher than those associated with the other groups because Jewish respondents would number only 40–60, reflecting the percentage of Jews in the overall population (the sample would contain 350–400 Catholics and about 1,000 Protestants). To compare across religious and gender groups simultaneously, the researcher would divide the same sample into six categories: male Protestants, male Catholics, male Jews, female Protestants, female Catholics, and female Jews. The sampling error associated with these classifications would be even larger. In general, as the original sample is subdivided into smaller and smaller subsets, the sampling error becomes larger and larger.

Scores of polls were conducted throughout 2003 on Americans' views of the war in Iraq and its aftermath. In many of the releases that polling organizations provided and in many news media accounts of the polls, the typical lead focused on the overall levels of support for the war and for the president and how those numbers had changed since the last poll. Then some of the releases and news stories would examine the opinions of subsets of Americans, defined by political party affiliation or gender, less often by age, and even less frequently by race. Many of these polls had a sample size of 1,000 or fewer respondents and a typical overall sampling error of about 4 percent. Thus, when the sample was subdivided by political party affiliation, defined by Democratic, Republican, and independent, or by gender, defined by male and female, there were still several hundred respondents in each of the subcategories, and the sampling error had not increased too much. Depending on how many age categories were used, the number of respondents in each subcategory became smaller, and the sampling error grew. Finally, with respect to race, defined (for ease of exposition) as white, black, and other, the number of cases in the nonwhite categories became very small, and the sampling error increased to as much as 10 percent in some cases. Typically the polling data showed substantial differences among Democrats, Republicans, and independents, particularly in the postwar era, with Republicans most supportive of Iraq policy and the president, Democrats least supportive, and independents falling somewhere in between. The age breakdown typically showed that older Americans were less eager to go to war and were less supportive of the war overall. Finally, in those relatively few instances when polling results were broken down by race, there were sharp differences between white and black Americans, with the latter much more opposed to the war. Throughout these releases and media reports, relatively little attention was given to the sampling error associated with the various subgroups. One might speculate that one reason why the dramatic black/white differences received so little attention was that the percentages for black citizens had a large sampling error associated with them. To address this, the polling organizations and news media could have noted whether the racial differences were apparent in many polls rather than just in the one they happened to be reporting on at the time. If so, that would provide good evidence that there were genuine differences between white and black Americans that were not simply a function of sample size and sampling error.

Total versus Actual Sample Size

When a sample of citizens is interviewed, not every question is answered by every respondent. Some respondents may refuse to answer, other respondents may be screened out because of nonattitudes, and still others may have no opinion on the matter. In some instances there may be a substantial difference between the total sample size and the actual number of people responding to a particular question, whose responses thus are the basis of the reported results.

Consider the hypothetical situation in which 1,500 Americans are asked about their vote preferences one month before an election. Perhaps only 80 percent of the sample is registered to vote, and only 60 percent of those registered will actually vote on election day. If the investigator wants to report the vote preferences of likely voters only, and is able to identify that group (a difficult task), then the effective sample has shrunk from 1,500 to 720 (0.80 x 0.60 x 1,500), with an attendant increase in sampling error. Of these 720, 3 percent might refuse to reveal their preference, and another 22 percent might be unsure, thereby reducing the 720 to 540 likely voters with definite vote preferences, or just 36 percent of the original sample of 1,500. The 540 voters then are the actual sample out of the total sample. Of the 540 likely voters, 300 may intend to vote Democratic, and 240 Republican, a 56 percent to 44 percent split. In reporting this split, the pollster also should describe the subset of the sample from which it is calculated.

A real-life example of the importance of reporting actual sample size is provided by a July 1985 ABC News/*Washington Post* poll on President Reagan's Strategic Defense Initiative, also known as "Star Wars." The three questions and responses were

Q. Have you read or heard about plans by the Reagan administration to develop weapons in outer space that could destroy nuclear missiles fired at the United States by the Soviet Union or other countries? Reagan calls the research on these weapons SDI, for Strategic Defense Initiative, and some people refer to it as "Star Wars."

Yes, have read or heard	84%
No, have not read or heard	16%
Don't know or no opinion	1%

Q. Supporters say such weapons could guarantee protection of the United States from nuclear attack and are worth whatever they cost. Opponents say such weapons will not work, will increase the arms race, and the research will cost many billions of dollars. How about you: would you say you approve or disapprove of plans to develop such space-based weapons?

Approve	41%
Disapprove	53%
Don't know or no opinion	5%

Q. [For those who approved] Currently the United States and the Soviet Union have an anti-ballistic missile treaty that prohibits both nations from developing certain weapons. Suppose the U.S. had to violate or abandon that treaty in order to develop the space-based weapons. Would you still favor development of those space-based weapons or not?

Yes, would still favor	63%
No, would not still favor	32%
Don't know or no opinion	5%

Fortunately, *Post* writer George Lardner Jr. (1985) was very careful in his reporting of the responses to the last question, for without the appropriate qualifications, citizens might interpret the result as showing strong support for development of the weapons even if the United States had to scrap the treaty. Note that the 63 percent favoring SDI represents only 26 percent (0.41 x 0.63) of the original sample of 1,506 and only 22 percent (0.41 x 0.63 x 0.84) of those respondents who had read or heard about the plan initially. It would, then, be misleading and unscrupulous to release only the results of the last item without the necessary qualifiers. Unfortunately, advocates of causes have at times been highly selective in their use of poll information, with the conscious aim of swaying the public to their position.

Response Rates

A growing concern among pollsters is the problem of nonresponse—meaning that some citizens selected for the sample either refuse to participate in the interview or cannot be contacted. Refusals are attributed to several reasons, including growing hostility to legitimate public opinion polling because of the excesses and intrusiveness of the telemarketing that bombards Americans. Moreover, reaching people is now more difficult because of the proliferation of technological barriers and cellular phones. According to Piekarski, Kaplan, and Prestgaard (1999), 50 percent of households have answering machines, 25 percent have "Caller ID," and 6 percent have voice mail. By 2003, Caller ID use had grown to close to 40 percent, although there was some indication that its popularity among subscribers was waning since many calls are never identified (Howe 2003). Bierma (2002) mentions instances in which telephone poll response rates have fallen substantially—from 60 percent and higher down to 30 and 40 percent. Nagourney (2002) cites pollster Whit Ayres, who argued, "I can't fathom 20 years from now the telephone remaining the primary means of data collection. This industry is in a transition from telephone data collection to Internet data collection. In the meantime, we've got to get people to answer the phone."

Also contributing to the increased difficulty in contacting respondents is the growing tendency of pollsters to conduct overnight polls on salient political topics such as presidential candidates' debate performance or the "bounce" produced by a national nominating convention. In overnight polls there is insufficient time to do the multiple callbacks that may be needed to contact a member of the sample who was not at home or was otherwise unavailable when the first telephone call was made. As Kagay (1999) points out, most reputable pollsters make multiple calls to households over the multiple days that the poll is in the field to contact the designated respondent. These repeat calls are made at different times of the day to enhance the probability of a response. In many instances, interviewers leave phone messages explaining why they are calling and try to arrange a more convenient time to interview the respondent. Many polling organizations also field specially trained interviewers to re-contact respondents who had originally refused to participate to try to convert their refusals into completed interviews. But none of these special measures can be applied to an overnight poll, in which the actual interviewing period might be four hours or less. And all of these measures add to the cost of polling.

The American Association for Public Opinion Research has called on polling organizations to provide more systematic and comparable information about response rates for telephone, in-person, and mail surveys. For example, for telephone interviews AAPOR advocates that the disposition or outcome of telephone calls be made available to the users of polls so that they can better evaluate the product. The outcomes would be (1) a successful interview with an eligible case; (2) an eligible case that was not interviewed (for example, a refusal); (3) a noneligible case (for example, a fax line or a nonworking number); and (4) a case of unknown eligibility (for example, a constant busy signal). AAPOR recommends that survey organizations calculate and present response rates, cooperation rates, refusal rates, and contact rates. Traditionally, pollsters and media reports of polls have provided little information about response rates. An exception is the *Columbus Dispatch*'s reporting of its mailed election surveys, which have an outstanding record of accuracy in election predictions (see chapter 7) despite low response rates. In a September 2000 mail survey on the presidential race in Ohio, the *Dispatch* listed as one of many sources of error "nonresponse bias," which it defined as the possibility that those who responded to the mail survey might not reflect the views of those who did not respond. The *Dispatch* then told its readers that the response rate was 22 percent. The scant attention given to response rates is also unfortunately reflected in major academic social science journals. Examining issues of some leading political science, sociology, and survey research journals published between 1998 and 2001, Smith (2002) found that in 73 percent of the cases, political science journals provided no information about response rates, compared with 59 percent for sociology journals, and 53 percent for survey research publications.

What difference do lower response rates make in the accuracy of a public opinion poll? Fortunately there is some research, albeit far from definitive, that suggests that lower response rates do not necessarily result in bias or inaccuracy in the results. For example, researchers have examined what happens to the properties of a sample when respondents who initially refused to be interviewed are converted to a successful interview through repeated callbacks and other methods. Wiese (1998) found that the inclusion of "converted refusals" does not make the sample more representative of the population from which it was drawn and that such respondents provide less-complete information than respondents who were successfully interviewed on the first try. In a study by Curtin, Presser, and Singer (2000), few differences were found in the Index of Consumer Sentiment among respondents who required varying numbers of telephone calls to complete a successful interview. Teitler, Reichman, and Sprachman (2003) found some differences between nonrespondent and respondent fathers in a national longitudinal survey of new parents, but they also argued that the efforts and resources required to convert nonrespondents into respondents reached a point of diminishing returns.

One of the most ambitious efforts to assess the effects of differential response rates was a study in which two national random-digit dialing surveys were conducted using identical questionnaires (Keeter et al. 2000). The first survey was conducted over a five-day period and used a sample of adults who were at home when the interviewer called. The second was conducted over an eight-week period that allowed for greater efforts to contact mobile and reluctant respondents. The first survey had an overall response rate of 36 percent; the second, a 60.6 percent response rate. Despite the large difference in response rates, the two surveys produced very similar results across a wide variety of questions. What differences there were tended to occur on demographic items and not on attitudinal and opinion questions.

What conclusions can be drawn about the problem of response rates? Certainly it is important to monitor them. AAPOR's recommendations, if followed, will be very helpful here. Declining response rates are less of a problem for those reputable survey organizations that work harder to secure completed interviews through multiple callbacks and other tactics. But for the overnight polls, low response rates can be a serious problem and need to be recognized as such. Much more research is needed on the fundamental question of whether survey respondents are indeed representative of nonrespondents. Obviously, high response rates are better than low rates, but lower rates do not automatically indicate that a poll is inaccurate.

As America's telecommunications technology continues to advance and as individual concerns about the intrusiveness of telemarketing and protection of privacy continue to grow, the problem of response rates will become an even greater challenge for public opinion polling, and methods of data collection other than by telephone may become more prominent.

Weighting the Sample

Although pollsters select their samples to be representative of the population from which they are drawn, sometimes they must adjust a sample before analyzing and reporting the results of a poll. The adjustments may be made for substantive reasons or because of biases in the characteristics of the selected sample. An example of an adjustment made for substantive reasons would be the pollster's attempt to determine who the likely voters will be and to base election predictions not on the entire sample but on that subset of likely voters.

Weights are used to correct for biases—that is, to make the sample's demographic characteristics more accurately reflect the population's overall properties. Because sampling and interviewing involve statistics and probability theory, as well as the logistical problems of contacting respondents, a sample may contain too few blacks, or too few men, or too few people in the youngest age category. Assuming that the true population proportions for sex, race, and age are known, the researcher, using weights, brings the sample numbers into line with the overall population values. For example, if females constitute 60 percent of the sample but 50 percent of the overall population, the researcher might weight each female respondent by five-sixths, thereby reducing the percentage of females in the sample to 50 percent (five-sixths times 60 percent).

A 1986 *Columbus Dispatch* preelection poll on the gubernatorial preferences of Ohioans illustrates the consequences of weighting. In August 1986 the *Dispatch* mailed a questionnaire to a sample of Ohioans selected from the statewide list of registered voters. The poll showed that incumbent Democratic governor Richard Celeste was leading former GOP governor James Rhodes, 48 percent to 43 percent, with independent candidate and former Democratic mayor of Cleveland Dennis Kucinich receiving 9 percent. An "undecided" alternative was not provided (Curtin 1986a). Fortunately, the *Dispatch* report of its poll included the sample size for each category (unlike the practice of the national media). One table that the paper presented showed the following relationships between political party affiliation and gubernatorial vote preference (Curtin 1986b):

Gubernatorial preference	Democrat	Republican	Independent
Celeste	82%	14%	33%
Rhodes	9	81	50
Kucinich	9	5	17
Total %	100	100	100
(N)	(253)	(245)	(138)

Given the thrust of the news story, that Celeste was ahead 48 to 43 percent, the numbers in the table were surprising. Rhodes was running almost as well among Republicans as Celeste was among Democrats, and Rhodes had a substantial lead among independents. Based on the numbers provided, one could calculate the actual number of Celeste, Rhodes, and Kucinich votes in the sample as follows:

Celeste votes = .82(253) + .14(245) + .33(138) = 287
Rhodes votes = .09(253) + .81(245) + .50(138) = 291
Kucinich votes = .09(253) + .05(245) + .17(138) = 58

The percentages calculated from these totals show Rhodes slightly ahead, 46 to 45 percent, rather than trailing. At first I thought there was a mistake in the poll or in the party affiliation and gubernatorial vote preferences. In rereading the news story, however, I learned that the sample had been weighted. The reporter wrote, "Results were adjusted, or weighted, slightly to compensate for demographic differences between poll respondents and the Ohio electorate as a whole" (Curtin 1986b). Although the reporter informed readers that the data were weighted, nowhere did he say that the adjustment affected who was ahead in the poll. The adjustment was statistically valid because the poll respondents did not include sufficient numbers of women and blacks, two groups that were more supportive of the Democratic gubernatorial candidate. However, nowhere in the news story was any specific information provided on how the weighting was done. This example illustrates that weighting can be consequential, and it is typical in terms of the scant information that citizens receive about weighting procedures.

One ongoing problem in polling is the tendency of selected samples to overrepresent females and underrepresent males. This problem can be easily corrected by weighting the sample so that the proportion of male and female respondents in the sample reflects the overall population distribution. This solution, however, assumes that sampled males are representative of unsampled males. Males may be undersampled for several reasons. First, there are simply more female-only households than there are male-only households. Moreover, because fewer men live in male-only households and a higher proportion of men live in mixed households, the probability of a male's being selected in the sample is lower than for a female. The second factor relates to how the actual respondent to be interviewed is determined. Typically, interviewers (in telephone polling) ask the person who answers the phone if they can speak with the oldest female, or the second-oldest male, or some other designated person in the household. Sometimes the person who answers the phone is unwilling to transfer the interviewer to the household member requested. Because women are more likely to answer the phone in the first place and are less willing than men to bring their spouse to the phone, the number of male respondents is diminished. Finally, daytime calls are more likely to obtain female respondents because of the higher proportion of males who work outside the home.

Conclusion

For many Americans, sampling is the most problematic feature of public opinion polling. Many citizens doubt whether the "small" samples reported in the media can adequately represent the population of whatever entity is being studied. And if the response rates noted are low, citizens are likely to be even more skeptical. They may question the wording of a poll, but it is difficult for individuals to offer informed criticism of sampling procedures unless the polling organization provides sufficient information about such matters as the size of the sample, sampling error and confidence levels, the dates of the interviews, response rates, and the method of interviewing. And even with this information, many people will still be unsure about the quality of the sampling procedures, which seem to be technical and statistical matters beyond the layperson. Even when the sampling is statistically and scientifically sound, sampling problems may undermine the substantive results and interpretations of public opinion polls. Normally, however, citizens must trust the polling organization to select a good sample.

Exercises

1. In exercises 1 and 2 in chapter 1, you kept a log of newspaper and newsmagazine public opinion polls. Now reexamine those same polls and look for information related to sampling. In particular, look for information about sample size, size of sample subset (where appropriate), sampling error, sampling error of sample subsets (where appropriate), response rates, and the use of weights. What type of information was

provided most often? What type of information was provided least often?

2. Assume that you must select a sample of college students who live in officially sanctioned university housing, whether residence halls, fraternity and sorority houses, or university-run, off-campus housing. Design a sampling scheme based on all these housing units. Design another sampling scheme based on telephone numbers; feel free to make assumptions about the university phone system for students. Finally, design a sampling scheme based on the printed student directory.

5 Interviewing and Data Collection Procedures

The interviewer's role in measuring public opinion is critical. Because polling organizations generally provide the public with little or no information about the interviewing process, the consumers of polls cannot make independent judgments and must assume that the interviews were conducted competently. That is a safe assumption with respect to the major polls. Nevertheless, when I have agreed to be a respondent in public opinion, market research, and academic research surveys, I have been surprised by the clear disparities in the training and competence of the interviewers I encountered.

Often, when I am a respondent, I ask the interviewer what a certain question means or complain about the range of alternatives available to me. Some interviewers are well trained to handle such reactions, but others are not. One interviewer agreed with my frustration about a particular item and informed me that there had been many complaints about the survey. Another interviewer—when I strenuously objected to the alternatives offered—pleaded with me to pick one of the given choices because he did not know how to handle volunteered responses. In yet another situation the interviewer told me that she would place my aberrant response in the category in which she thought it would best fit.

In some surveys there is no live interviewer. The most familiar example is the self-administered, mailed questionnaire, typically in paper-and-pencil format. Gaining popularity are the computerized self-administered questionnaire (CSAQ) and computer-assisted self-interviewing (CASI), which give pollsters greater flexibility. Finally, there is the growing phenomenon of Web-based Internet polls, which are typically self-administered and raise a variety of issues about sampling, representativeness, and the like.

The purpose of this chapter is to alert the consumers of polls about the potential effects of the interviewing process on poll results. The first section describes the methods used to collect data and the advantages and disadvantages of different approaches. That section is followed by a closer look at the interview situation and factors—such as the sex, socioeconomic status, race, and ethnicity of the interviewer—that can affect responses. The chapter ends with a discussion of the advantages and limitations of Web-based Internet surveys.

Methods of Collecting Polling Information

There are three basic ways to collect polling information: self-administered questionnaires, telephone interviews, and personal interviews.

Self-Administered Questionnaires

Organizations with access to good mailing lists are especially frequent users of mailed questionnaires, whose main advantage is their low cost. As discussed in chapter 1, interest groups often use mailed surveys in conjunction with their fund-raising efforts. Because mailed surveys are self-administered by the respondent, no interviewers must be trained and supported, dramatically reducing costs. Interviewer bias does not affect results. Moreover, the privacy in which they can complete a mailed survey may reassure respondents about the anonymity and confidentiality of their responses and encourage them to respond more frankly, particularly on sensitive topics. For example, a study by Aquilino (1994) showed that self-administered questionnaires used in the context of a personal interview generate a higher level of admitted illicit drug and alcohol use than does a telephone or personal interview without a self-administered questionnaire. Indeed, an extensive body of literature generally shows that self-administered questionnaires are more likely to produce higher estimates of illicit, illegal, or controversial behaviors than modes of data collection in which an interviewer directly interacts with respondents (Tourangeau and Smith 1996). Krysan et al. (1994) demonstrated that a mail questionnaire revealed more negative views among white respondents to questions about racial integration and affirmative action than did personal interviews. The explanation given for this finding was straightforward: white respondents were more open and honest about their views in the privacy of the self-administered mail questionnaire. In a personal interview the pressure to be socially and politically correct came into play, resulting in responses more supportive of civil rights.

These advantages of mailed questionnaires are typically outweighed by their limitations, foremost of which is that response rates tend to be lower for mailed surveys than for telephone and personal interviews. However, this disadvantage may be lessening, in part because of the higher re-fusal rates in personal and telephone interviews and improved techniques for generating satisfactory response rates to mailed questionnaires (Goyder 1985).

Researchers continue to investigate ways to improve response rates for mail surveys, and there is a solid body of scholarship on the topic. A study by Fox, Crask, and Kim (1988) found that university sponsorship (as opposed to private business sponsorship) of a mail survey increased the re-sponse rate, as did notifying respondents about the survey beforehand by letter, sending the survey by first class mail, using a postcard follow-up, and providing return postage. Another significant factor was the color of the paper on which the questionnaire was printed. According to James and Bolstein (1990), a monetary incentive to return the survey, along with fol-low-up mailings urging respondents to complete the questionnaire, increases response rates. Yammarino, Skinner, and Childers (1991) and Church (1993), who reviewed a large number of studies of the factors that affect response rates, found similar results.

Ascertaining the extent to which respondents represent the actual population is a particularly acute problem when the response rate is low. A study by Bernick and Pratto (1994) concluded that it can be worthwhile to expend the extra resources to enhance response rates; simply weighting or adjusting the respondents obtained from smaller samples in their study would not have fully resolved the problem of response bias in a small sample. On the other hand, if the respondents are representative of the broader population even when the response rates are low, there is less need to incur the costs required to increase the response rate.

Another limitation of mailed surveys is that much information cannot be collected through self-administered surveys. For example, one cannot be sure who actually completes a mail questionnaire—a serious limitation when surveying elite populations, such as members of Congress or state legislators who, because they are bombarded with questionnaires, may have a staff person fill out the survey form. Also not available is informa-tion about respondents' reactions to a survey or the environment in which a survey is completed. Because no interviewer is present to assist respon-dents who have difficulty with a questionnaire, instructions must be explicit and questions must be as unambiguous as possible. There is no opportu-nity for clarification.

Mailed questionnaires must not be too burdensome for respondents, or the response rate will plummet. Whenever I receive a questionnaire in the mail, I first check the number of open-ended questions that would require me to write mini-essays. If there are many, I'm likely to toss the question-naire into the circular file, unless it addresses a topic of particular interest to me. Mailed questionnaires encourage response when they are largely limited to highly structured, fixed-alternative questions. However, even the structured items are often annoying to citizens, particularly to political elites, who complain that the political world is too complicated, and their own opinions are too complex, to be captured in a fixed-alternative item.

The burdens that a mailed questionnaire imposes are not uniform across the population. Poorly educated respondents will have more difficulty with a mailed survey, and illiterate persons may simply have to ignore it. In addition, there is no way of knowing the order in which any particular respondent answered the questions. The questionnaire may elicit different responses from individuals depending on the order in which they approach the questions. Finally, mailed questionnaires are inappropriate if an investigator needs a quick response on a topic such as a presidential debate or foreign policy crisis. Experienced researchers allow several weeks for questionnaires to be returned.

One response to some of the limitations of self-administered mailed questionnaires is computer-assisted self-interviewing (CASI), in which respondents answer survey questions on a computer. CASI permits more flexibility in questionnaire design. For example, it allows branching, in which respondents are presented with different survey questions depending on their responses to previous ones. CASI eliminates some of the errors that occur in the usual paper-and-pencil format and allows quick identification of any internal inconsistencies in item responses. Yet it maintains many of the privacy benefits of self-administered mailed questionnaires. Indeed, CASI appears to perform better than mailed questionnaires in generating accurate responses on sensitive topics. Studies of drug use (Wright, Aquilino, and Supple 1998) and sexual behavior (Harmon 1998) suggest that computerized administration of polls may make respondents feel more certain of privacy and therefore freer to offer honest responses about socially unacceptable and possibly illegal behavior.

A study by Epstein, Barker, and Kroutil (2001) found mode effects on another sensitive topic, respondents' reports of how often they experienced various mental health problems. Epstein and her colleagues compared two modes of data collection—audio computer-assisted self-interviewing (ACASI) and interviewer-administered, paper-and-pencil (I-PAPI) procedures. With I-PAPI, an interviewer asked respondents about mental health symptoms, the respondents answered, and the interviewer recorded their replies. With ACASI, respondents can listen to questions through a headset or read them on a computer screen and then enter their responses directly on the computer; they have greater privacy. It turned out that respondents cited more mental health problems with ACASI than with I-PAPI procedures, again suggesting that pollsters and investigators collecting sensitive information must be aware that the mode of data collection they employ can affect their results.

Telephone Interviews

Unlike mailed questionnaires, telephone surveys can be completed quickly (often in only two to four days and sometimes in a single evening), providing an almost instantaneous reaction to a political event. Another advantage, as detailed in chapter 4, is that by using random-digit dialing techniques, researchers can pick a representative sample with a higher response rate than is possible with self-administered questionnaires, although lower than with personal interviews. Telephone interviews cost more than mailed questionnaires but less than personal interviews. In some situations telephone interviewing may succeed where other methods can fail, perhaps because of the sensitivity of a topic or because respondents will not allow a stranger in their home to conduct a personal interview.

Telephone interviews also have shortcomings beyond the dropping response rates discussed in the last chapter. Respondents become fatigued more quickly in a telephone interview than in a personal interview, and that limits the scope of a telephone survey (although recent experience indicates that telephone surveys can be lengthier than was originally thought). Training interviewers, to avoid unwanted effects from the interviewing process, adds to the cost of a project. Finally, use of the telephone eliminates the possibility of using visual aids during the interview unless materials are sent to respondents in a preliminary mailing.

Telephone interviews are now faster, more efficient, and more accurate thanks to recent advances, the foremost of which is computer-assisted telephone interviewing (CATI). With CATI, interviewers sit at video display terminals and feed responses directly into a computer, thereby eliminating a separate keypunching step. A computer program controls the overall flow and logic of the interview. Among other things, the program ensures that questions are asked in the correct sequence and that responses are consistent with the question(s) being asked (Frey 1983, 144–145). Running totals are easily generated with CATI, so that survey results are available almost instantaneously. As CATI systems become more sophisticated, investigators who use them can save money, particularly as the sample size grows larger.

Personal Interviews

Personal interviews generally provide the richest and most complete information in public opinion polling and tend to have the highest response rates. Respondents are willing to participate in lengthy personal interviews, particularly if the interviewer is skillful in developing a rapport with them. The presence of the interviewer is also helpful in other ways. He or she can assess respondents' problems with and reactions to the survey and can directly record not only the verbal responses of the interviewee but also nonverbal behavior such as fidgeting, nervousness, and other signs of unease or lack of interest in the interview situation. Moreover, the interviewer has more opportunities to ask follow-up questions and to probe in a personal interview than in a telephone survey. Holbrook, Green, and Krosnick (2003) compared the merits of telephone and personal interviewing and found that telephone respondents were not as forthcoming as face-to-face interviewees. Telephone respondents were less cooperative and less engaged in the interview, more suspicious about the interview itself, and more likely to offer socially desirable responses.

The obvious drawbacks of personal interviews are their high cost and the danger of introducing substantial interviewer effects and biases. The cost of training interviewers, supporting them in the field, often with housing, meals, and transportation allowances, and paying their salary is steep. Because the interview is a social situation, poorly trained interviewers may alter its interpersonal dynamics and thereby influence respondents' answers in undesirable and often unpredictable ways.

Interviewer Effects in Public Opinion Polling

Interviewer effects can emerge in both telephone and personal interviews, although they are likely to be more pronounced in personal interviews because of the face-to-face interaction between the interviewer and the respondent. For most respondents, the personal interview is a new experience, with all the attendant uncertainties and ambiguities of unfamiliar activity. Unsure of how to behave, respondents may look to the interview situation for cues. The two most important sources of cues are the survey instrument itself (the questionnaire) and the person who administers it, the interviewer. The cues that the survey instrument provides are direct (even if the questions are flawed); the cues that the interviewer provides may be far more subtle. If interviewers are inconsistent in the cues they give to different respondents, the reliability of the survey results may be undermined. At minimum, interviewers must not change the question wording, question order, or their voice intonation from respondent to respondent. And because most polls use more than one interviewer, the interviewing process must be standardized as much as possible, which requires careful training of interviewers.

This emphasis on consistency and uniformity in the interviewing process reflects a concern with the *reliability* of the measuring instrument.

One type of reliability measure is based on *equivalence,* the extent to which different investigators applying the same measuring instrument to the same individuals obtain consistent results. Ideally, the identity of the interviewer should not affect the responses that the questionnaire generates in the interview.

The reliability of an instrument can be distinguished from its *validity,* the extent to which the instrument measures what it is supposed to measure. For example, consider one of the political efficacy items discussed in chapter 3: "Voting is the only way that people like me can have any say about how the government runs things." A "disagree" response to this item is considered an efficacious reply; it presumably means that the respondent believes that he or she can be influential in ways other than voting. But what if a respondent rejects this statement out of a belief that there is no way (not even by voting) that people can have influence? In this case, a "disagree" response signals a lack of efficacy, and the item itself is not a valid indicator of the underlying concept of political efficacy. Because of the problem with validity, this item has been eliminated from the American National Election Studies.

Interviewer Skills and Demeanor

An interviewer's general demeanor, competence, and performance have much to do with the success of the interview. Interviewers must be able to make respondents feel at ease and receptive to the survey. If such a rapport is not established, respondents may refuse to cooperate or fail to provide complete and accurate information to interviewers. Ideally, interviewers are well informed about the purposes of the research and the intention of specific questions so that they know whether a respondent has answered a question fully and how to ask follow-up questions for clarification. They should not, however, inject themselves into the interviewing process by making editorial comments about respondents' replies.

Although they must follow instructions carefully and ask all appropriate questions, interviewers also should be able to handle the unexpected, such as a respondent who volunteers additional information. Equally important, interviewers must record and transcribe responses as accurately as possible, even when the answers do not fall neatly into one of the predetermined response categories.

How difficult an interviewer's job is depends on the nature of the questionnaire as well as the characteristics of the respondents. For example, highly structured survey items require less guidance and judgment from an interviewer; relatively unstructured instruments require more. For interviews of political elites that use open-ended questions, an interviewer must not only be a good listener and prober who takes few or no notes during an interview, but he or she must be able to write up the results after the question-and-answer session has ended. Sometimes such interviews are taped, which eliminates the need to take extensive notes, but taped interviews must be transcribed to be usable.

Gender and Status

In addition to demeanor and skills, the personal characteristics of an interviewer can affect responses to a poll. For example, many interviewers are middle-aged women because this group is least threatening to both male and female respondents, particularly in a personal interview in a home. Also, female interviewers often are able to establish a rapport more successfully than men.

Morin (1990) cites research that shows that men and women answer poll questions differently depending on the gender of the interviewer. In a poll on abortion conducted by the Eagleton Institute, women were much more likely to give pro-choice responses to female interviewers than to males; the response pattern for men was weaker. For example, when given the statement, "The decision to have an abortion is a private matter that should be left to the woman to decide without government intervention," 84 percent of the female respondents interviewed by women agreed, compared with only 64 percent of women interviewed by men. Seventy-seven percent of the male respondents interviewed by women agreed with the statement, compared with 70 percent of those interviewed by men.

A growing body of research indicates that women are more likely to give traditional, nonfeminist responses to male interviewers and more feminist responses to female interviewers. Likewise, men are somewhat more likely to give feminist responses to female interviewers than to males. Kane and Macaulay (1993) found that both men and women were likely to express more egalitarian gender-related attitudes and more criticism of gender-related inequalities to female interviewers than to male interviewers. Huddy and Bracciodieta (1992) obtained similar results in their research, except that they also found gender-of-interviewer effects on topics such as party identification and authoritarian attitudes, which are not directly related to gender. For example, both men and women gave more feminist, Democratic, and anti-authoritarian responses when interviewed by a female than when interviewed by a male. Therefore, on gender-related survey topics such as abortion, and perhaps even on gender-neutral topics, researchers must be sensitive to the potential for interviewer-gender effects.

Just as personal characteristics can, the social distance between interviewers and respondents can influence an interview. If an interviewer appears to be of higher social status than a respondent, the respondent may tend to defer or acquiesce to the interviewer by providing answers intended to win approval. Even an interviewer's manner of speech can affect a respondent's replies because a person's speech may reflect his or her geographical origin, social class, age group, or level of education.

Race and Ethnicity

An interviewer's race and ethnicity are additional factors that can affect responses to a poll (Schuman and Converse 1971; Hatchett and Schuman 1975–1976; Campbell 1981; Weeks and Moore 1981; Cotter, Cohen, and Coulter 1982; Meislin 1987). When black respondents are queried about the American political and judicial system, they are more likely to give supportive, positive answers to white interviewers than to black interviewers. Likewise, white respondents are less likely to reveal attitudes of racial hostility when interviewed by blacks than when interviewed by whites.

In late 1993 and early 1994 a major national telephone survey of African Americans was conducted using only black interviewers (Morin 1995b). A comparison of the answers of respondents who correctly believed they were being interviewed by blacks (76 percent) with those of respondents who incorrectly thought they were interviewed by whites (14 percent) revealed substantial differences. For example, only 17 percent of the respondents who thought they were queried by African Americans agreed with the statement, "American society is fair to everyone," compared with 31 percent agreement by those who believed their interviewer was white. Davis (1997) found that black respondents in a survey were likely to be more accommodating and deferential to white interviewers, even to the point of taking contradictory stances in evaluations of political figures and political parties.

Similar patterns of race-of-interviewer effects occurred in a 1989 ABC News/*Washington Post* poll (Morin 1989b). On a number of race-related questions, white responses shifted about 5 to 10 percentage points depending on the race of the interviewer. For some questions the effect was greater. For example, 62 percent of whites interviewed by whites said that most of the problems now faced by blacks were "brought on by blacks themselves"; only 46 percent of white respondents interviewed by blacks gave that response. A study by Anderson, Silver, and Abramson (1988) found that "blacks interviewed by whites were much more likely to express warmth and closeness toward whites than were blacks interviewed by blacks" (289). Finally, in a study by Finkel, Guterbock, and Borg (1991) of race-of-interviewer effects in a poll prior to the 1989 Virginia gubernatorial contest between black Democrat Douglas Wilder and white Republican

Marshall Coleman, white respondents interviewed by black interviewers were more likely to state a preference for Wilder (52.2 percent) than those queried by white interviewers (43.8 percent). This pattern was particularly pronounced among white Democrats and among whites who were less sure of their vote intention.

Davis and Silver (2003) identified a different kind of race-of-interviewer effect in a study in which they found that African American respondents answered fewer factual knowledge items correctly when queried by white interviewers than when queried by black interviewers. The researchers speculate that "respondents who belong to racial minorities may experience added anxiety when they risk being uninformed in the presence of the dominant racial group" (43), and this anxiety may lead to poorer performance in answering a battery of knowledge items.

A study by Reese and colleagues (1986) on the effects of interviewer ethnicity—white versus Hispanic—found that ethnicity also affected the responses to certain questions, especially items that related to the culture of the interviewer. When Anglos were asked questions by Hispanics about aspects of Mexican American life, they responded more sympathetically than when they were asked the same questions by fellow Anglos. Why? The general explanation is that respondents try not to give answers that might offend an interviewer, particularly on matters that relate to the interviewer's race and ethnicity.

Internet Polling

Pollsters would benefit greatly from using the Internet to conduct public opinion polls of representative samples of citizens. First, they could interview large numbers of people quickly and economically. Moreover, they could provide respondents with audio and video materials as part of the interviewing process. Internet surveys could be self-administered, but an interviewer, either live or recorded, also could participate. Finally, Internet polling would permit researchers to tabulate and analyze data very rapidly.

With all these potential advantages, what is preventing the widespread use of Internet polling? The most obvious factor is access. Lenhart et al. (2003) report that about 42 percent of Americans say that they do not use the Internet, although they may formerly have been Internet users or have relationships with the Internet through family or household members. About 24 percent of Americans are truly disconnected from the Internet in that they have no experience, direct or indirect, with going online. The rate of growth in Internet access flattened between 2001 and 2003, resulting in about 57 to 61 percent of the population having Internet access. And even though Internet use has grown among all segments of Americans, users are still more likely to be younger, better educated, more affluent, white, and residents of suburban and urban areas. But this description is likely to change rapidly in the not-too-distant future. Some observers compare the Internet today to the early days of the telephone and believe that just as telephone access became almost universal in American households, so too will Internet availability. Today there are demographic differences between citizens who go online and those who do not. According to Lenhart and colleagues, 56 percent of non-Internet users believe they will never go online; they tend to be poorer, older, female, retired, white, and living in rural areas.

Even if Internet access and use were universal, the most significant flaw in many Internet polls is that respondents are not selected through a scientific sampling procedure. Instead, respondents are self-selected—they choose to participate. Obviously, such respondents may not be representative of the overall population, perhaps because they are more interested in the topic of that particular survey or because they have been stimulated by various groups to take part. Then there is the problem of respondents who participate in a survey more than once. Internet surveys with self-selected or voluntary samples are nonprobability samples, and that means that sampling error cannot be calculated. Nor can probability statements be made about the relationship between the sample results and the true population parameters. There is simply no sampling list from which a probability sample can be collected. This problem, however, is not inevitable. One can create Internet polls that are probability samples or that have elements of probability sampling. Couper has presented the following typology of Web surveys (2000, 477):

Types of Web Surveys	
Nonprobability Methods	Probability Methods
1. Polls as entertainment	4. Intercept surveys
2. Unrestricted self-selected surveys	5. List-based surveys
3. Volunteer opt-in panels	6. Web option in mixed-mode surveys
	7. Pre-recruited panels of Internet users
	8. Pre-recruited panels of full population

On the nonprobability side, the first two methods are what we commonly think of when we talk about self-selected Internet polling, with large numbers of respondents, many of whom may participate multiple times. These are typically not particularly useful polls, even if it is fun to participate and read about the results. The third category of nonprobability Web polls is more interesting, and we will discuss one specific application shortly.

On the probability side, the intercept poll simply entails sampling people who visit a particular Web site, with features built in to account for multiple hits by the same people. Here the sample reflects the overall population that visited that Web site, but results cannot be generalized to broader populations. The next category—list-based sample of high-coverage populations—takes advantage of the fact that there are certain populations, such as those on university campuses, in which access to computers, e-mail, and the Internet is universal and comprehensive lists of the population exist. These circumstances make Internet polling of representative samples of university populations very feasible and enable one to generalize from the sample to the overall population from which it was drawn (assuming appropriate response rates and the like). The mixed-mode design simply offers the Internet as one way of participating in a poll; some respondents might use the Web, while others might participate over the telephone or through filling out a mail questionnaire.

The final two categories both involve using probability sampling methods such as random-digit dialing to identify a representative sample, then contacting them, identifying those with Internet access, obtaining their e-mail address, and trying to recruit them to participate in a Web survey. The major difference between the pre-recruited panels of Internet users and the pre-recruited panels of the full population is that in the former case, only those citizens who are already Internet users can be selected as part of the sample. In the latter case, those who currently are not Internet users are provided Internet access and training; thus one can conduct an Internet survey of a sample from the entire population.

Two of the most creative and ambitious examples of Internet polling have been conducted by Harris Interactive, using volunteer opt-in panels, and Knowledge Networks, using pre-recruited panels of the full population. Harris Interactive puts together a large (over 7 million in 2000) national, online panel of willing respondents. As described by Taylor et al., "the panel was recruited through multiple sources, including banner advertisements and sweepstakes that have run across the web, the Harris/Excite daily poll, product registrations on Excite and Netscape, and telephone surveys" (2001, 38). This results in a panel of Americans who already use the Internet, but it is not representative of all Internet users or of the total American population. Hence, statistical sampling and weighting procedures are used to adjust for the differential likelihood of different respondents being included. As early critics (e.g., Mitofsky, 1999) of the Harris sampling procedures worried about representativeness and low response rates, a major test of this type of online polling occurred in the 2000 presidential election. The Harris Interactive online poll had Bush and Gore tied, a more accurate prediction than the telephone polls sponsored by other organizations produced. Moreover, the individual-state-level predictions made by Harris Interactive were twice as accurate as all other telephone polls (Taylor et al. 2001, 38).

In contrast to Harris Interactive, Knowledge Networks tries to obtain a representative sample of all Americans whether or not they initially have Internet access. This is accomplished by using random-digit dialing techniques to select a large panel (sample) from all households having a phone. These households are then contacted to recruit them to participate in online surveys. Households that agree to participate are provided Web access and Internet equipment. Thus, citizens who previously did not use the Internet are included in the sample. Various studies (Greenberg and Rivers 2001; Smith 2003) comparing Knowledge Networks online polls with telephone and with face-to-face polls indicate that the Knowledge Networks Internet surveys often yield reasonably similar results, although some notable differences were observed. For example, there tends to be a higher incidence of "don't know" responses in Knowledge Networks polls, perhaps because they provided an explicit "don't know" option and perhaps because it is easier to probe and elicit a response from people in phone and personal interviews. Based on his own research, Smith offered a cautionary note about the accuracy of online polling:

> [I]t cannot automatically be expected that even Internet surveys based on probability samples and general populations will produce results equivalent to those from non-Internet surveys. Internet surveys intrinsically differ from standard, non-Internet surveys in format and respondent-demand characteristics and will often differ on other characteristics such as population coverage, response rate, and the use of panels. These factors will usually combine together to produce notable differences between Internet and non-Internet surveys. (2003, 175)

My own view is that whatever the current shortcomings of Internet polling, it will continue to grow, particularly as the challenges facing telephone polling continue to get more daunting. On grounds of cost, speed, the availability of large samples, and the ability to incorporate audio and visual elements in polls, Internet polling is increasingly attractive. For many practitioners, the information collected in Internet polling is useful even if it cannot be generalized to larger populations. And even though there are questions about the accuracy of specific, one-time estimates obtained in Internet polls, such surveys should do a good job of tracking trends over time. Technical and statistical developments and expanded access to the Internet will serve to make Internet surveys more scientific and more representative in the future. In the meantime, the results of Internet surveys should be viewed with caution, particularly if they are conducted by entities with an agenda to promote. The National Council on Public Polls (NCPP), skeptical about the reliability of many Internet surveys, has provided journalists with ten questions they should address before reporting the results of Internet polls. According to the NCPP, if an Internet survey is not designed to be representative, and if there is no evidence that it is representative, its results should not be reported. The NCPP also essentially dismisses self-selected, call-in polls. Yet despite the NCPP's admonitions to journalists and the news media to be careful about publicizing and reporting Internet polls, Web-based surveys are becoming more prominent, and many are even sponsored by the news organizations themselves.

Conclusion

The method of interviewing and the actual conduct of the interview measurably affect the responses to a public opinion poll. In most instances consumers of polls are in a weak position to evaluate these effects, mainly because pollsters provide little information about interviewing procedures. Nevertheless, consumers might raise a number of questions about the interviewing process, particularly if they have been selected to be respondents in a poll. For example, consumers who refuse to complete a mailed questionnaire might ask themselves why. Is it because the subject matter is of no interest, because the questions are too simplistic, or because the questionnaire is too time-consuming? Consumers who choose to participate in a survey might examine their reactions to question wording and question order, to the overall experience itself, or to other specific elements of the questionnaire.

One question that poll consumers will never be able to answer is whether the same results would have been obtained had a different interviewing method been used. Some research suggests that the choice of interviewing method can affect the responses because of the different interpersonal dynamics that characterize different interviewing modes. For example, in two studies on substance use, personal interviews found higher levels of alcohol and drug use by respondents than did telephone interviews (Johnson 1989; Aquilino and Losciuto 1990).

Respondents to personal or telephone polls also should make some mental notes about the skill of the interviewers. How effective was the interviewer in establishing a good climate for the interview? How well did the interviewer handle the respondent's questions and problems? Did the interviewer do or say anything that seemed to lead the person to respond in certain ways? Did the interviewer have any characteristics or traits that either facilitated or hindered the interview? The answers to these and other questions should alert poll respondents to biases that can influence the interviewing process and the answers it generates.

Exercises

1. Go to the Web site of the American National Election Studies, Gallup, or the Program on International Policy Attitudes and download an actual questionnaire. Then assume that you are an interviewer who will administer that questionnaire (or a subset of it) in a face-to-face setting. Find five friends who are willing to serve as respondents and administer the survey to each of them separately. What problems did you encounter in conducting the interviews? How did the fact that you were interviewing friends affect the interpersonal dynamics of the interview situation? How do you think the experience would have differed if you were interviewing strangers?

2. Design a ten-item Internet survey to be self-administered on your college campus. How might your survey differ if you were to interview the respondents directly (in person or on the phone) rather than use the Internet?

6 The Media and the Polls

Newspapers and television are the major sources of what Americans learn about polls. Most citizens do not have direct access to reports that polling organizations prepare. And because newspapers and TV are the sources Americans rely on most, citizens need to recognize that many of the organizations that sponsor surveys try to manipulate those media to cover poll results in ways that promote the organizations' objectives. Candidates for office also often try to obtain advantageous media coverage of private campaign polls by selectively leaking the results

Moreover, the national television networks and their local affiliates, the major newsmagazines, and newspapers throughout the country themselves sponsor some of the most publicized and widely disseminated public opinion polls. Thus the media generate much of the public opinion data that in turn become the subject matter for the news stories that they present. For some observers, this situation raises questions about a conflict of interest—meaning that the definition of what is newsworthy may be unduly influenced by media-sponsored polls on particular topics. In addition, the fact that these news organizations make substantial investments in developing their capability for public opinion polling may result in a tendency to use that capability even when it is not appropriate to the topic at hand.

Because of the media's pivotal role in developing citizens' awareness of polling, this chapter evaluates the media's reporting of public opinion polls, both the ones they sponsor and those sponsored by other organizations. The discussion focuses on two distinct aspects of poll coverage—the treatment of the polls' technical features (for example, sampling error and question wording) and the presentation of substantive results and interpretations based on the polling data. It concludes with some caveats about the reporting of polls.

Standards for Reporting Results

Because media reporting of polls may not always be reliable, various organizations have adopted standards to govern the disclosure of poll results to citizens. For example, the National Council on Public Polls (NCPP), a group of polling organizations, has adopted the following Principles of Disclosure:

All reports of survey findings of member organizations, prepared specifically for public release, will include reference to the following:

—sponsorship of the survey
—dates of interviewing
—method of obtaining the interview
—population that was sampled
—size of the sample
—size and description of the subsample, if the survey report relies primarily on less than the total sample
—complete wording of questions upon which the release is based
—the percentages upon which conclusions are based

The recommendations go on to state:

When survey results are released to any medium by a survey organization, the above items will be included in the release. . . .

Survey organizations reporting results will endeavor to have print and broadcast media include the above items in their news stories and make a report containing these items available to the public upon request.

Both the American Association for Public Opinion Research (AAPOR) and the Council of American Survey Research Organizations (CASRO) have codes of conduct that specify standards for disclosure of how a poll was conducted. Both organizations specify two sets of standards for disclosure, one a minimum and the other more encompassing. Both organizations recognize that it is difficult to expect the media, polling organizations, and the like to devote substantial time and attention to the methodological aspects of a poll, but they both agree that there is at least a minimum body of information that must be disclosed. For example, AAPOR advocates that at the minimum the following items be disclosed:

1. Who sponsored the survey and who conducted it.
2. The exact wording of questions asked, including the text of any preceding instruction or explanation to the interviewer or respondents that might reasonably be expected to affect the response.

3. A definition of the population under study and a description of the sampling frame used to identify that population.
4. A description of the sample selection procedure, giving a clear indication of the method by which the respondents were selected by the researcher, or whether the respondents were entirely self-selected.
5. Sizes of samples and, if applicable, completion rates and information on eligibility criteria and screening procedures.
6. A discussion of the precision of the findings, including, if appropriate, estimates of sampling error, and a description of any weighting or estimating procedures used.
7. Which results are based on parts of the sample, rather than on the total sample.
8. Method, location, and dates of data collection. (AAPOR 1986)

Effectiveness of the Standards

But how much protection do these standards provide for consumers of public opinion research, assuming that polling organizations adhere to them? The answer is that they provide less protection than is apparent at first glance, although they have contributed to improved media coverage of the polls. One reason why the standards are not as effective as they appear is that they apply primarily to survey organizations and pollsters who release results rather than to the news organizations that are covering the results. In cases when the survey organization and the disseminator of the results are part of the same news organization, the coverage is usually more in line with the NCPP and AAPOR standards.

Here is an example of how the standards may be applied when the survey organization and the disseminator of the results are the same. Reports of the results of a CBS News/*New York Times* poll may emanate from four distinct sources: (1) the story that appears in the *New York Times*; (2) the report presented on the *CBS Evening News*; (3) a news release issued by the *New York Times*; and (4) a news release prepared by CBS News. The first two sources are readily available to citizens; the latter two are not. Normally, the news releases prepared by CBS News and by the *New York Times* and the news story in the *Times* comply closely with the NCPP and AAPOR standards; the story presented on the *CBS Evening News* is less complete because airtime is limited.

If the organization reporting the poll is different from the group that sponsored it, the poll release and the actual news story may show major discrepancies in meeting the NCPP, CASRO, and AAPOR recommendations. For example, most newspapers do not conduct their own polls. Instead, they rely on syndicated polls from organizations such as Gallup or on news releases in the public domain that are issued by polling organiza-

cathy® by **Cathy Guisewite**

tions. In these situations the NCPP recommends that the sponsoring organization attempt to ensure that the medium that reports its results conforms to the NCPP standards. But there really is no way to enforce this recommendation with news organizations once the poll release has become public. Moreover, the interests of the sponsoring organization may not be well served by full disclosure of the technical features of the poll, particularly when the sponsoring organization has manipulated the poll to generate a desired set of results. Overall, then, compliance with the standards is voluntary, and that diminishes their effectiveness.

Another reason the NCPP, CASRO, and AAPOR standards are less effective than they might be is that they do not specify reporting of all the technical aspects of a poll that can markedly affect the results. For example, the NCPP standards recommend reporting the "complete wording of questions on which the release is based." Complete wording is not necessarily identical to the complete questionnaire—that is, without the entire survey instrument it is difficult to ascertain whether question order and placement have influenced the results reported in a release. Likewise, the second AAPOR standard is a very subjective recommendation. Different polling organizations might very well disagree about the meaning of "instruction or explanation . . . that might reasonably be expected to affect the response." For the major news organizations, whether this standard has been met is of less concern because their releases typically include entire questionnaires, showing the order in which the items were asked. Moreover, the television networks and major newspapers are willing to distribute complete poll releases to interested citizens.

A more serious problem arises, however, when a news organization prepares a news analysis based on a subset of items from a questionnaire and does not inform readers or viewers about item selection, question wording, and question order. Then the news analysis may or may not accurately represent the content of the entire survey. Obviously, the items chosen for analysis and the perspective taken on them can dramatically affect the resulting coverage.

The NCPP and AAPOR minimum standards ignore other technical specifications. For example, NCPP standards do not require reporting of adjustments made to a sample, such as weighting (used to achieve demographic representativeness—see chapter 4) or filtering (e.g., used to identify likely voters within a sample). A poll release will often state that weighting and filtering have been done, but in most cases it will not tell how. As a result, the poll consumer, ill equipped to assess the soundness of the poll, is at the mercy of the decisions made by the news organizations. For example, pollsters identify likely voters using different methods that can generate divergent predictions of election outcomes (see chapter 7).

Finally, the NCPP and AAPOR minimum standards do not address response rates or the procedures, such as callbacks, that were used to increase them. Poor response rates may require adjusting the interviewed sample to make it representative of the broader population. If respondents who are called back multiple times in order to complete an interview differ in systematic ways from those who are interviewed on the first attempt, then the decision on whether to use multiple callbacks can affect the substantive findings of the poll. Unfortunately, in most situations poll consumers receive little if any information about response rates and related matters.

Observing the Standards

How closely do the media actually conform to these professional standards in their reporting of polls? An early study by Miller and Hurd (1982) examined how well three newspapers—the *Chicago Tribune,* the *Los Angeles Times,* and the *Atlanta Constitution*—followed the AAPOR guidelines. In a sample of 116 polls reported between 1972 and 1979, compliance was highest for sample size (reported 85 percent of the time) and sponsorship (reported 82 percent of the time), and lowest for sampling error (reported only 16 percent of the time). Miller and Hurd found that compliance with the AAPOR standards on sampling error was better for election polls than for nonelection surveys. In general, compliance on sampling error was better when newspapers reported on their own polls than on polls provided by external sources, a finding repeated in a study of major newspaper performance in the 2000 general election (Welch 2002).

Overall, Miller and Hurd did see signs that newspaper reporting of polls had improved over the years. The improvement can be attributed to increased collaboration between journalists and social scientists, the availability of readable books on polling, and the increased frequency of in-house polls (newspapers do a better job of reporting their own polls because of local interest in them and because reporters have greater access to information about their technical aspects).

The positive findings of that study must be tempered by the fact that it dealt with major daily newspapers of reasonably high quality. One expects such papers to be competent in reporting polls. Moreover, many of the polls the researchers analyzed were election surveys, which are more likely to report information such as sample size and sampling error than are nonelection surveys. A different study found that reports of nonelection polls were more descriptive of question wording and method of interviewing than were election polls (Salwen 1985a). That finding was speculatively attributed to the fact that question wording and interviewing method are more self-evident in election polls and therefore need not be reported. In smaller daily and weekly newspapers, without the resources to conduct their own polls or employ their own survey research experts, poll coverage is probably much poorer.

If newspaper reporting falls short of the NCPP and AAPOR standards, what must television coverage be like? Newspapers have obvious advantages in reporting polls. One is that they provide the reader with hard copy that can be reread and referred to, in contrast to the television message, which (unless taped) "disappears" as soon as it is presented. Another is that newspapers can more easily present a lot of information, such as full question wording.

Paletz and colleagues (1980) conducted one of the few empirical studies of the treatment of polls by network television. They examined every poll reported on the CBS and NBC evening news shows and in the *New York Times* in 1973, 1975, and 1977, years deliberately chosen to avoid presidential elections. Their conclusion was that the television networks generally did a poorer job of reporting details about polls than did the *Times,* although the latter's performance was not stellar. Among the findings was that the sponsor of a poll was almost never mentioned on the networks and mentioned only about 25 percent of the time in the *Times.* Sample size was presented in two-thirds of the *Times* stories but in only 26 percent of the television reports. The time of interviewing was given in 43 percent of the *Times* accounts and in 30 percent of the television reports. And in only 30 percent of the *Times* stories and 5 percent of the television reports was the complete wording of particular questions provided. Beyond these details, the reports provided virtually no other technical information about the polls (Paletz et al. 1980, 504–505).

One recent study focused on how well the television networks treated sampling error in their coverage of the polls in the 2000 general election campaign. Larson (2003) found that although more than half the television stories included mention of sampling error, a major improvement over what used to be the case, the coverage often demonstrated a lack of understanding of how the sampling error was to be applied to the reported percentages. Too often, the news report compared the sampling error directly with the percentage gap between Gore and Bush, rather than applying the sampling error (plus and minus) to the Gore and Bush percentages, concluding incorrectly that the margin separating the candidates was statistically significant. Larson also found that when the news reports talked about subsets of poll respondents, the stories generally failed to acknowledge that the margin of error for the subgroup was higher than for the overall sample. This finding was echoed by Langer (2000), who found that media coverage of the presidential preferences of subgroups (such as Hispanics) often ignored the fact that the sampling error was so great that no definitive statements about the patterns of voter movements could really be made.

The available evidence suggests that the media could do a much better job of adhering to the NCPP and AAPOR standards in reporting poll results, especially for surveys not conducted in-house. If they did, citizens could become more proficient in evaluating poll results. Methodological sophistication in poll reporting is increasing as journalists, political practitioners, and even media audiences acquire survey research skills. Moreover, as more news organizations conduct their own polls and ignore those from other sources, the overall quality of poll reporting will probably improve.

In 1994 two examples of excellent reporting of the mechanics of a poll appeared in the *Columbus Dispatch*. That year, the newspaper conducted its own in-house mail surveys and commissioned the Gallup Organization to conduct statewide telephone polls on the 1994 elections in Ohio. About its own poll, the *Dispatch* said:

> The *Dispatch* poll was based on returns from 1,456 registered Ohioans who intend to vote Nov. 8. *The Dispatch* bought a computerized list of all registered Ohio voters. A *Dispatch* computer randomly chose those to receive ballots, modeled as closely as possible after the state's official ballot layout. Voters receiving the ballots were asked to describe themselves by party affiliation, age, sex, race, education, income, religion, union membership and how they voted for president in 1992 and governor in 1990. Ballots of different colors were sent to various regions of the state so *The Dispatch* could ensure that each area was represented in proportion to its actual voting strength. The areas, patterned on groupings of the state's media markets, are: northeast (20 counties); central (20 counties); southwest (8 counties); northwest (12 counties);

west (14 counties); and southeast (14 counties). The standard margin of sampling error in a scientific poll of the size conducted by *The Dispatch* is plus or minus 2.5 percentage points in 95 out of 100 cases. This means that if a scientific poll is conducted 100 times, in 95 cases the result will not vary by more than 2.5 percentage points from the result that would be obtained if all registered voters in Ohio were polled and responded. Error margins are greater for poll subsamples. Like all polls, *The Dispatch* Poll is subject to possible error other than sampling error. Other sources of error can be unintentional bias in the wording of questions, data entry error or nonresponse bias. Nonresponse bias means that those who responded to the poll may not necessarily reflect the views of those who did not participate. The response rate was 19 percent. The results were adjusted slightly to compensate for demographic differences between poll respondents and the Ohio electorate as a whole. Although precautions are taken to ensure that the sample reflects the demographic characteristics of the Ohio electorate, precise estimates for total possible error cannot be calculated. The poll was designed, conducted and financed by *The Dispatch*. (*Columbus Dispatch* 1994a, 5)

About the Gallup poll, the *Dispatch* reported the following information provided by the Gallup Organization:

The results of the Gallup survey are based on telephone interviews with a randomly selected statewide sample of 803 registered voters, conducted Tuesday through Thursday. Data were weighted to ensure appropriate representation by age, sex, education, race and geographical location. Household telephone numbers were generated by a computer to ensure that all areas of the state were represented in proportion to the actual population in that area. This method ensures that both listed and unlisted telephone numbers are included in the sample. Respondents were asked whether they were registered to vote in their precinct or election district. For all respondents—registered or not—information was obtained on their gender, age, education and race, so that the overall sample of registered and unregistered adults could be weighted to conform to the census statistics. Registered voters also were asked their likelihood of voting and how interested they were in the election. These two questions were used to compute a "likely voter" category, which includes 483 respondents. For results based on the statewide sample of 803 registered voters, one can say with 95 percent confidence that the error attributed to sampling and other random effects could be plus or minus 4 percentage points. For results based on the "likely voter" category, the margin of error is plus or minus 5 percentage points. In addition to sampling error, question wording and practical difficulties in conducting surveys can introduce error or bias into the findings of public opinion polls. (*Columbus Dispatch* 1994b, 2)

Note that in addition to the standard information about sampling error and confidence levels, both of these descriptions discussed weighting or adjusting the data and mentioned the different sampling error for subgroups. They also mentioned other sources of error, although they did not develop these points. It is to the credit of the *Dispatch* that it commissioned an outside poll for results that could be compared with the results of its in-house surveys.

Substantive Interpretation of Polls

Without access to the complete results of polls, citizens cannot easily evaluate how well the news media report the technical aspects of polling. It is even more problematic for them to evaluate how well news organizations describe and interpret the substance of public opinion polls. Because interpretation of polling data can be highly judgmental and value laden, it may be difficult to demonstrate that one particular interpretation is superior to another except in cases where obvious misreadings of the data have occurred or blatant biases have been built into the analysis. Even a simple description can pose a problem if a news story covers only a subset of the items on a topic because there is insufficient time or space.

In this section I will present several examples illustrating how the news media use and interpret polls and how much leeway they have in deciding which parts of a poll to emphasize. A good example of the choices that face the analyst is Adam Clymer's *New York Times* story on attitudes toward abortion, based on a survey of Americans conducted in late 1985. Though there have been countless surveys on abortion attitudes since the one that Clymer discussed in his article, it remains rare to see a reporter explicitly point to the deep complexity of public opinion on a topic. In Clymer's view, the wording of questions about abortion has a tremendous impact on the responses, and that is a "clear indication of uncertainty and conflict" in the public's attitudes on the topic (Clymer 1986b). Three items in the survey illustrate the complexity of popular attitudes:

What do you think about abortion? Should it be legal as it is now, legal only in such cases as saving the life of the mother, rape or incest, or should it not be permitted at all?

Legal as is now	40%
Legal only to save mother, rape or incest	40%
Not permitted	16%
Don't know, not ascertained	4%

Which of these statements comes closest to your opinion? Abortion is the same thing as murdering a child, or abortion is not murder because a fetus isn't really a person.

Murder	55%
Not murder	35%
Don't know, not ascertained	10%

Do you agree or disagree with the following statement? Abortion sometimes is the best course in a bad situation.

Agree	66%
Disagree	26%
Don't know, not ascertained	8%

A journalist could write markedly different stories based on this survey, depending on which items are emphasized and how particular items are interpreted. By focusing only on the first item, a reporter could write a pro-choice story that points out that 40 percent of Americans favor the current abortion law, another 40 percent favor legalized abortion in limited circumstances, and only 16 percent oppose abortion outright. Another reporter could write an antiabortion story based on the first item, by stressing that 56 percent of the sample (40 percent plus 16 percent) favor limiting somewhat the current availability of abortion. Likewise, the second item could be used to document an antiabortion story that emphasizes that a majority of Americans think abortion is murder. But a story based only on the third item would suggest that a strong majority of Americans think abortion is sometimes the best course of action. The article that Clymer wrote reflects the complex and even contradictory nature of popular attitudes on abortion (1986b). Imagine the advocacy piece he could have written if he had adopted a blatantly pro-choice or antiabortion perspective.

News articles in the *New York Times, Washington Post,* and other major newspapers that include polling data usually integrate the polling information into the body of the article, often presenting detailed breakdowns of the data and a reasonable amount of information about the poll and its characteristics. Newspapers not only use polls to supplement a news story but also print articles whose subjects are the polls themselves. By contrast, newsmagazines such as *Time* and *Newsweek* often commission polls to use as sidebars to news stories, the results shown in a separate box, with little reference made to them in the accompanying story.

The following examples suggest that media reports of polls conducted by other organizations are particularly susceptible to misinterpretation and faulty reporting. Krosnick (1989) investigated the *New York Times* coverage of a poll commissioned by Aetna Life and Casualty on the public's attitudes toward the civil justice system and tort reform; the poll was conducted by Louis Harris and Associates. Aetna had a vested interest in tort reform. When the poll was completed, Aetna issued a press release that began, "An overwhelming majority of Americans support a number of specific reforms to improve the nation's civil justice system." Throughout the press release and the Harris report of the survey results were assertions that Americans supported and favored many changes. The survey questions themselves, however, did not ask respondents whether they supported or favored those changes; instead, the questions asked whether respondents found the changes acceptable. Clearly, finding something acceptable is not the same thing as supporting or favoring it. Nevertheless, the news story on the poll that appeared in the *New York Times* failed to recognize this distinction and made strong claims that the poll results demonstrated "broad public support for *changes* in the civil justice system" and "reflected the public's *demand* for reform" (Krosnick 1989, 108). As Krosnick concluded, the *Times* coverage of the poll results most likely overstated public support for the changes that Aetna desired.

Another example, one with serious international ramifications, of media misreporting and misinterpreting of polls occurred in the late 1970s as the U.S. Senate considered ratification of the treaties that would lead to Panamanian control of the Panama Canal. Smith and Hogan (1987) found that as the debate progressed in the Senate, many media organizations were reporting that public opinion was shifting toward support of the treaties—a finding that, if true, would obviously make it easier for senators sympathetic to the treaties to vote for ratification. But when Smith and Hogan examined the myriad poll results from the period, they found a pattern of stable opinion (which was hostile to the treaties), not one of change. They attributed the misleading interpretations to the variety of questions asked by different polling outfits, flaws in these questions, misinterpretation of key findings, and other factors. Here, though, the key point is the researchers' evaluation of how different news organizations actually reported the polls. They wrote:

> In general, CBS and the *New York Times* provided accurate and perceptive accounts of public opinion on the treaties. But the *Time, Newsweek,* and NBC stories . . . display serious flaws. During the crucial period of Senate deliberation (January through April 1978) all claimed a massive shift in approval based on comparison of responses to different questions asked, in most cases, by different pollsters. Furthermore, the coverage is littered by errors of fact and inference and shows little understanding of the complex issues involved. . . .

> Equally disturbing are certain common omissions. After January 1978, most findings of continued public opposition were simply ignored. . . . Also omitted were the methodological details that would have allowed an educated reader or viewer to discover the misinterpretations embedded in the media coverage. Only two articles, both in the *New York Times,* provided the complete text of a question; only one, also in the *Times,* included all of the information required by the American Association for Public Opinion Research (AAPOR) Standards of Disclosure for poll reports. In *Time* and *Newsweek* almost no information was given. (Smith and Hogan 1987, 27)

Morin (1998b) has pointed out that much of the media coverage (including some of his own) of the U.S. role in Bosnia in the late 1990s ignored poll results indicating strong support for some form of multilateral involvement and instead emphasized public opposition to U.S. involvement.

The coverage of domestic policy issues also is often flawed. Morin (1997d) cites the work of Jacobs and Shapiro (1995; 1995–1996), who investigated how the media use polls to report on entitlement programs. Their conclusions are very critical, claiming that news stories often fail to provide context and background from which to interpret survey data. They also point out that polling on topics such as entitlements is focusing increasingly on the politics (for example, the performance of various political actors) of the issue rather than the substance. Certainly it is possible that the way the media portray public opinion on controversial issues such as the canal treaties or Bosnia or entitlements may affect the public policy decisions that are ultimately made.

The above examples focus on media coverage of polls conducted by other organizations. But the media can also stumble in reporting their own commissioned polls. In 2002, the state of Ohio was addressing the issue of science education in public schools. A controversy arose about the teaching of evolution versus other explanations of life including "intelligent design," a perspective supported by creationism advocates. The *Cleveland Plain Dealer* sponsored a poll to ascertain Ohioans' attitudes about what should be taught in science education and ran a major, page one story on the results titled "Poll: Teach More Than Evolution" with the subtitle, "A majority of those surveyed want evolution, intelligent design to get equal time in school" (Stephen and Mangels 2002). And in the second paragraph of the story (on the first page of the paper), the reporters wrote, "A clear majority of the state's residents—59 percent—favor teaching evolution in tandem with intelligent design in public school science classes." The evidence for that conclusion was the following poll question and responses:

Currently, the Ohio Board of Education is debating new academic standards for public school science classes, including what to teach students about the development of life on Earth. Which position do you support?

Teach only evolution	8%
Teach only intelligent design	8%
Teach both	59%
Teach the evidence both for and against evolution, but not necessarily intelligent design	15%
Teach nothing about human development	9%
Not sure	1%

The thrust of the story was that Ohioans were very supportive of teaching intelligent design, and its proponents cited the *Plain Dealer* as evidence for their position. But a very different story could have been written had the reporters chosen to focus on other questions in the survey and had they adopted a different analysis strategy. For example, one item asked respondents,

Which of the following is the best place to teach about beliefs regarding the development of life that differ from evolution?

In a science class	23%
In a class other than science	17%
At home or in a religious setting	51%
Not sure	9%

Based on these responses, a different story lead might have been that Ohioans overwhelmingly preferred that intelligent design be taught somewhere other than in a science class and that a majority of them preferred that intelligent design be taught outside the school altogether.

One might also question whether Ohioans responding to the poll even knew what evolution and, especially, intelligent design were. Respondents were asked about their familiarity with intelligent design and evolution. Eighteen percent said they were very familiar with intelligent design, 37% said "somewhat familiar," and 45% said "not that familiar." The comparable percentages for evolution were 42, 43, and 15. Perhaps the reporters should have replicated their analysis for those respondents who were at least somewhat familiar with intelligent design and evolution. Doing so would undoubtedly have eliminated some nonattitudes and might provide a more accurate portrait of Ohio public opinion.

Sometimes the news media use pseudopolls of self-selected respondents to embellish a news story in a misleading way. In one example, ABC used a pseudopoll in its coverage even though genuine polling data were available (Morin 1996a). ABC's newsmagazine show *20/20* devoted a segment to "physical attraction"—that is, whether women were satisfied with their physical appearance and what aspects of the physical appearance of women were most important to men. ABC's own scientific survey on these topics had found that the vast majority of women were satisfied with their physical attributes. The show decided, however, to build its story about physical attractiveness around a pseudopoll conducted by *Self* magazine, and it went on to report that 50 percent of the women who completed the magazine survey and mailed it in said that "they were inadequate because of their breast size." But the genuine poll that ABC itself conducted found quite different results: only 23 percent of respondents had ever wished their breasts were a different size, and contrary to the thrust of the *20/20* segment, with its emphasis on breast enlargement, more than half of the dissatisfied women in the genuine poll had wished that their breasts were smaller, not larger. In this case, entertainment values overrode any responsibility to use appropriate polling data.

The statistical analysis that poll stories most commonly present is simple percentage distributions for individual questions in the survey—something that most adults understand. Sometimes reports include a breakdown by demographic subgroups, such as men and women or blacks and whites, but they seldom offer a cross-tabulation that shows the relationship between two survey items. Measures of association, correlation analysis, and multivariate statistical analyses almost never appear in news stories, probably out of the media's fear of intimidating and alienating the audience. It is fair to say, however, that news organizations' use of statistics is reasonably accurate, as far as it goes, in part because the data analysis is not very ambitious given media executives' perceptions of what audiences want and are able to comprehend.

Media, Polls, and the News Reporting Emphasis

The media are frequently criticized for elevating polls to such a position of prominence that the polls themselves become regular topics f or news stories. Indeed, some observers complain that the media, in their role as sponsors of polls, have gone into the business of creating the news rather than simply reporting it. More and more news organizations have developed their own polling capabilities, and to justify this sizable expenditure they may increasingly report poll-based stories that are not newsworthy in the traditional sense. Fitzgerald, Rule, and Bryant (1998) documented the rise of poll-based reporting on television news and the growing tendency of the networks to use their own polls. Consider this hypothetical example: A news organization conducts a poll on American attitudes toward mass transportation. Even though this topic is not on the national agenda and not a focal point for public debate, the news organization publishes a story reporting the results of the survey. Such a story comes very close to being news that is created by the media rather than news that is coverage of real events. The media also come close to generating news in their constant reporting of presidential popularity polls, in that the latest blip in the trend line of presidential popularity becomes a news story.

Another concern is that as more news organizations develop their own polling capabilities, they will less and less cover polls conducted by their rivals. Most of the media pollsters query citizens on matters such as presidential election trial heats, but usually their news reports do not mention the competition's results, particularly when those results disagree with their own.

The media's treatment of election polls has received especially harsh criticism. The most common complaint is that the news organizations treat elections as sporting events—the comparison is usually to horse races (see chapter 7)—and use the polls to handicap the outcome. Indeed, Fitzgerald, Rule, and Bryant (1998) found that between 1969 and 1996 only four topics accounted for 90 percent of the poll-based stories on TV news, and number one on the list was candidates and elections. These stories frequently emphasize candidates' relative standing as measured by the polls (Broh 1980; Asher 1992), rather than their stances on the issues. As Robinson and Sheehan argue,

> The main problem with polling . . . is that it is objective and so "newsworthy" (at least for the moment) that it drives out all other forms of news. Polls have a higher priority in the newscast than most other forms of campaign reporting. And, of course, polls tend to be among the least substantive kinds of political journalism. (1983, 252)

In the 1988, 1992, 1996, and 2000 presidential campaigns, much of the criticism of presidential election polls focused on their frequency, their intrusiveness, their inconsistency, and the quality of media coverage of them. For example, Elving (1989) notes that in August 1988 fourteen major polls on the Dukakis-Bush presidential contest had results that varied by nineteen percentage points, a situation that generated confusion and annoyance with the polls. In defending their enterprise, many pollsters shifted blame to the media:

> "Did I see [1988] polls that annoyed me? No, but I did see reporting on them that did," says Linda DiVall of American Viewpoint Inc. "I wish the

press had less desire to be conclusive and say the race is over when it's 10 points and it's May."

Ed Goeas, president of Tarrance & Associates, says newspaper polls can be manipulated by the campaigns. "When newspaper polls are in the field the campaign can learn of it and do things to pump their guy up."

But, Goeas contends, the real problems come when the data are in hand: "Newspapers are hurting the credibility of the industry because they are not prepared to analyze the data correctly." . . .

"They're getting better, but I am always amazed at how many reporters are covering polls . . . without training or background," says Bud Lewis, the veteran pollster for the *Los Angeles Times.* "It's like sex— everybody thinks they're good at it automatically."(Elving 1989, 2187)

The 1992 elections offer another example. In the preconvention period, different polls had either George Bush or Ross Perot ahead (though not by large margins). The media coverage of these polls was often very dramatic and definitive, giving little recognition to how unstable early presidential preferences can be (Morin 1992d). Harwood (1992) argues that the media then did a poor job of accounting for dramatic postconvention swings in polled support for Bill Clinton and Bush, often simply attributing them to convention "bumps," when in fact much of the fluctuation might have stemmed from the limitations inherent in the polls themselves.

A similar situation occurred in the preconvention period in the 1996 presidential campaign. Most polls in May 1996 showed Clinton with a sizable double-digit lead over Bob Dole. Most of the next round of poll results, in mid-June, showed Clinton still ahead by a double-digit margin but a smaller one than in May. Of the June polls, the one that received the greatest media attention was the survey that showed the smallest gap between Clinton and Dole; the *Time*/CNN survey revealed that Clinton's lead had dropped from 56 percent to 34 percent, to 49 percent to 43 percent. Why did the news media focus on the *Time*/CNN poll when other polls showed Clinton with a larger lead? The probable answer is twofold: First, the media love a close horse race that generates excitement, and that is what the *Time*/CNN poll showed. Second, the *Time*/CNN poll showed the greatest fluctuation over time, which intrinsically made it more interesting to those who report the news.

In the 2000 election, the Bush-versus-Gore poll results bounced around substantially through the Republican and Democratic conventions, past Labor Day, and into the presidential debates in October. This volatility perplexed some observers and led others to be critical of the media for their breathless reporting of slight changes in poll standing.

Other problems inherent in public opinion polling by news organizations reflect the structural characteristics of the polling and news-reporting enterprises. Ladd questions whether polling and journalism can ever fit together well, given that *newsworthiness* for the media entails speed and timeliness, whereas good polling, despite the current technology for quick assessments of public attitudes, requires "extensive, time-consuming explanation and exposition" (1980, 576). This conflict is exacerbated by the space and time constraints that news organizations face, which often do not allow them to present a poll-based story that includes complete details about the poll itself plus substantive background and context. Ladd also argues that good reporting is generally sharply focused with relatively unambiguous conclusions; good survey research, however, usually reveals uncertainty, ambiguity, and low levels of public information and interest on matters of public policy. Often the portrait of public attitudes that polls reveal is a complex, contradictory one that may not make a "good" news story.

News treatment of polls also is shaped by the capabilities of journalists to analyze and report on the polls. Because of changes in the curriculum of university journalism programs and the availability of specialized training programs, reporters are becoming increasingly skillful in reporting on polls. Even so, Crespi argues that journalistic requirements affect polling in both positive and negative ways:

Positive	Negative
Journalistic requirements place a high value on factual documentation of poll results, in the form of actual percentages rather than fuzzy generalizations.	There is a preoccupation with reporting numbers, the "objective" poll results, with a corresponding lack of interest in their underlying meaning or patterning.
Subjective editorializing is devalued insofar as poll reports are concerned, reducing the likelihood that the personal views of pollsters will introduce bias.	Superficiality and lack of analysis too often characterize coverage of even the most complicated issues.
Attention is focused on opinion regarding specific events and issues, thereby making poll results relevant to the real-life experiences and problems of the public, and to the political process.	Topics that can be expected to create front-page headlines dominate, leading to a spasmodic coverage of the agenda of public concerns.
Sensitivity to changes in public opinion, resulting from the effects of events, is enhanced.	There is limited continuing coverage of long-term trends, and background news is often neglected. (1980, 473)

Conclusion

The relationship between polling and the media can be difficult and complex. But if poll sponsors recognize both the uses and limitations of polls, the relationship also can be beneficial and informative for citizens. News organizations need to take whatever steps are necessary to ensure that they provide their audiences with sufficient information to make informed judgments. Reporting sample size and sampling error is the beginning of good poll coverage, not the end. Standard practice should include presenting question wording and question order, factors that can have a much greater effect on the responses than can sampling error.

Beyond this, the journalism profession must be more sensitive to and reflective about the possible links between polls and news coverage. The media can easily play an agenda-setting role by bringing certain issues to the public's attention through news reporting, sponsoring and conducting polls on those issues, and reporting the results, activities that will reinforce the visibility of an issue to the electorate. Indeed, citizens can become highly concerned about an issue even though its prominence is largely due to media coverage and media-sponsored polls. For example, Morin (1994a) says that public concern about drugs in the late 1980s and fears about crime may have been largely driven by media coverage of those issues and of polls about them. He points out that in January 1989, only 19 percent of poll respondents cited drugs as the most important problem facing the nation. By October of the same year, the percentage had increased to 53. But less than a year later, only 16 percent of Americans named drugs as the country's major problem. He attributes much of the rise and fall in the public's concern about drugs to the news media's heavy attention to the problem, which subsided as news organizations turned their attention elsewhere.

Journalists also need to be more perceptive about the frailties and limitations of polls and about how the reporting of polls can influence people in unintended ways. Gawiser and Witt, in a pamphlet sponsored by the National Council on Public Polls, compiled a list of twenty questions that journalists should ask about poll results. Their elaborations of and answers to the following questions should be required reading for journalists:

1. Who did the poll?
2. Who paid for the poll and why was it done?
3. How many people were interviewed for the survey?
4. How were those people chosen?
5. What area: nation, state, or region—or what group: teachers, lawyers, Democratic voters, etc.—were these people chosen from?
6. Are the results based on the answers of all the people interviewed?
7. Who should have been interviewed and was not?

8. When was the poll done?
9. How were the interviews conducted?
10. What about polls on the Internet or World Wide Web?
11. What is the sampling error for the poll results?
12. Who's on first?
13. What other kinds of mistakes can skew poll results?
14. What questions were asked?
15. In what order were the questions asked?
16. What about "push polls"?
17. What other polls have been done on this topic? Do they say the same thing? If they are different, why are they different?
18. So I've asked all the questions. The answers sound good. The poll is correct, right?
19. With all these potential problems, should we ever report poll results?
20. Is this poll worth reporting?

The *New York Times* and the *Washington Post* usually do a good job of informing their readers about the technical features of their surveys. For example, a *Times* article on the presidential candidates in 2000 included the following polling information:

The latest *New York Times*/CBS News Poll is based on telephone interviews conducted Wednesday through Sunday with 1,462 adults throughout the United States. Of these, 1,131 said they were registered to vote.

The sample of telephone exchanges called was randomly selected by a computer from a complete list of more than 42,000 active residential exchanges across the country.

Within each exchange, random digits were added to form a complete telephone number, thus permitting access to both listed and unlisted numbers. Within each household, one adult was designated by a random procedure to be the respondent for the survey.

The results have been weighted to take account of household size and number of telephone lines into the residence, and to adjust for variations in the sample relative to geographic region, sex, race, age, and education.

Some findings regarding voting are additionally weighted in terms of an overall "probable electorate," which uses responses to questions dealing with voting history, attention to the campaign, and likelihood of voting in 2000 as a measure of the probability of respondents' turning out in November. The method assumes approximately 50 percent turnout in November. In theory, in 19 cases out of 20 the results based on such samples will differ by no more than three percentage points in either direction from what would have been obtained by seeking out all American adults.

For smaller sub-groups, the margin of sampling error is larger.

In addition to sampling error, the practical difficulties of conducting any survey of public opinion may introduce other sources of error into the poll. Variations in the wording and order of questions, for example, may lead to somewhat different results. (Berke and Elder 2000)

Note that in addition to the standard items, the *Times* briefly explained random-digit dialing, explicitly stated that the data had been weighted, directly acknowledged and explained that some findings were based on a subset of respondents called "the probable electorate," discussed sampling error for the entire sample and for subgroups, and mentioned other sources of errors in polls. Overall, this is a thorough yet concise statement of the factors that can influence poll results. Moreover, a comparison of this disclaimer to the one that the *Times* used ten years earlier reveals that the paper had begun providing much more information. But even if some news organizations are becoming more responsible and thorough in reporting some of the technical details of polls, one must wonder whether readers actually read and can understand this information. The person who wishes to be a discerning consumer of polls must take some responsibility for using the technical polling information that the paper provides. And when the news media (or other polling outfits) do not provide basic information about their polls, the consumer should be wary. Finally, even when a news organization provides technical information about its polls, it still must ensure that the substance of the story accurately reflects the polling data. Only conscientious, well-trained reporters and editors can guarantee that.

Exercises

1. Take the *New York Times* description of the technical details of its polls on page 122 and try to determine whether five friends of yours can actually understand what the *Times* is saying. Do this by constructing a brief questionnaire that attempts to determine whether people know what sampling error, random-digit dialing, weights, question order, and other technical aspects of polls actually are. Then administer your questionnaire to the five friends and draw some conclusions as to how helpful the *Times* discussion is.
2. Try to find one news story about a poll whose tone, thrust, or emphasis you disagree with. That is, try to find one example where you would have written a different story than the reporter did, even though both of you were looking at the same data. To do this you will likely need to track down the actual question wording used in the poll.

3. Find five reports of public opinion polls, either news articles or releases from polling organizations, that adhere to the AAPOR minimum standards for disclosure. Now find five additional reports in which the guidelines are not followed. Can you make any generalizations from these ten reports about which outlets are most likely to adhere to the AAPOR standards? Feel free to use the Web sites listed on page 202 to find the reports.

☑ 7 Polls and Elections

Election surveys are probably the polls that are most familiar to Americans. Like surveys on presidential performance, election surveys receive substantial and continuing news coverage. They also generate the most controversy, particularly when preelection polls incorrectly predict the election day outcome. Although the most prominent election polls focus on the presidential contest, polling has expanded to congressional contests as well as many state and local races. Indeed, American-style campaigns, replete with polling, media ads, and "spin doctors," have spread throughout the world, even to countries such as Russia that are in transition from authoritarian to democratic regimes, where their accuracy is spotty.

Sponsors of Election Polls

A variety of organizations and individuals, such as candidates for office, political parties, and news organizations, sponsor election polls . The candidates and parties use polls as research tools, collecting information to devise winning campaign strategies. Typically, candidate-sponsored polls survey citizens on their sociodemographic characteristics, their perceptions of the candidates, and their views on issues. The candidates can then determine how well they are running overall, how their campaigns are going within important subgroups, and how campaign events and advertising affect their standing among the voters.

As for the mass media, election polls are a central focus of their election coverage, and they have been criticized for treating elections as if they were horse races, emphasizing not what the candidates say on the issues but their relative standing in the polls (Asher 1992, 273–278): Who's ahead? Who's behind? Who's gaining? Who's falling back? Yet polls also often go beyond recording levels of support for the candidates and address topics such as patterns of support for the candidates among groups of voters defined by their demographic characteristics and issue stances.

This chapter describes the types and uses of polls common to election campaigns. It examines candidates' and parties' attempts to use polls for purposes other than research and to manipulate media coverage of polls. It addresses the role of polling during the presidential primary season, as well as the general election campaign, and how and why polls can go wrong in making election predictions. The chapter concludes with some thoughts on how polls can affect the way citizens vote.

Types of Election Polls

The many kinds of election polls differ less in their methods than in the purposes they serve. For example, some of the candidate- and party-sponsored polls, such as tracking surveys, serve as the private tools of a campaign; media-generated surveys, such as exit polls, often become topics of public controversy. It is important for consumers of public opinion polls to be aware of the different kinds of surveys and what they can say about elections.

Benchmark Surveys

A candidate usually commissions a benchmark survey at the time he or she decides to seek office. It collects standard information about the candidate's public image and positions on issues and about the demographics of the electorate to provide a baseline for evaluating the progress of a campaign. Three important pieces of information often gathered in a benchmark survey are the candidate's name-recognition level, the candidate's electoral strength vis-á-vis that of opponents, and citizens' assessments of an incumbent officeholder's performance.

One problem with a benchmark survey is its timing. The earlier it is done, the less likely it is that the respondents will know anything about the challenger and the more likely it is that the political and economic situation will change dramatically as the election nears. Nevertheless, useful information can be collected about voters' perceptions of the strengths and weaknesses of the incumbent, their perceptions of the ideal candidate, and their views on major policy issues. The results of a benchmark survey normally are not publicized or leaked unless they show the candidate doing surprisingly well.

Reprinted by permission of MIKE THOMPSON *Detroit Free Press.*

Trial Heat Surveys

Technically, a trial heat survey is not a survey but a question or series of questions within a survey. Trial heat questions pair competing candidates and ask citizens which they would vote for in such a contest.

Typically, a trial heat question reads, "If the election were held today, would you vote for X or Y?" Sometimes questions are asked about hypothetical matches, particularly in the earlier stages of the presidential selection process. For example, in September 2003, a *Newsweek* poll conducted by Princeton Survey Research Associates paired a number of declared Democratic candidates, such as Wesley Clark, Dick Gephardt, John Kerry, Howard Dean, and Joe Lieberman, against President Bush in trial heat questions, asking Americans whom they would vote for if the 2004 presidential election were held that day. The results of these trial heat questions facilitate the "horse race" emphasis in media coverage of election campaigns; they are fun and often become the grist for interesting political speculation and gossip.

Several caveats apply, however, to the results of trial heat questions, the most important of which is that much can change between the time a question is asked and the actual voting on election day. This observation is best illustrated by the dramatic fluctuations in support for the presidential candidates in 2000. For example, a Reuters/MSNBC/Zogby poll in early August of that year gave Bush a seventeen-point lead over Gore; by early October the poll was indicating that Gore had a four-point lead. Equally dramatic changes can occur in a much shorter time. For example, a *New York Times*/WCBS-TV poll less than two weeks before the 1993 New Jersey gubernatorial contest showed incumbent Democratic governor Jim Florio with a 49 percent to 34 percent lead among registered voters over his Republican opponent Christine Todd Whitman (and an even larger lead among likely voters). But on election day Whitman was the victor. In California's 1994 gubernatorial race Democratic challenger Kathleen Brown was more than twenty points ahead of the Republican incumbent, Pete Wilson, in trial heat polls conducted months before the election. But Wilson defeated Brown by a fifteen-percentage-point margin.

Trial heat questions asked far in advance of an election measure name recognition more than anything else, particularly in less-prominent election contests. The consumers of such surveys must be careful not to view trial heat placements as immutable, nor should they be surprised when the standings of the candidates change dramatically over the course of the campaign. Moreover, because the results of a trial heat question depend on how the question is constructed, consumers must be careful in assessing the results. For example, when the political party affiliation of the candidate is given, the outcome is bound to be affected. With well-known candidates it makes little difference whether party affiliation is mentioned, but in races between less well-known candidates, it can make a substantial difference if the question is phrased, "Mary Doe versus Joe Blitz" or "Mary Doe, the Democrat, versus Joe Blitz, the Republican."

Tracking Polls

Tracking polls provide the most up-to-date information on which to base changes in campaign strategy and media advertising. A tremendous resource for candidates, these polls are often conducted on a daily basis near election day to monitor closely any late shifts in support. Because tracking polls are expensive, they rely on rolling samples. For example, samples of 100 different people may be collected on four consecutive days. Although an N of 100 is small and has a large sampling error, an N of 400 is much more reliable. But much can happen between the first and fourth day of interviewing, perhaps making the oldest interviews less interesting to the campaign. Thus on the fifth day another 100 people are interviewed and added to the sample, and the first 100 responses are discarded. And on the sixth day another 100 people are interviewed, and the 100 interviews done on the second day are eliminated. This procedure guarantees an overall sample of 400 that includes 100 new interviews each day, thereby allowing a close and timely monitoring of voters' reactions to the campaign. One danger of tracking polls is that any single day's interviews could be highly aberrant; the candidate and campaign must be careful not to overreact to what might be only a statistical blip.

Tracking polls were prominent in the 2000 presidential campaign. As election day approached, the results of various media-sponsored tracking polls converged to yield predictions very close to the actual election outcome. But throughout the campaign one particular tracking poll—that conducted by the Gallup Organization for CNN and *USA Today*—showed dramatic fluctuations over very short time periods. For example, one set of results showed Gore ahead by eleven points, yet two days later Bush was up by seven. This substantial volatility surprised observers, who questioned the accuracy of the Gallup results. It turned out that one reason for the results was dramatic variation in the proportions of Democrats and Republicans in their samples over short periods of time (Morin and Deane 2000). When the sample had relatively more Democrats, Gore did better, and vice versa. Gallup argued that the short-term fluctuations in the distribution of partisanship were genuine. Other polling organizations made different decisions and weighted their results so that the proportion of Democrats and Republicans did not vary as much with each night's sampling, and thus their results did not show as much volatility. This example demonstrates the effect of weighting on poll results (see chapter 4).

While tracking polls are typically conducted either by campaigns or by news organizations, the 2000 presidential election saw the most ambitious and extensive use of rolling samples to measure the dynamics of the presidential campaign. The National Annenberg Election Survey (Romer et al. 2004) entailed a complex research design. At its core were interviews conducted daily between December 14, 1999, and January 19, 2001, permitting researchers to study campaign dynamics over a lengthy period to ascertain what voters learned about the candidates and how their views changed over time in response to particular campaign events and media coverage.

Cross-Sectional versus Panel Surveys

When the major polling organizations conduct multiple polls over time on an election contest, they generally use a *cross-sectional design* in which different samples of citizens are selected for each round of interviewing. For example, in the 2000 presidential contest a CBS News/*New York Times* poll conducted in mid-October showed Bush ahead of Gore 46 percent to

44 percent, with 4 percent for Ralph Nader and 1 percent for Pat Buchanan—both minor-party candidates. Another CBS News/*New York Times* survey conducted in early November showed Bush ahead 47 percent to 42 percent, with 5 percent for Nader and 1 percent for Buchanan. Each of these surveys provides a picture of where the electorate stood at a single point in time, and each is based on a different sample. A comparison of the two surveys reveals that the Bush lead went from 2 percent to 5 percent (subject to sampling error) and that the net gain for Bush was 3 percent. But what pattern of movement produced this net gain? Perhaps 1 percent of Gore supporters moved to Bush and another 1 percent of Gore supporters shifted to Nader. But perhaps 10 percent of Gore supporters moved to Bush and 1 percent of Gore supporters went to Nader, while 9 percent of Bush supporters changed to Gore. Both of these hypothetical scenarios yield a net gain of 3 percent, but the total percentage of citizens who changed their preferences varies dramatically—2 percent in the first instance and 20 percent (10 + 1 + 9) in the second case.

Unfortunately, cross-sectional surveys reveal only the net change; they cannot tell poll consumers about the gross change or about the pattern of individual changes that produced the net result. Thus cross-sectional surveys are fine for revealing net changes in the relative standing of the candidates, but a *panel design* is needed if the total volatility of voters' attitudes and preferences is the chief concern.

In a panel survey, the same individuals are interviewed two or more times—a more costly and difficult process because the same respondents must be located repeatedly, no easy task in view of the mobility and mortality of respondents. For example, panel surveys of college students conducted over a period of months or years can be burdensome because of the high mobility of that group. Another problem is that respondents may not be willing to participate in multiple interviews; moreover, respondents who do agree to be reinterviewed may differ in distinct ways from those who do not. A final problem with panel surveys is that the experience of being interviewed at one point in time may affect the respondent's answers at the next interview. Despite these difficulties, panel surveys provide better information about the dynamics of the campaign and of voter decision making than do cross-sectional surveys.

Focus Groups

Focus groups can be an important campaign tool even though voters may never hear of them. Technically, focus groups are not polls but in-depth interviews with a small number of people (usually ten to twenty) who often are selected to represent broad demographic groups. A focus group might watch a candidate debate and offer reactions, thereby helping the candidate to prepare better for the next debate. Or a group might be asked to react to a political commercial, so that campaign managers can gain some insight into its effectiveness before spending money to air it. Focus group discussions also are useful in raising and developing questions that later may be incorporated into a public opinion poll.

The effectiveness of focus groups was illustrated most famously in the 1988 election, when the Bush campaign team called on a group to identify the "hot button" issues that it later used with devastating effect against Bush's Democratic opponent, Massachusetts governor Michael Dukakis, in the general election. The campaign team invited two dozen New Jersey residents to a local hotel to talk about the candidates. Many of the participants were blue-collar and Catholic Democrats who had supported Reagan but intended to vote for Dukakis even though they knew little about him. Because these Reagan Democrats were seen as critical to a Bush victory, the focus group leader pushed until issues emerged that moved participants away from support for Dukakis. The issues turned out to be Dukakis's opposition to the death penalty, his opposition to a bill requiring Massachusetts schoolchildren to recite the Pledge of Allegiance, and his support of a weekend furlough program for prisoners (among them the infamous Willie Horton). The reactions of the focus group participants told the Bush team that it had found the issues it needed to undermine the Dukakis campaign. It would have been much more difficult to generate this information through a public opinion survey. As Bush campaign manager Lee Atwater commented, "Focus groups give you a sense of what makes people tick and a sense of what's going on with people's minds and lives that you simply don't get from reading survey data" (Grove 1988b).

Morin (1992e) has pointed out that focus groups have become very popular with newspapers and television networks, which frequently commission them. Although Morin applauds focus groups as another tool for journalists, he warns that the media often fail to recognize the limitations of this method. Certainly one caveat is that focus groups are not mini-public opinion surveys. Focus groups may suffer from problems of external validity—that is, the results of the focus group may not be generalizable to any broader population because the participants may not be representative. Nevertheless, the process of intensive discussion within a focus group may provide insights into what factors are motivating citizens, insights that a standard public opinion survey does not readily reveal. In the early 1990s a report prepared for the Kettering Foundation relied heavily on focus group methodology (Harwood Group 1993). Titled "Meaningful Chaos: How People Form Relationships with Public Concerns," the report argued that if political leaders really want to engage citizens in key public policy concerns, they and the media may need to devise new ways to reach that goal. Among the report's recommendations was a call for more "mediating institutions" where citizens can interact directly and discuss the issues of the day. Sensitive to the limitations of the focus group method, the Kettering report stated in its appendix on methodology,

> There are, of course, limitations to group discussions. The research is qualitative. Thus, the observations detailed in this report should not be mistaken for findings from a random sample survey. They are, technically speaking, hypotheses, or insights, that would need to be validated by reliable quantitative methods before being considered definitive. Still, the insights are suggestive of how citizens view public concerns and their relationships to them. (49)

In observing focus group sessions dealing primarily with local government topics, such as the quality of city services or the performance of the local school system, I have been struck by how often the sessions take a critical and negative turn. One focus group participant relates a horror story, leading others to join in with their own awful anecdotes. Soon the focus group becomes a gripe session. Would public opinion polls on the same topics elicit as much intensely negative content? I doubt it. A 1996 book on gender relations by Roberta Sigel, who employed both focus groups and surveys in her work, supports my speculation. In general, Sigel's focus group data—more than her survey information—showed women to be angry about gender discrimination and mistreatment they had endured as women. Sigel attributed the differences in the focus group responses and the survey responses in part to the different modes of data collection. In other words, focus groups do not yield the same kinds of information as surveys and polls. Focus groups are fine research tools for certain purposes, but citizens should be wary of accepting general descriptions and explanations of people's attitudes and behavior based solely on a focus group.

Deliberative Opinion Polls

A deliberative opinion poll combines elements of both the focus group and the standard public opinion poll—that is, it brings together a representative group of citizens, provides them with information and the opportunity for discussion on issues, and then polls them on those issues. Fishkin sets out the rationale and need for deliberative polls (1992, 1996), arguing that public opinion surveys measure what the public thinks, but not what people would think if they had the opportunity to meet and become immersed in the issues through discussion and study. A deliberative poll is an expensive and challenging undertaking because it requires bringing together a representative sample and providing fair and balanced materials about the issues at hand.

The first major deliberative poll in the United States took place in Austin, Texas, in January 1996 in the context of the presidential election (Merkle 1996; Winkler 1996). A representative sample of Americans were surveyed about their opinions in three main issue areas: foreign policy, the economy, and family concerns. Then a subset of the sample attended the National Issues Convention in Austin, where, after extensive presentations and discussions on the same issue domains, members of the subset were polled again to determine whether and how their views had changed. Attitude changes did occur. For example, support for U.S. military engagement abroad rose, and support for a flat income tax declined. The respondents' views about the biggest problems facing American families moved toward economic concerns and somewhat away from the breakdown of traditional family values.

The key question rising from this deliberative poll is to what extent its users can generalize its conclusions to the broader population. Fishkin (1996) would argue that because the sample was representative, similar attitude changes might be expected in the population at large. But one of the major criticisms of Fishkin's claim is that citizens in the real world and the election campaign itself do not operate in the same way as the National Issues Convention (Mitofsky 1996). Most people do not take the time to learn, nor are they exposed to information about the issues or candidates in such a concentrated and thorough way. Even though small group discussions may occur in the real world, much of what citizens experience and learn comes directly from campaign ads, news coverage, and the like. Moreover, critics faulted the representativeness of the 1996 sample, as well as the intrusive effects of television, which heightened the awareness of the respondents that they were participating in a very special event. That awareness might have unduly influenced participants' reactions to the deliberative polling experience.

Even if the real-world prospects for deliberative polling are less than its adherents believe, the rationale for the enterprise is clear. Traditional public opinion polls capture what is immediately on the voters' minds, and as noted in chapter 2, they often are plagued by nonattitudes. Moreover, candidates tend to treat citizens' opinions as something to manipulate through political advertising and campaign rhetoric. A deliberative poll, by contrast, can reveal what citizens think once they are informed about an issue. Whether such results would ever constrain candidates or influence politics and elections remains doubtful.

Interest in deliberative polls waned in the 2000 election, but a fascinating example of a deliberative poll occurred in January 2003 (Fishkin, Luskin, and Brady 2003). A scientifically selected sample of 343 Americans were polled by phone on topics such as Iraq, international security issues, and foreign aid. The respondents were then brought together to experience the deliberative process and subsequently re-interviewed on the same topics. Participants in the deliberative process became more likely to see Iraq as a threat, but they also grew more skeptical about the United States going it alone on Iraq and other matters. They became more supportive of U.S. rebuilding of Iraq once the prospective war was over. And they became generally more positive about the United States taking a leadership role in world affairs and being more generous in providing foreign aid to other nations. That the results of this deliberative process received little media attention was frustrating to the sponsors of the deliberative poll. They argued that their results were important and worthy of news coverage because they showed what citizens' preferred policies were once they had become informed on the issues.

Exit Polls

Exit polls, as noted in chapter 1, are interviews with voters as they leave polling places. These very visible and controversial polls typically ask voters whom they voted for. They also collect some information on the issue positions and demographic characteristics of the respondents. The most prominent exit polls are conducted by the major news organizations to predict and explain presidential election outcomes as well as the results of congressional and major state-level races.

Exit polls have several advantages and uses. First, they are polls of actual voters, and so they avoid the enduring problem that preelection surveys face of determining who will actually vote. Second, exit poll samples are collected in many states, allowing state-by-state analysis of the presidential election—an endeavor not feasible with national surveys of 1,500 respondents, which are not amenable to breakdowns by state. (For details on how exit poll samples are selected, see Levy 1983.) Third, exit polls can be tabulated quickly, allowing almost instantaneous predictions and descriptions of election outcomes. Indeed, this advantage became a central selling point for exit polls as the television networks competed with each other to be the first to call an election. Finally, exit polls generate rich information that enables both journalists and social scientists to understand better the factors that help to shape the voters' choices.

Exit polls are generally accurate, although recent developments in the mechanics of how Americans vote might affect their predictive ability. For

Jeff MacNelly © 2001, Tribune Media Services, Inc. Reprinted with permission.

example, numerous states are making it easy to vote by absentee ballot, and some are experimenting with voting prior to election day. Stein (1998) notes that since 1988, eight states have given their citizens the opportunity to cast their votes in person up to three weeks before the general election and the state of Oregon has moved to conduct elections through the mail. Election day exit polling will not capture these votes. Moreover, there is evidence that exit polls overrepresent the well educated and affluent because they are more willing to fill out the exit poll forms (Morin 1994e).

Occasionally exit poll results are inaccurate. For example, an exit poll in the 1989 Virginia gubernatorial race showed the black Democratic candidate, Douglas Wilder, winning by 10 percent of the vote, when he actually won by less than 1 percent. The explanation for this inaccuracy is that some white respondents in the exit poll indicated that they had voted for Wilder when they had not (Traugott and Price 1992). As another example, the exit poll in the 1992 GOP presidential primary in New Hampshire showed George Bush with only a six-point margin over Republican challenger Pat Buchanan, when his lead in the actual vote count was sixteen points. The discrepancy was attributed in part to the greater intensity of Buchanan supporters and their greater willingness to participate in the exit polling (Mitofsky 1992; Morin 1992b).

Exit polls created a storm of controversy on election night in 1980 and again in 2000. Although the national preelection polls had indicated a close race between Jimmy Carter and Ronald Reagan in 1980, the results from the eastern time zone revealed that a Reagan landslide (especially in the Electoral College) was developing. What troubled many observers was that within minutes after the polls closed in a state, the television networks would declare—on the basis of exit polls and not official election returns—that Reagan had carried that state. By 8:30 p.m. Eastern Standard Time (EST), it was clear from exit poll results that Reagan had won enough states to ensure his election, no matter what happened in the states west of the

Mississippi, where the polls were still open (strong Reagan states in any event). Thus the networks declared Reagan the victor while parts of the country were still voting. Moreover, Carter conceded the election before all of the polls had closed. Understandably, many concerns were raised about the effects of news media declarations of victory when some voters had not yet cast their ballots. There were reports that voters in line at polling booths left when they heard that the presidential race was already decided and that other citizens decided not to go to the polls at all. In 1984 Democrat Walter Mondale wisely waited until the polls were closed on the West Coast before conceding, as did Michael Dukakis in 1988.

Did the early call of the 1980 presidential election actually deter citizens from voting? The empirical evidence is mixed (Jackson and McGee 1981; Jackson 1983; Epstein and Strom 1984; Delli Carpini 1984; Sudman 1986). It is clear that the early projections had no significant impact on the outcome of the presidential race in 1980, but in state and local contests turnout effects, no matter how small, could have been much more consequential. In those elections fewer votes are cast, and the margin between victory and defeat is sometimes very small.

In the 2000 election, the major television networks twice made predictions about the outcome of the presidential contest in the key state of Florida that never should have been made. Early on election night, the networks projected Vice President Gore as the winner. Much later in the evening, they projected that Governor Bush had won Florida—another forecast that had to be withdrawn but one that nonetheless gave Bush a major strategic advantage in the postelection Florida recount battle. Mitofsky (2001) explained that the incorrect Gore prediction may simply have been a case of the sampled precincts yielding a bad estimate, whereas the later, Bush prediction was less a problem with exit polling than a case of flawed communications among entities tabulating the vote.

Election night in 2002 witnessed a computer programming problem with respect to the exit polls. It led the networks to ignore exit polls in their election night coverage and rely instead on the actual vote tabulations (Torry 2002; Kurtz 2002; Plissner 2003). The problems in 2000 and 2002 led six news organizations to disband the Voter News Service, which had been the umbrella organization responsible for collecting exit polling data, and create a new consortium called the National Elections Pool, which will have the responsibility for constructing an exit polling capacity for the 2004 elections (Associated Press 2003). (For a comprehensive discussion of the exit polling fiasco in 2000 and how the Voter News Service performed, see the "Review Symposium: Election Night 2000 in Perspective," a collection of articles in the spring 2003 issue of *Public Opinion Quarterly*.)

Projecting election results for a state before that state's polls are closed raises concerns about the behavior of broadcast news organizations. Although there is some dispute about how late in the day exit polls must be taken to obtain a representative sample and make accurate projections (Busch and Lieske 1985), it is clear that if the polls close in a state at 7:30 p.m., exit polls could in most cases accurately predict the winner by late afternoon. Yet widespread reporting of such projections by the broadcast media could measurably depress turnout within a state. The television networks claim they are very careful not to make projections about a state until after its polls have closed, but a 1983 study by the League of Women Voters and the Committee for the Study of the American Electorate pointed to numerous instances in which 1982 election projections were broadcast while the polls were still open. In 2000, there were deliberate leaks of exit poll results while the polls were still open in some of the early key early primary states. Only the threat of lawsuits prevented certain media outlets from prematurely leaking exit poll results during the general election. Even some of the major television news anchors have become careless about revealing exit poll results for a state before that state has completed voting and all too often are heard speculating on election night that the early exit poll results suggest that it will be a good evening for a particular candidate.

The opposition to exit polls has been fierce in many circles. Newspaper columnist Mike Royko once urged readers to lie to exit poll interviewers, thereby undermining the usefulness of the entire enterprise. Some pollsters have been critical of exit polls and early projections. Although Roper (1985) and others believe that exit polls have few if any effects on elections, they argue that their use should still be curtailed because most citizens believe that exit polls can influence election outcomes. Exit polls, they claim, cause citizens to lose confidence in the electoral process and become increasingly suspicious of the mass media.

Congress and state governments have sharply criticized exit polls as well. The House Task Force on Elections conducted hearings in 1985 on the news industry's use of exit polls and called for voluntary restraint (Swift 1985). The state of Washington went further. Recognizing that it would be difficult to prohibit the reporting of election projections and results, the state legislature passed a law making it a misdemeanor to conduct any exit interviews within 300 feet of the polls (Abrams 1985), the obvious intention being to make the collection of exit data far more difficult. The law was ultimately invalidated in federal court. In 2001 congressional committees again held hearings, and state legislatures again considered legislation that would restrict the conduct and/or reporting of exit polls.

The controversy surrounding exit polls will likely continue to heat up every two years. The television networks argue strenuously that government-imposed limitations on the reporting of exit polls would be a form of censorship and a violation of their First Amendment rights. Also, the news organizations note that if the polls were open simultaneously for twenty-four hours in all fifty states, the problem of early projections would be resolved. State officials reject that option as too expensive and point out that the networks could still make premature projections for those states for which they had sufficient information. Broder (1984) has proposed the Canadian solution: the networks could begin their election coverage by time zone from east to west, beginning each regional broadcast just as polls in that region are closing. Thus the networks might begin election coverage in the East at 8:00 p.m. EST, in the Midwest at 9:00 p.m. EST, in the Mountain States at 10:00 p.m. EST, and on the Pacific Coast at 11:00 p.m. EST.

Consumers of exit polls should carefully evaluate the news reports throughout election day. Any news about patterns of vote choice among various groups is most likely based on the exit polls completed to that point. Consumers should ask themselves whether such reports might affect their likelihood of voting or their choice of candidate. They also should note the time of the announcement of any election projections. If the projection is made before the polls have closed, then it is based on exit polls and not on official election returns, which are not available until after the polls close. The next question is whether the projection is for a state contest or a national race. If the latter, consumers should note whether the polls are still open in some states. Finally, consumers should try to keep a mental list of the number of early projections that subsequently are contradicted by the actual vote totals.

It is unlikely that exit polls will ever be regulated except by the self-policing of the networks themselves. In the early days of exit polling, the television networks, aiming to beat the competition and to improve ratings, invested heavily in the technology of polling and election coverage. (The polls play a somewhat different role for newspapers, which are not in a competition to predict election outcomes on election night. Instead, newspapers use exit polls primarily to describe voting patterns and to explain why the election turned out as it did.) Beginning with the 1990 midterm elections, however, the competition was somewhat mitigated when ABC, NBC, CBS, and CNN decided to conduct one joint exit poll under the auspices of the Voter News Service. The major reason for the change was financial; exit polling is very expensive. But as Schneider (1989) has pointed out, when different exit polls have been conducted for the same election, the results have differed; multiple polls enabled investigators to compare the results and decide which were more likely on target.

Push Polls

Push polling gained notoriety in the 1996 elections, even though the practice had been around for years, particularly in U.S. House races and in some state and local contests. As push polling has become more common, the American Association for Public Opinion Research and the National Council on Public Polls have condemned the practice. AAPOR has described push polling as follows:

> a telemarketing technique in which telephone calls are used to canvass potential voters, feeding them false or misleading " information" about a candidate under the pretense of taking a poll to see how this "information" affects voter preferences. So-called "Push polls" are not polls at all. They are a form of political telemarketing whose intent is not to measure public opinion but to manipulate it—to "push" voters away from one candidate and toward the opposing candidate. Such polls defame selected candidates by spreading false or misleading information about them. The intent is to disseminate campaign propaganda under the guise of conducting a legitimate public opinion poll. (1997)

The National Council on Public Polls further explains the difference between legitimate political polls and push polls:

> [Legitimate political polls] use samples representative of all voters. "Push Polls" use telephone banks to canvass large numbers of voters. Legitimate polls may seek out weaknesses of candidates and attempt to ascertain the impact on voters of knowledge of these weaknesses, as well as issues and other facets of a political campaign. "Push Polls" attack selected candidates. The intent of legitimate polls in each case is research; a sample is interviewed, not a canvass, and the survey is not designed to deceive. . . . The results of "Push Polls" should never be reported by the media, but the use of such polls by a candidate may, of course, be a legitimate news story. (1995)

In 1996 a push poll was used in a Republican congressional primary in Texas (Clymer 1996). Representative Greg Laughlin was the preferred choice of the Republican Congressional Committee, which financed a push poll designed to hurt the other two contenders, Ron Paul and Jim Deats. About 30,000 calls were made. If respondents said they preferred Ron Paul, they were asked if they would still support him if they knew that Paul supported legalization of drugs, pornography, and prostitution. Likewise, if respondents said they favored Deats, they were asked how strong their support was given his campaign debt of $200,000 and four previous unsuccessful attempts for office. The information provided to respondents was misleading, however, and designed to push them away from Paul and Deats and toward Laughlin. In the 2000 presidential primaries, a major controversy emerged in the South Carolina Republican primary when the McCain campaign accused the Bush team of engaging in massive push polling. The Bush campaign denied the charge, pointing out that the thousands of phone calls being made were simply advocacy calling, not done under the guise of a poll. The intent, the Bush camp said, was to disseminate negative information about Sen. John McCain to South Carolina voters.

It is perfectly legitimate in survey research to present respondents with information to see how it affects their opinions. For example, in surveys about support for a balanced budget, respondents who favor a balanced budget might be asked whether they would still support a balanced budget if it meant reductions in spending on Social Security or Medicare or some other program. Likewise, in surveys about support for American military engagement abroad, respondents who support such involvement might be asked whether they would still support it if it cost American lives or a substantial amount of money. What makes the push polling enterprise so objectionable is that the information provided to the respondents is most often inaccurate and argumentative, and sometimes inflammatory. Moreover, the push polling is conducted as if it were a legitimate public opinion survey trying to ascertain citizens' attitudes, when in fact it is trying to influence voters' attitudes and behavior.

Given that push polling and legitimate survey research may seem very similar on the surface, how can citizens protect themselves from push polls? The American Association of Political Consultants, another organization that has denounced push polling, has provided some advice for spotting such polls. First, reputable polling begins by providing the name of the sponsor of the research or the organization conducting the research; push polls typically do not provide that information. Second, legitimate telephone surveys usually last at least five minutes and often much longer; the typical push poll is less than a minute in duration. A third sign of a push poll, more apparent to news reporters than the average citizen, is the number of calls made in a particular election contest. The fact that thousands and thousands of calls have been made to citizens about a particular race is a clear sign that push polling is under way, because most genuine polls require fewer than a thousand respondents. Indeed, when the news media hear of such an activity they should publicize and condemn it. And citizens who believe they have been called as part of a push poll might tip off their local media in the hope that a news organization would investigate and expose the situation. Because push polling is more likely to be used in less-visible, lower-level elections, where media scrutiny is often less extensive, it is important that citizens be particularly vigilant in those circumstances.

Uses of Polls by Candidates

Candidates use polls to test the political waters in a variety of ways. Prospective candidates might commission a private poll and also examine public polls to assess their chances. How they assess the results can steer their expectations and actions. For example, bad poll news might lead to a decision not to seek office. In 1986 New Yorker Geraldine Ferraro decided not to run for the U.S. Senate against incumbent Republican senator Alphonse D'Amato in part because poll results showed her trailing substantially. A party organization with the financial resources to conduct polls and to provide other election services may use this capability to provide services to recruit candidates. At the national level the Republican Party has been much better able than the Democrats to offer such assistance to its candidates and would-be candidates because of its more successful fund-raising operations based on computerized direct mail.

Sometimes candidates use positive poll results to generate campaign contributions or to deter contributions to their opponents. In 1985 Idaho's Democratic governor, John Evans, sent the results of a poll he had conducted to many political action committees (PACs) and potential contributors. The poll showed Evans in a virtual tie with the state's Republican U.S. senator, Steve Symms, in a trial heat for Symms's Senate seat. Evans's action was clearly a signal to contributors that he had a good chance of unseating Symms in the 1996 election and therefore was worthy of their donations (Rothenberg 1985, 11). Evans ultimately lost, however, by a narrow margin.

Often when published polls show a candidate running poorly, the candidate may try to minimize the potential damage to fund-raising and volunteers' morale by attacking the credibility and relevance of the poll. "The only poll that counts is the poll taken on election day," the candidate might argue, citing examples of the polls' having been wrong in the past. In a systematic analysis of the reactions of the 1992 Bush campaign to negative poll results, Bauman and Herbst (1994) found three dominant responses. First was the (often valid) assertion that it was too early to give much credence to poll results. Second was an attack on the pollsters themselves and the journalists who reported the polls. Finally, the campaign tried to counter the results of published polls with the results of its own private polls. In other instances, the attack on a poll may be more method related, challenging the sample, question wording, or question context.

Whatever the merits of these criticisms, it is clear that a candidate "harmed" by polls has a strong incentive to cast doubt on their credibility so that a campaign is taken seriously. If a campaign is not taken seriously, it will have difficulty raising money and attracting other resources, such as free media coverage.

Sometimes candidates deliberately manipulate aspects of their campaign or the polling process to generate poll results that will advance their candidacies. For example, in the four-way contest for the Republican nomination for governor of Ohio in 1982, one of the candidates, Seth Taft, scheduled his early television advertising to go on the air before the Ohio Republican Party conducted a statewide poll assessing the standing of the candidates. The poll showed Taft running first, thereby enhancing his credibility. Undoubtedly, his famous last name and the skillful timing of his commercials gave Taft an early advantage in the polls, but he eventually lost the primary. To demonstrate greater electoral strength than they actually have, candidates often schedule television commercials and mailings in conjunction with party- and media-sponsored polls.

Candidates and campaign managers are also very skillful in selectively leaking information from in-house, private polls. Sometimes in-house polls are deliberately designed to generate the desired results. For example, before asking a trial heat question about the contenders, pollsters might ask a series of issue questions or candidate qualification items that will predispose the respondent to support one candidate over another. But in leaking the results of the trial heat item to the media, the campaign will not include information about the questions that preceded it. A candidate can also try to control poll results through sample selection. For example, if a candidate is thought to be more popular among women than men, interviewing might be conducted mainly during the day to obtain a predominantly female sample. When the results of the poll are leaked, however, the pollsters will not mention the gender composition of the sample, thereby inflating the standing of the candidate.

Voters and reporters should be wary of such selective leaking. One tip-off is refusal by a campaign to reveal additional information about a poll, such as question wording and question order. Although this kind of manipulation is not widespread, many campaigns use whatever tactics they believe will work because the objective of most campaigns is to win the election. "Good" poll results—whether valid or not—can make fund-raising easier, generate more serious media coverage, and invigorate the campaign team and volunteers. Consumers can only endeavor to exercise good judgment in evaluating election poll results and hope that reporters and other journalists will not be easily victimized by manipulative campaigns.

Polls in the Presidential Selection Process

Polls pervade all stages of the presidential selection process. During the primary season, media polls in key states are common, as are national polls measuring the presidential preferences of Democrats and Republicans throughout the nation. During the general election campaign, the major news organizations and the campaigns themselves regularly conduct polls. When a major campaign event occurs, such as a televised debate among presidential contenders, a slew of polls follow immediately assessing the effect of the event.

One result of the ubiquity of polls in presidential campaigns is the increasing prominence of pollsters. Over the past two decades, individual pollsters such as Pat Caddell, Richard Wirthlin, and Stanley Greenberg achieved celebrity status during the Carter, Reagan, and Clinton campaigns. Today pollsters are part of individual candidates' core strategy groups that decide on themes and tactics, media advertising, public speaking schedules, and other key aspects of the campaign.

Polls do much more than simply reflect the current standing of the candidates in the presidential contest. The polls and the reporting of them shape the very course of the campaign. They also have been instrumental in campaign fund-raising, although their impact has lessened in that area. Since 1976, presidential campaigns in the general election have been publicly funded, leaving major party nominees free from worry that poor poll performance will cut off the flow of money to their campaigns. In 1968, however, many Democrats complained that the early polls showing Hubert Humphrey losing the election badly hindered fund-raising, so that even when it became clear near the end of the campaign that Humphrey had a chance to win, the money available for the final push was inadequate. In contrast to the general election, during the primary season eligible candidates receive only partial public funding, and the amount of public matching money they receive depends on their ability to attract private financial support. Bad poll results, as well as poor primary and caucus showings, may deter potential donors from supporting a failing campaign.

The Caucus and Primary Season

The combined effect of polls and media coverage of polls is particularly critical during the caucus and primary season for at least two reasons. First, many candidates may seek a party's presidential nomination. In 1988, for example, six Republicans and seven Democrats sought party nominations. As of September 2003, ten Democrats were seeking their party's 2004 presidential nomination. Unable to cover all candidates equally, the media give more attention to the most serious and viable candidates, with viability defined foremost by candidates' standings in the polls and how much money they have raised.

Second, the caucuses and primaries are a sequence of elections in which news media coverage of the outcome in just one state can dramatically affect later polls and primaries. For example, in 1984 John Glenn's campaign conducted a poll in New Hampshire about one week before that state's primary. The actual interviewing was conducted around the time of the Iowa precinct caucuses, in which Glenn did much worse than expected. The media coverage of the Iowa results stressed how badly the Glenn campaign was hurt there. Glenn's New Hampshire survey then showed that interviews completed before the reports of his poor finish in Iowa had him running much more strongly in New Hampshire than did interviews completed after the reports of the Iowa results. The combined effect of media coverage and the polls is particularly significant in Iowa and New Hampshire, the states in which the formal process of selecting delegates to the parties' national nominating conventions begins. The "winners" in Iowa and New Hampshire almost invariably enjoy a sizable gain in support in the national polls because of the positive and extensive media coverage they receive.

The presidential primary season is something of a sequential, psychological game in which the perception that a candidate is running strongly, as reflected in good poll results, makes it easier for the campaign to attract money, volunteers, and media coverage; bad poll results have the opposite effect. But strong performance in the polls is itself a function of the amount and content of media coverage that a candidate receives. That is why Iowa and New Hampshire are so critical. Because they are small states in which both a personal and a media campaign can be conducted, they enable a relatively unknown or underdog candidate—such as Jimmy Carter in 1976, Gary Hart in 1984, Bill Clinton in 1992, or John McCain in 2000—to do better than expected and thus receive substantial media coverage. The coverage can move a candidate higher in the public opinion polls, which in turn enhances the candidate's media coverage and credibility.

During the primary season candidates appeal for support on the grounds that they are more electable than their opponents, as demonstrated by the polls. Probably the best examples of this phenomenon occurred in 1976 and earlier in 1968. In 1976 Gerald Ford and Ronald Reagan were locked in a tight battle for the Republican presidential nomination; the winner would most likely face former Georgia governor Jimmy Carter in the general election. The Ford campaign conceded the South to Carter no matter who won the GOP nomination but argued, citing public opinion polls, that Ford was much the stronger candidate to run against Carter nationwide (Phillips 1976). In 1968 Nelson Rockefeller's campaign to win the GOP nomination also depended heavily on the public opinion polls because Rockefeller knew he would have great difficulty winning presidential primaries and caucuses. Rockefeller challenged Richard Nixon, the front-runner, to cosponsor fifty state polls to see which candidate was the strongest. He also commissioned and released polls of states whose electoral votes were key that showed him running better than Nixon against Democratic candidate Hubert Humphrey (Crossley and Crossley 1969, 7). Rockefeller hoped to sway Republican delegates to his cause by the argument that he was the strongest candidate the party could offer.

Presidential Debates and the General Election

The interaction between poll results and media coverage is well illustrated by the treatment of the presidential and vice-presidential debates before the general election. Often polls taken immediately after a debate produce very different results than ones taken a few days later. The difference is attributable to the dominant media message in the interim. For example, in the Ford-Carter debate in 1976, President Ford mistakenly asserted that Eastern Europe was not under the domination of the Soviet Union, when in fact, at the time, Soviet troops were stationed in Poland and the Polish government, among others in the region, was following the dictates of Moscow. Telephone polls immediately after the debate showed Carter winning, but only by a narrow margin. When Ford received negative media coverage after the debate for his mistake, his campaign officials did not display much skill at putting the matter to rest. As a result, Carter's narrow margin burgeoned in the follow-up polls, which showed that Americans overwhelmingly viewed him as the winner of the debate.

"Winning" a debate may be a function less of a candidate's actual performance than of the media's coverage and interpretation of that performance. That is why the call-in poll that the ABC News organization sponsored after the Carter-Reagan debate in 1980 was particularly offensive. ABC News invited its viewers to call one of two numbers to indicate whether they thought Reagan or Carter had won; the call cost fifty cents. Despite the self-selection and economic biases inherent in this procedure and the technical difficulty many citizens experienced in trying to complete their calls, ABC News announced that Reagan had won the debate by a two-to-one margin over Carter. Ideally, Americans should have dismissed this instant poll as foolish and unsound. Unfortunately, because it was the first large-scale reaction to the debate to be publicized, the poll and ABC's reporting of it shaped subsequent perceptions of who won the debate. After the first Bush-Gore presidential debate in 2000, scientific polls generally showed Gore to be the victor, albeit by a small margin. Many Internet and radio call-in polls, however, characterized by self-selected and unrepresentative samples, showed Bush the big winner. Fortunately, when the news media discussed the debate polls, they focused on the scientific ones. Broadcasters were criticized, however, for their reliance on instant and overnight polls.

As polling has become an integral part of media coverage of major campaign events such as convention speeches and presidential debates, news organizations have increasingly incorporated overnight and instant polls into their coverage. The NCPP, however, has urged caution:

> One issue where news values and good polling methods clash is the media's appetite for "instant" polls which provide an immediate reaction to dramatic events. . . .
>
> A key question for poll watchers, and the media who report polls, should always be *"How many days was the survey in the field?"* In general, the quality of the sample improves the longer the survey is in the field. . . .
>
> All surveys fail to interview many people . . . because they are on vacation, on a business trip, visiting, shopping, eating out or just too busy to take the call. That is why the most reliable telephone surveys make three, four or more calls, on different days, to try to complete an interview. Obviously, this is not possible for polls that are conducted overnight or over a few hours, and their response rates are much lower.
>
> Given the very real possibility that those who are not interviewed, because they are not available, have even slightly different opinions than those who are interviewed, overnight polls, with their very low response rates, are much more likely to have substantial biases than polls with multiple call-backs over several days. (2000)

Polls also play a big role in determining which candidates are allowed to participate in presidential candidates' debates. In 1980, the League of Women Voters, the sponsor of the debate, decided to invite candidates whose popular support in public opinion surveys was more than 15 percent. The real issue at the time was whether independent candidate John Anderson would meet the 15 percent test. In 1996, unlike 1980, all independent and minor-party candidates were excluded from the debates. Ross Perot and other candidates asked the courts to overturn the decision, but to no avail. The decision had been made by the Commission on Presidential Debates, a ten-person body of five Republicans and five Democrats, which determined the debates' format and who would participate. The Democratic and Republican nominees (Clinton and Dole) were automatically included, but the candidates of other parties had to demonstrate that they had a realistic chance of being elected president to be invited to participate. That is, they had to show evidence of a national organization, national newsworthiness, and national enthusiasm for their candidacies (Hernandez 1995). One indicator of national enthusiasm was a candidate's standing in the public opinion polls. The commission, after judging that Ross Perot's low standing in the polls, along with other evidence, made it unlikely that he could win, excluded him from the debates.

Presidential debates should not be cluttered with numbers of mostly frivolous candidates, but was the decision to exclude Perot appropriate? After all, Perot was on the ballot in all fifty states, he had received 19 percent of the popular vote in 1992, and he had more than $20 million in public funding to finance his 1996 campaign. Although the polls the commission used to exclude Perot showed him with the voting support of only about 5 percent of the American people, other polls showed that more than 70 percent of Americans wanted Perot included in the debates. Moreover, although Perot's 5 percent in the polls when the commission made its decision in 1996 was close to his support level at a comparable point in the 1992 election campaign, he ultimately took almost a fifth of the vote in 1992. As Perot learned, using poll standing to exclude a candidate from the presidential debates creates a self-fulfilling prophecy. If a candidate is showing poorly in the polls, excluding that candidate from the most visible event of the presidential campaign can only further erode that candidate's support as the campaign moves into its critical final weeks.

A similar situation occurred in 2000 when the presidential debate commission again decided to use poll standing as one criterion for determining who could participate in the presidential debates. The commission chose a floor of 15 percent in a set of polls conducted shortly after Labor Day. The two most prominent minor-party candidates—Ralph Nader and Pat Buchanan—could not meet that standard and thus were excluded. This situation was particularly frustrating to Buchanan who, as the nominee of the Reform Party, had received $12 million in public funding based on the Reform Party's performance in the 1996 election.

When and Why Election Predictions Are Wrong

The vast majority of polls are on target. Nevertheless, pollsters have made some notorious mistakes, such as in the *Literary Digest* poll of 1936 (discussed in chapter 4) and the 1948 presidential election polls that indicated that Republican Thomas Dewey would beat Democrat Harry Truman. The bad call in 1948 is widely attributed to the quota method of sampling that the polls employed and, more important, to the fact that polling stopped too far in advance of the election and therefore did not reflect the movement of many Democratic defectors back to Truman. In fact, the last polls showed Dewey with only a five-point lead over Truman, and the trend had been one of a declining Dewey advantage.

National polls have been off target in other important races. In 1980, for example, they failed to predict the magnitude of Reagan's victory. Most polls showed a very tight race, but Reagan beat Carter by ten percentage points. Again the poor predictions were attributed to the fact that many polls did not continue right through to the end of the campaign and thus did not capture the last-minute surge to Reagan by the undecideds and independents. The state-level polls in 1980 were far more accurate in predicting a sizable Reagan victory.

In 1992 the general election presidential polls were quite accurate overall, although critics expressed concerns about the deluge of some-times-conflicting polls and the way the news media reported them. One set of criticisms focused on the tracking polls that Gallup conducted toward the end of the campaign. Those polls, which received substantial media attention (Traugott 1992), generated concerns about the selection of respondents, the method by which undecided voters were allocated to candidates, and most important, a shift in poll analysis from registered voters to likely voters, which created confusion among the media and the public as to how much the gap between Clinton and Bush had actually narrowed.

In 1996 the preelection polls correctly predicted that Clinton would be reelected, but some of them substantially overestimated his margin of victory. Among polls seeking to predict the makeup of the House of Representatives, even the ones conducted just before the election yielded widely varying estimates, with some predicting a sizable Democratic victory, others a smaller Democratic win, and others a narrow GOP victory. Political scientist Everett Carll Ladd described 1996 as a very bad year for pollsters—"an American Waterloo" (1996). Ladd criticized the polls for overstating Clinton's margins and blamed the polls and the news media for contributing to the low voter turnout by dampening interest in the outcome with their predictions of a major Clinton win. Pollsters defended the polls; Newport (1997) and Morin (1997a) found the 1996 polls generally on target.

Perhaps the real problem with election polls is not their accuracy but how they are reported. Too many polls dominate news coverage of the election and contribute to the horse race mentality. Small changes in poll standing often are given too much attention, becoming the subject of breathless news stories when there really is no news. In the meantime, the subtleties of poll interpretation frequently are lost, particularly those related to the polls' methodological aspects. And the media tend to focus on their own polls and ignore those of the competition.

The performance of the polls in 2000 was generally good, with most of the national polls converging toward the end of the campaign to show a very close contest between Bush and Gore. Even so, of eighteen national preelection polls conducted right at the end of the campaign, thirteen indicated a Bush lead, three estimated a tie, and only two had Gore ahead. Gore received 48.6 percent of the popular vote, compared with 48.3 percent for Bush (Traugott 2001). And some of the polls that had Bush ahead showed him with a lead over Gore of 5 to 7 percent. Although the national polls generally performed well in 2000, Rademacher and Smith (2001) found that 79 state-level telephone polls were, on average, not as accurate. Probably the worst experience for the pollsters in 2000 (other than the Florida fiasco) was the New Hampshire Republican primary, where John McCain scored a landslide victory over George W. Bush when most polls were showing a much closer contest. Part of the problem for pollsters in New Hampshire was that independents could vote in either party's primary, and many of them voted for McCain in the GOP primary. Moreover, as Smith and Hubbard (2000) note, the turnout among the "undeclared" or independents was much higher than normal in 2000.

The accuracy of predictions depends on several factors. The rest of this section examines four of them: the timing of preelection polls, the treatment of undecided voters, the estimation of voter turnout, and the changing political and economic climate.

Timing of Polls

The closer to the election a preelection poll is conducted, the more accurate its results are likely to be (Felson and Sudman 1975). Late polls can capture the effects of last-minute events and campaign activities that may influence outcomes. By contrast, early polls primarily reflect name recognition and perceptions of incumbents' performance. When voters initially have little information about the candidates, their attitudes are highly likely to change once they acquire some new information about the contenders. For that reason, presidential primary polls often are less accurate than the general election polls. In the primaries, especially the early ones with a large field of candidates, information levels are low and voters' commitments to candidates are weak.

In a comprehensive analysis of the factors affecting the accuracy of preelection polls, Crespi (1988) found that the most important factor was how close to election day the preelection poll was conducted. The next most important factor was margin of victory, and then either turnout or whether the election was a primary. These findings suggest that polls would be more accurate if they did a better job of identifying likely voters and monitoring trends in voters' preferences in the latter stages of a campaign. This suggestion is directly relevant to the failure of the polls to predict George H. W. Bush's comfortable win in the 1988 New Hampshire

Republican primary. Why were most of the polls so wrong? The Gallup Organization explained that it stopped polling too early (by 4 p.m. on Sunday
before the Tuesday election) and therefore did not capture late-breaking developments (Grove 1988a). The one poll that correctly predicted Bush's
victory was the CBS survey, which involved a tracking poll on the Sunday
and Monday before the election (Morin 1988a) and thus reinforces
Crespi's advice to poll as close to the election as possible. Clearly, if there
is a late-breaking development in a campaign, such as an international crisis or a revelation about scandalous behavior, only polls conducted after
those events can capture their impact on citizens' vote choices. Lau's analysis of the accuracy of the 1992 presidential polls found that polls conducted
over multiple days were more accurate than overnight polls (1994). Lau
also found that tracking polls were more accurate than standard polls and
that polls that interviewed on both weekdays and weekends were more accurate than weekday-only polls.

Treatment of Undecided Voters

When respondents claim to be undecided they can mean different
things. Some genuinely cannot choose among the candidates because they
do not have enough balanced information to make a choice, but that is
probably unusual. Others may know very little about one or more of the
candidates and therefore be unwilling to make a choice. On the other hand,
"undecided" may be a safe answer for those who do not want to reveal
their election choices to the interviewer.

Evidence for this third possibility comes via the secret ballot technique
that the Gallup Organization has long used. In this procedure respondents
are given a ballot by the interviewer, asked to mark their choices, and then
requested to drop the folded ballot into a box. Perry (1979) points out that
this approach yields an undecided rate that is about one-third to one-fourth
as large as that obtained when respondents are asked their vote preference
by means of a standard survey item. (Note that the secret ballot technique
can only be used with personal interviews.)

Pollsters can simply ignore undecided respondents and tabulate results
only for those who have already made up their minds, but that is a highly
flawed procedure if the undecideds differ in major ways from the decideds.
Another way of handling the undecideds is to report their numbers but then
to assume that they will split in the same way that the decideds already have.
Thus if 60 percent of decideds vote Democratic, 60 percent of the undecideds will be allocated to the Democratic Party. This is probably a reasonable rule when both candidates are equally well known and when there is no
reason to suspect that anything unusual is going on among the undecideds.

When one candidate is well known and the other is not, however, the treatment of the undecideds is more problematic. In a race between a well-known, longtime incumbent and a relatively unknown challenger, an undecided vote can reflect poorly on the incumbent. In 1978 Ohio state representative Charles Kurfess challenged incumbent governor James Rhodes for the GOP gubernatorial nomination. Rhodes had already served three, four-year terms and was seeking a fourth; he was the well-known warhorse of the Ohio Republican Party. The benchmark survey conducted for the Kurfess campaign showed that respondents favored Rhodes over Kurfess by 66 percent to 6 percent, with 28 percent undecided. The final election results were 67 percent to 33 percent in favor of Rhodes. Without panel data it is impossible to conclude definitively that most of the undecideds moved to support Kurfess, but it seems plausible in this case that the undecided vote was actually a negative comment on the incumbent. In response to another question, the undecideds overwhelmingly preferred a new candidate for governor.

The behavior of undecided voters also partially accounts for the failure of preelection polls to mirror closely the outcome of the two prominent contests of 1989—those for mayor of New York City and for governor of Virginia. Although polls accurately predicted the winners, David Dinkins in New York and Douglas Wilder in Virginia, the poll estimates of their margins of victory were much too high. Wilder won in Virginia by less than 1 percent, whereas the preelection polls were suggesting a double-digit margin. In New York Dinkins won by about 2 percent, even though the polls had shown him between fourteen and twenty-one points ahead (Balz 1989). The contests received a lot of media coverage because both Dinkins and Wilder would be the first black Americans to be elected to their respective positions. If, as pollsters increasingly believe, whites who are undecided in a contest between a black and a white candidate vote heavily for the white candidate, then one reason for the polling errors in the Dinkins and Wilder contests was the behavior of the heavily white undecided voters. Other factors contributing to poll discrepancies in the Dinkins and Wilder victories were race-of-interviewer effects, turnout effects, and last-minute changes in voter preferences. The fact remains, however, that many white voters gave an "undecided" response to an interviewer querying on a black-versus-white contest even though they had already decided to support the white candidate.

Estimating Turnout in Elections

Probably the most difficult task pollsters face is estimating which of their respondents will actually vote. If the preferences of voters and nonvoters were identical, that task would not be a problem. But often there are marked differences between the two groups.

Pollsters use a variety of means to predict whether a person will vote. The Gallup Organization has used a subsample of likely voters from the overall sample of all possible voters (Perry 1979, 320–321). Among the items in the survey are the respondents' stated intention to vote, registration status, reported frequency of past voting, awareness of where to vote, interest in politics in general, interest in the particular election, and intensity of candidate preference. Thus in Gallup's final survey for the presidential election in 1976, when all respondents were considered Carter led Ford 48 percent to 43 percent; Eugene McCarthy and others received 4 percent; and undecideds and those who refused to participate amounted to 5 percent. But when the survey considered only likely voters, Carter led 48 percent to 46 percent; the other candidates received 2 percent; and undecideds or those refusing to respond to the poll made up 4 percent. Morin (2001b) notes that the index used by the Gallup Organization to identify likely voters appears to work as well today as it did decades ago.

Other pollsters use similar procedures. For example, Peter Hart has used respondents' reports of registration status, past voting in other races and current intention to vote, interest in the election and estimate of its importance, and awareness of the candidates and where to vote (Goldhaber 1984, 49). In 1998 a CBS News/New York Times poll identified likely voters as those who said they voted in either 1996 or 1994, who said they were paying attention to the current campaign, and who said they would definitely vote in November. Respondents who voted in both 1994 and 1996 were defined as "more likely voters" (Kagay 1998). One interesting result of the CBS News/New York Times classification was that the more likely a respondent was to vote, the more that person tended to be pro-Republican. For example, registered voters in the 1998 poll preferred Democratic to Republican congressional candidates by a margin of 45 percent to 37 percent. But among likely voters the Democrats led by only 47 percent to 42 percent, and among the most likely voters Republicans led 48 percent to 44 percent.

After tracking polls did not correctly predict the outcome of the 1988 New Hampshire primary, ABC News/Washington Post pollsters changed the way they determined who the likely voters would be (Morin 1988b). In their New Hampshire polling, the ABC News/Washington Post pollsters had simply asked self-described registered voters if they were certain to vote, would probably vote, if the chances were 50–50, or if they would probably not vote. Anyone who said that he or she was certain to vote was considered a likely voter. This method produced a sample whose projected turnout rate was twice as high as the real percentage because people often say they will vote even when they will not; they want to portray themselves as good citizens. Therefore ABC News/*Washington Post* decided to establish multiple criteria for determining a likely voter. For example, the respondent had to say that he or she was certain to vote and had to have voted in 1986. Other factors also were considered, including strength of commitment to a candidate. This more stringent test of likely voters generated more accurate results but also resulted in more interviews with registered voters being tossed aside when election predictions were made.

A somewhat different approach has been taken by the *Columbus Dispatch,* which uses mailed questionnaires. As discussed in chapter 4, mailed questionnaires have low response rates, and the representativeness of the people who do reply is uncertain. The *Dispatch* partially corrects for these problems by mailing questionnaires to samples selected from lists of registered voters. In 1994 and 1995, the paper used its mailed questionnaires but also commissioned telephone surveys by the Gallup Organization. Overall, the *Dispatch* results were much more accurate than the Gallup telephone polls, most likely because the mail poll did a better job of estimating the likely electorate. Anyone who completes a mailed questionnaire probably has a level of motivation indicative of a likely voter; the Gallup screen for likely voters simply consisted of registered voters who said they were likely to vote.

Visser et al. (1996) conducted an extensive comparative analysis of the performance of the *Dispatch* mail poll and the telephone polls conducted by the University of Akron and the University of Cincinnati in Ohio elections between 1980 and 1994. Overall, the election predictions of the final *Dispatch* poll were much more accurate than those generated by the telephone surveys. Numerous reasons were given for the superiority: a larger sample size, a questionnaire that closely resembled the actual ballot, response categories that minimized undecided answers and eliminated the need to allocate undecided respondents, and sampling and response procedures that produced more representative samples. Thus, contrary to conventional wisdom, mail questionnaires with an average response rate of only 25 percent were more accurate than telephone surveys. Even more surprising, for the final preelection *Dispatch* polls the deadline for receipt of the mailed surveys by the newspaper was typically the Thursday before election day. Therefore no information was gathered over the last weekend before the election, a time when sizable shifts in voter preference might occur, and yet the *Dispatch* polls were still more accurate. The *Dispatch* experience may lead some pollsters to rethink some of the conventional wisdom.

The Changing Political and Economic Climate

Surveys predict best when there is a normal voter turnout pattern. This observation applies to the polls of 1982. They performed poorly because they consistently underestimated the Democratic turnout, which was higher than expected that year because of the deepening economic recession and effective efforts by labor unions and black organizations to mobilize participation among their members. Moreover, although voter turnout is usually low among the unemployed, the 1982 election may have been atypical because many of the newly unemployed had been regular voters, and they participated at a higher-than-expected rate (Rothenberg 1983, 8).

The 1982 contest that probably did the most damage to the polls' reputation was the Illinois gubernatorial election. Most polls predicted that incumbent Republican governor James Thompson would score a fifteen-to-twenty-point victory over Democrat Adlai Stevenson III. But when the votes were tabulated, Thompson won by less than 0.2 percent.

Kohut (1983) and Day and Becker (1984) tested numerous hypotheses about the inaccuracy of the Illinois polls. They ruled out some, such as last-minute shifts in preference that the polls missed; polls were conducted to the very end of the campaign, and they still showed Thompson winning by a large margin. A poor estimate of the likely voters also was ruled out. Instead, the polls' poor performance seems to have been caused mainly by an upsurge in straight-ticket voting among Democrats, including some who preferred Thompson to Stevenson but still cast a straight Democratic vote. In Chicago the Democratic organization had devoted its resources to a "Punch 10" (that is, vote straight Democratic) media campaign, an effort that was particularly effective in black areas where it was part of an overall anti-Reagan theme (Kohut 1983, 42; Day and Becker 1984, 613). Thus a good part of the Illinois poll debacle stemmed from political organization and mobilization, developments that are difficult to anticipate and assess by means of a poll.

A more recent example of inaccuracy occurred in the 1994 midterm elections, in which the Republican victory was more sweeping than had been indicated by the polls conducted weeks before the elections. Perhaps part of the discrepancy was attributable to the difficulty of estimating the likely Democratic and Republican turnout, but events in the ten days before the elections also may have affected the results. The extensive and visible campaigning by President Clinton, for example, may have served to nationalize many of the local contests to the advantage of the GOP. The polls conducted right before election day were largely on target in predicting the Republican sweep, as many races broke in favor of the GOP over the final weekend of the campaign. A similar situation occurred in the 2002 midterm congressional elections, in which the election day results evidenced greater Republican success than had been expected based on polls conducted weeks earlier. Some attribute the GOP's strong performance to effective and extensive campaigning by President Bush and the greater ability of the Republican Party to frame the key issues of the election.

How Preelection Polls Affect Voters

Speculation about how polls affect voters has been widespread and contradictory. Some observers argue that polls that show one candidate ahead of another increase the incentives for supporters of the trailing candidate to change their preference and climb on board the winning candidate's bandwagon. Others emphasize underdog effects: sympathetic voters, they claim, rally around the candidate the polls show to be losing. Little strong evidence supports either of these views. The bandwagon effect would require that leading candidates consistently increase their margin, and the underdog effect predicts that the losing candidate will inexorably gain on the leader. These kinds of simple effects have not shown up consistently in surveys.

An experimental study by de Bock (1976) found some evidence that reports of disheartening poll results weakened support and motivation to turn out among a candidate's adherents. However, this finding seems to have been influenced by the experimental design itself, in which exposure to the negative polls was much more direct than would be the case in the real world. Other experimental studies have shown that polls can encourage support for the underdog, although the effects are not strong (Marsh 1984).

A 1985 ABC News/*Washington Post* poll attempted to address the effects of polls on voter choice. The survey asked a sample of Americans whether they knew whom the polls had favored in the 1984 election and whether the polls had influenced their voting behavior (Sussman 1985f). Seventy-eight percent correctly knew that the polls had picked Reagan to win, 7 percent said Mondale, and 15 percent did not know or remember what the polls had said. Among the 78 percent who knew the polls had predicted a Reagan victory, 4 percent said it helped them decide for Reagan, 4 percent said it helped them decide for Mondale, and 93 percent said it had no effect. Sussman concluded that the preelection polls could not have had any significant impact on the vote split because the pro-Mondale and pro-Reagan effects almost canceled each other out.

Anyone using Sussman's study, however, should weigh three factors. First, asking people to recall their views seven months after the election is risky—people simply forget. Second, Sussman's procedure required

You Can't Fool Us...

Jeff Danziger © 2003, Tribune Media Services, Inc. Reprinted with permission.

people to remember explicitly that the polls had influenced them; polls can influence voters even though they may not be aware of it. Third, some people might not be willing to admit that the polls affected their vote lest they appear to be making decisions on inappropriate grounds. Despite these reservations, Sussman's conclusion seems plausible in general and certainly so for the 1984 election.

Bandwagon and underdog effects can and do occur, but their magnitude is small and probably inconsequential. Polls may have an indirect effect on voters through their impact on campaign contributors, campaign workers, and media coverage. In addition to affecting voting behavior, polls can influence public opinion itself, a topic addressed in chapter 9. For example, if people become aware of changes in public opinion on an issue, that information may lead them to support the position favored by the trend. Or if they learn that their views are not shared by their fellow citizens, they may become unwilling to express their views. The very act of polling people can sensitize them to politics and campaigns in general and can encourage them to seek out information or become more involved. Given the prominence of polls in elections and in political discourse in general, it is important for citizens to understand both the positive and the manipulative uses made of polls, regardless of the original intent.

Conclusion

By and large, election polls in the United States are very accurate, particularly those conducted and sponsored by reputable media and polling organizations. In nations where the history of polling and free elections is much shorter, the track record of polls is far less impressive. For example, in December 1993, in the first multiparty election ever held in Russia, the pollsters' performance was abysmal. Shlapentokh (1994) recounts that the pollsters failed to predict the victorious party and even the order in which the parties would finish. In some countries polling is problematic for several reasons, some of them technical and some cultural. For example, it may be very difficult to pick a good sample: telephone ownership may not be widespread, and other information about residential units, especially in rural areas, may be flawed. Citizens in countries with traditions of totalitarian governments and repression may be wary about being interviewed by strangers and therefore may not participate in polling or give answers that reflect their true views. As one Russian analyst commented about the difficulties of polling in the former Soviet Union, "You are talking about sampling 30,000 villages and more than 1,000 cities. You must go to places that have for decades despised authority and then ask people their most personal fears about the future. And they are supposed to tell people they have never met what is on their mind" (Specter 1996).

Fortunately, these technical and cultural problems are less prevalent in the United States, and the track record of American election polls is impressive. Of greater concern is how the polling enterprise affects the behavior of citizens in a democratic nation. We return to the issue of how the polls affect citizens and society in the last chapter.

Exercises

1. First examine the national-level preelection polls conducted between Labor Day and election day by two different polling organizations in the 2000 or 2004 presidential election. Note changes in the relative standings of the Democratic and Republican candidates and the minor party candidates over this time period. Try to link specific campaign occurrences to changes in the candidates' poll standings. Then compare how similar or dissimilar the results of the two polling organizations were over the Labor Day to election day period.

   Next, pick two states and follow the state-level polls for the same time period. Pick one state in which the presidential contest was very close and a second state in which the contest was lopsided. Trace the fluctuations in the poll results in both states. How does sampling error affect your description of how the presidential contest was unfolding in each of the states you selected?

2. Pollsters often query Americans about what they think is the most important problem facing the nation and which political party can better address that problem. Find one polling organization that has asked these types of questions and trace the responses of the American people between early 2001 and 2004. How did citizens' responses change over that time? What do the patterns you uncovered suggest to you about possible Democratic and Republican campaign strategies and messages in presidential and congressional elections?

8 Analyzing and Interpreting Polls

Thus far we have considered how public opinion surveys are conducted, how they are reported in the media, and how they influence elections and campaigns. This chapter focuses on the end products of public opinion surveys—the analysis and interpretation of poll data.

Interpreting a poll is more an art than a science, even though statistical analysis of poll data is central to the enterprise. An investigator examining poll results has tremendous leeway in deciding which items to analyze, which sample subsets or breakdowns to present, and how to interpret the statistical results. Take as an example a poll with three items that measure attitudes toward arms control negotiations. The investigator may construct an index from these three items, as discussed in chapter 3. Or the investigator may emphasize the results from one question, perhaps because of space and time constraints and the desire to keep matters simple or because those particular results best support the analyst's own policy preferences. Another possibility is to examine results from the entire sample and ignore subgroups whose responses deviate from the overall pattern. Again, time and space limitations or the investigator's own preferences may influence the choices. Finally, two investigators may interpret identical poll results in sharply different ways depending on the perspectives and values they bring to their data analysis: the glass may be half-full or half-empty.

The analysis and interpretation of data entail a high degree of subjectivity and judgment. Subjectivity in this context does not mean deliberate bias or distortion but simply professional judgments about the importance and relevance of information. Certainly, news organizations generally interpret their polls in an unbiased fashion. But biases can slip in—sometimes unintentionally, sometimes deliberately—when, for example, an organization has sponsored a poll to promote a particular position. Be-

FRANK & ERNEST reprinted by permission of Newspaper Enterprise Association, Inc.

cause this final phase of polling is likely to have the most direct influence on public opinion, this chapter presents several case studies to illustrate the judgmental aspects of analyzing and interpreting poll results.

Choosing Items to Analyze

Many public opinion surveys deal with multifaceted, complex issues. For example, a researcher querying Americans about their attitudes toward tax reform might find initially that they overwhelmingly favor a fairer tax system. But if respondents are asked about specific aspects of tax reform, their answers may reflect high levels of confusion, indifference, or opposition. And depending on which items the researcher chooses to emphasize, the report might convey support, indifference, or opposition toward tax reform. U.S. foreign policy in the Middle East is another highly complex subject that can elicit divergent reactions from Americans, depending on which aspects of the policy they are questioned about.

Some surveys go into great depth on a topic through multiple items constructed to measure its various facets. The problem for an investigator in this case again becomes deciding which results to report. Moreover, even though an extensive analysis is conducted, the news media might publicize only an abbreviated version of it. In such a case, the consumer of the poll results is at the mercy of how accurately the media portray the overall study. Groups or organizations that sponsor polls to demonstrate support for a particular position or policy option often disseminate results in a selective fashion that enables them to put the organization and its policies in a favorable light.

In contrast with in-depth surveys on a topic, *omnibus surveys* cover many subjects superficially in a single survey. Here the problem for an investigator becomes ensuring that the few questions directed to a specific topic really do justice to that topic's substance and complexity. It is left to the consumer of both kinds of polls to judge whether they receive the central information on a topic or whether other poll items might yield different results.

The issue of prayer in public schools is a good example of how public opinion polling can be incomplete and potentially misleading. Typically pollsters ask respondents whether they support a constitutional amendment that would permit voluntary prayer in public schools. In response, more than three-fourths of Americans say they would favor such an amendment. But this question misses the mark. Voluntary prayer by individuals is in no way prohibited; the real issue is *organized* voluntary prayer. Yet many pollsters do not include items that tap this aspect of the voluntary prayer issue. Will there be a common prayer? If so, who will compose it? Will someone lead the class in prayer? If so, who? Under what circumstances and when will the prayer be uttered? What about students who do not wish to participate or who prefer a different prayer?

The difficulty with both the in-depth poll and the omnibus survey is that the full set of items used to study a particular topic is usually not reported, and thus the consumer cannot make informed judgments about whether the conclusions of the survey are valid. Recognizing this, individuals should take a skeptical view of claims by a corporate executive or an elected officeholder or even a friend that the polls demonstrate public support for or opposition to a particular position. The first question to ask is, What is the evidence cited to support the claim? From there one might examine the question wording, the response alternatives, the screening for nonattitudes, and the treatment of "don't know" responses. Then one might attempt the more difficult task of assessing whether the questions used to study the topic at hand were really optimal. Might other questions have been used? What aspects of the topic were not addressed? Finally, one might ponder whether different interpretations could be imposed on the data and whether alternative explanations could account for the reported patterns.

When people cite poll results, they may be tempted to seize on those that support their position and ignore those that do not. The problem is that one or two items cannot capture the full complexity of most issues. For example, Gallup polls conducted in early May 2003 illustrate how important the selective use and analysis of survey items could be in generating rather different impressions on the issue of gay rights. Fortunately, the Gallup Organization asked a range of questions and presented the results of all of them in a fair and unbiased fashion (Newport 2003a; 2003b). Among the questions Gallup asked were the following four:

Do you think homosexual relations between consenting adults should or should not be legal?

Should	60%
Should not	35%
No opinion	5%

Do you feel that homosexuality should be considered an acceptable alternative lifestyle or not?

Should	54%
Should not	43%
No opinion	3%

Would you favor or oppose a law that would allow homosexual couples to legally form civil unions, giving them some of the legal rights of married couples?

Favor	49%
Oppose	49%
No opinion	2%

As you may know, there has been considerable discussion in the news regarding the rights of homosexual men and women. In general, do you think homosexuals should or should not have equal rights in terms of job opportunities?

Should	88%
Should not	9%
No opinion	1%

If one focused on the second and third items, one might describe American public opinion as sharply split on the issue of gay rights. If one emphasized the first and last items, one would conclude that a substantial majority of Americans favor gay rights. Clearly, people promoting agendas on the issue of gay rights could easily select the items that favored their position. However, the Gallup Organization recognized that the attitudes toward homosexuality and gay rights are multifaceted, requiring multiple items to capture the complexity of public opinion.

The issue of government funding of faith-based initiatives further illustrates the importance of item selection and analysis in appreciating the complexity of popular opinion. A poll conducted by the Pew Forum on Religion and Public Life and the Pew Research Center for People and the Press in March 2001 found that 75 percent of Americans favored government funding of faith-based initiatives that provide social services, while 21 percent opposed the idea (Goodstein 2001; Morin 2001a). But support dropped dramatically when specific religious groups were mentioned as recipients of public money. Catholic and Protestant churches and Jewish synagogues still received substantial support at 62, 61 and 58 percent respectively, but Mormon churches, Muslim mosques, and Buddhist temples enjoyed the support of only 51, 38, and 38 percent of Americans respectively. In addition, respondents expressed concerns about religions' using public dollars to proselytize, about excessive government involvement with religious organizations, and about the fundamental issue of separation of church and state. Moreover, 78 percent of the respondents said that religious organizations that use government funds to provide social services should not be allowed to hire only people who share their religious beliefs. Thus, although there is widespread support—75 percent—for faith-based initiatives, there are important conditions and restrictions on that support.

Additional examples of the importance of item selection are provided by the polls taken to gauge Americans' attitudes about the Iraqi invasion of Kuwait in 1990, the war with Iraq in 2003, and the war against terrorism in the post–September 11 era. Early in the first Persian Gulf crisis, various survey organizations asked Americans, using different questions, how they felt about taking military action against Iraq. Not surprisingly, the organizations obtained different results:

Do you favor or oppose direct U.S. military action against Iraq at this time? (Gallup, August 3–4, 1990)

Favor	23%
Oppose	68%
Don't know/refused	9%

Do you agree or disagree that the U.S. should take all actions necessary, including the use of military force, to make sure that Iraq withdraws its forces from Kuwait? (ABC News/*Washington Post,* August 8, 1990)

Agree	66%
Disagree	33%
Don't know	1%

Would you approve or disapprove of using U.S. troops to force the Iraqis to leave Kuwait? (Gallup, August 9–12, 1990; qtd. in *Public Perspective,* September/October 1990, 13)

Approve	64%
Disapprove	36%

I'm going to mention some things that may or may not happen in the Middle East and for each one, please tell me whether the U.S. should or should not take military action in connection with it. . . . If Iraq refuses to withdraw from Kuwait? (NBC News/*Wall Street Journal*, August 18–19, 1990; qtd. in *Public Perspective*, September/October 1990, 13)

No military action	51%
Military action	49%

Note that the responses indicate varying levels of support for military action even though most of the questions were asked within two weeks of each other. The first question shows the most opposition to military action. This is easily explained: The question concerns military action *at this time*, and many Americans may have seen such a step as premature until other means had been tried. The next two questions indicate majority support for military action, and the final item shows a very divided American populace. It is clear which survey items proponents and opponents of military action would cite to support their arguments.

Throughout the Persian Gulf crisis, public opinion was highly supportive of President George Bush's policies; only in the period between October and December 1990 did support for the president's handling of the situation drop below 60 percent. For example, a November 1990 CBS News/*New York Times* poll showed the following patterns of response:

Do you approve or disapprove of the way George Bush is handling Iraq's invasion of Kuwait?

Approve	50%
Disapprove	41%
Don't know/NA	8%

An ABC News/*Washington Post*/poll in mid-November asked:

Do you approve or disapprove of the way George Bush is handling the situation caused by Iraq's invasion of Kuwait?

Approve	59%
Disapprove	36%
Don't know/NA	5%

Some opponents of the military buildup tried to use these and similar polls to demonstrate that support for the president's policies was decreasing—earlier polls had indicated support levels in the 60–70 percent range. Fortunately, the *Washington Post* poll cited above asked respondents who disapproved of Bush's policy whether the president was moving too slowly or too quickly. It turned out that 44 percent of the disapprovers said "too slowly" and 37 percent "too quickly." Thus a plurality of the disapprovers preferred more rapid action against Iraq—a result that provided little support for those critics of the president's policies who were arguing against a military solution.

In August 2003, the Gallup Organization (Newport 2003d) queried Americans about their views on aspects of American involvement in Iraq. Among the items in the survey were the following:

How would you say things are going for the U.S. in Iraq now that the major fighting has ended—very well, moderately well, moderately badly, or very badly?

Very/moderately well	50%
Very/moderately badly	49%

All in all, do you think the situation in Iraq was worth going to war over, or not?

Worth going to war	63%
Not worth going to war	35%

Do you approve or disapprove of the way that George W. Bush is handling the situation with Iraq?

Approve	57%
Disapprove	41%

Do you think the Bush administration does—or does not—have a clear plan for handling the situation in Iraq?

Does	44%
Does not	54%
No opinion	2%

Which comes closest to your view about what the U.S. should now do about the number of U.S. troops in Iraq—the U.S. should send more troops to Iraq, the U.S. should keep the number of troops as it is now, the U.S. should begin to withdraw some troops from Iraq, or the U.S. should withdraw all of its troops from Iraq?

Send more troops	15%
Keep as it is now	36%
Withdraw some troops	32%
Withdraw all troops	14%

Fortunately, we have all of the above items to capture the complexity of American public opinion about the situation in Iraq. But clearly very different portraits of public opinion could be generated if one focused selectively on only some of the items. For example, someone hostile to the Bush administration might focus on the fourth item, which indicates that a majority of the American people believed that the Bush administration did not have a clear plan for handling the situation in Iraq. A proponent of the Bush administration might focus on the second and third questions, which show that healthy majorities of Americans thought it was worthwhile to go to war with Iraq and approved the president's handling of the situation. Another observer might emphasize the first and last items and write that Americans were sharply divided on Iraq.

A FOX News/Opinion Dynamics poll in July 2003 included a number of questions about how safe Americans felt since the terrorist attacks of September 11 (The Polling Report, August 11, 2003):

How surprised are you that there has not been another terrorist attack in the United States since the 9/11 attacks?

Very surprised	21%
Somewhat surprised	30%
Not very surprised	27%
Not at all surprised	19%
Not sure	3%

How confident are you that U.S. intelligence agencies have now improved their procedures and will be able to prevent attacks like the 9/11 attacks in the future?

Very confident	17%
Somewhat confident	45%
Not very confident	20%
Not at all confident	13%
Not sure	5%

Do you think another major terrorist attack in the United States will happen within the next three months, within the next sixth months, in the next one to two years, more than two years from now, or never?

Within the next three months	4%
Within the next six months	10%
In the next one to two years	31%
More than two years from now	17%
Never	16%
Not sure	22%

Do you think there are members of the al Qaeda terrorist group in the United States today?

Yes	92%
No	4%
Not sure	4%

Do you think America is doing enough to secure the country's borders?

Yes	35%
No	57%
Not sure	8%

How safe and secure do Americans actually feel? Again, emphasizing different questions will produce different portraits of public opinion. For example, 62 percent of Americans (17 + 45) are either very or somewhat confident that U.S. intelligence agencies will be able to prevent future attacks, but 62 percent (4 + 10 + 31 + 17) believe there will be another major terrorist attack in the United States. Americans are split on whether or not they are surprised by the absence of another terrorist strike since September 11, but they are almost unanimous in their belief that al Qaeda members are in the United States. The lesson of this and the previous examples is clear: Constructing an interpretation around any single survey item can generate a misleading description of public opinion. And sometimes advocates of particular positions do that deliberately, using survey results selectively and misleadingly to advance their cause.

The political debate surrounding tax cuts in 2001 and 2002 often cited poll results to justify various positions. And certainly, all other things being equal, Americans would prefer to have lower taxes, a position that Republican tax cut advocates routinely cited. In the first round of tax cuts in 2001, the Bush administration claimed that the projected multi-trillion-dollar surplus would allow the United States to have tax cuts, pay down the national debt, and shore up Social Security and Medicare. But even under those circumstances, tax cuts were not a high priority for Americans. For example, a February 2001 CBS poll asked Americans the following question:

Some lawmakers are saying that there will be a budget surplus in the coming years. If that happens and you had to choose among the following things, how would you like the money to be used: (1) to cut income taxes, (2) to pay down the national debt, (3) to preserve programs like Medicare and Social Security, or (4) something else?

Cut income taxes	19%
Pay down debt	13%

Medicare/Social Security	48%
Something else	7%
Combination (volunteered)	12%
Don't know	1%

As the economy weakened and projected surpluses turned into actual deficits, opponents of the various actual and proposed rounds of tax cuts regularly cited poll results that showed that when tax cuts were paired against other public policy objectives, the desire for tax cuts declined markedly. For example, an NPR/Kaiser Family Foundation/Kennedy School of Government poll asked Americans in February and March 2003:

What's more important to you, having the government provide needed services, or cutting taxes?

Provide needed services	66%
Cut taxes	31%
Don't know	2%

In some ways this is a flawed question, since "needed services" could mean starkly different things to different respondents. But the question is representative of the typical pattern of responses obtained when the question of services versus tax cuts is presented to Americans. In a similar vein, a *Washington Post*/ABC News poll conducted in late summer 2003 found that about 60 percent of Americans were unhappy about the president's request to Congress to provide another $87 billion for the reconstruction of postwar Iraq and Afghanistan (although about the same proportion of the American public favored staying in Iraq). But when asked how the $87 billion should be generated, a plurality (41 percent) called for the repeal of recently passed tax cuts.

The obvious point of the tax cut example is that an accurate portrayal of American public opinion must take into account not simply a preference for lower taxes but also the trade-offs that might be involved in any tax cut, particularly when the federal budget is under great strain. Clearly, to capture the complexity and conditional nature of citizens' views, multiple items must be used. And when that is done, then the results of the multiple items should be made public, even if partisans on either side of the issue would prefer that only the results that support their position become public.

Schneider (1996) has provided an excellent example of how examination of a single trial heat question may give a misleading impression of the electoral strength of presidential candidates when the group includes the incumbent president. A better sense of the candidates' true electoral strength

Reprinted with special permission of King Features Syndicate.

is achieved by adding to the analysis information about the incumbent's job approval rating. For example, in a trial heat question in May 1980 incumbent president Jimmy Carter led challenger Ronald Reagan by 40 percent to 32 percent. Yet at the time Carter's job rating was quite negative: 38 percent approval and 51 percent disapproval. Thus Carter's lead in the trial heat was much more fragile than it appeared; indeed, Reagan went on to win the election. Four years later, in May 1984, President Reagan led challenger Walter Mondale by ten percentage points in the trial heat question. But Reagan's job rating was very positive: 54 percent approval compared with 38 percent disapproval. Reagan's ten-point lead thus looked quite solid in view of his strong job ratings, and he won overwhelmingly in November. Finally, in April 1992 incumbent president George Bush led challenger Bill Clinton by 50 percent to 34 percent in the trial heat question, a huge margin. But Bush's overall job rating was negative—42 percent approval versus 48 percent disapproval. Bush's lead over Clinton, then, was not as strong as it appeared, and Clinton ultimately won the election.

One of the anomalies of 1996 was the substantial number of Americans who were worried about the health of the economy at a time when by most objective indicators the economy was performing very well. Part of the answer to this puzzle was Americans' ignorance and misinformation about the country's economic health. For example, even though unemployment was substantially lower in 1996 than in 1991, 33 percent of Americans thought that it was higher, and 28 percent thought it was the same. The average estimate of the unemployment rate was 20.6 percent, when in reality it was just over 5 percent. Americans' perceptions of inflation and the deficit were similar; in each case people thought that it was much worse than it actually was. It is no wonder that many Americans expressed feelings of economic insecurity during good economic times: they were not aware of how strongly the economy was performing (Morin and Berry 1996).

Sometimes it is tempting to speculate broadly about citizens' opinions and policy preferences based on their responses to particular survey items. In many cases, the speculations and projections would be incorrect, but only additional polling questions would confirm the mistake. For example, in 1999 a survey conducted for CNN–*USA Today* by the Gallup Organization asked Americans, "Do you support the 'don't ask, don't tell' policy on homosexuality in the military?" Fifty percent of the respondents said they supported the policy, and 46 percent opposed it, suggesting a sharply divided citizenry with only the barest majority in favor of letting gays serve in the military. Fortunately, the survey posed a follow-up question to the 46 percent who opposed "don't ask, don't tell": "Do you oppose it because you think homosexuals should be able to serve openly in the military, or because you believe homosexuals should not be able to serve in the military under any circumstances?" In response to this question, the 46 percent broke down into 35 percent who said that gays should be able to serve openly, 8 percent who said they should never be able to serve, and 3 percent who cited no reason for their stance. Inclusion of the second item revealed a portrait of American public opinion that is much more supportive of gays serving in the military.

Two polls on abortion demonstrate that while support for the use of abortion may have weakened in recent years, one cannot conclude that citizens are therefore more likely to favor legally restricting it. A 2000 *Los Angeles Times* poll found that more than half of the respondents thought abortion should be either totally illegal or legal only in cases of rape, incest, or when the mother's life was in danger (Rubin 2000). Yet more than two-thirds said the decision to have an abortion should be left to the woman and her doctor. Even among the 57 percent of respondents who believed abortion to be murder, more than half agreed that the decision to have an abortion should be left to the woman. A 1998 *Columbus Dispatch* poll of Ohioans obtained similar results (Rowland 1998). Only 27 percent of Ohioans believed that abortion should be generally available; 15 percent said that it should be available but under stricter limits; 43 percent said that abortion should be against the law except in cases involving rape, incest, and the life of the mother; and 15 percent believed that abortion should not be permitted at all. Moreover, 51 percent of the respondents believed that abortion was an act of murder. These results might suggest that Ohioans would support government action to limit or prohibit abortions, but that was not the case. Ohioans were asked to agree or disagree with the following statement: "Even in cases where I might think abortion is the wrong thing to do, I don't think the government has any business preventing a woman from having an abortion." Fully 66 percent of respondents agreed with this statement, and only 27 percent disagreed. The lesson here is that one cannot presume to know citizens' policy prescriptions based on their opinions on an issue. Rather, one has to ask specific questions about both issue opinions and policy preferences. Some citizens do not like abortion but are unwilling to impose their views on others. Likewise, some citizens may reject gun ownership for themselves, but that does not mean that they would prevent their fellow citizens from owning guns. Some may oppose mercy killings and doctor-assisted suicides, but that does not mean that they support stiff criminal penalties to punish such actions.

The final example in this section focuses on how the news media select what citizens learn about a poll, even when the complete poll and analyses are readily available. *Sex in America: A Definitive Survey,* by Robert T. Michael and others, was published in 1994, along with a more specialized and comprehensive volume, *The Social Organization of Sexuality: Sexual Practices in the United States,* by Edward O. Laumann, Michael, and John H. Gagnon. Both books are based on an extensive questionnaire administered by the National Opinion Research Center to 3,432 scientifically selected respondents, a genuine public opinion survey on sexual behavior, unlike the sex pseudopolls discussed in chapter 1.

Because of the importance of the subject matter and because sex sells, media coverage of the survey was widespread. How various news organizations reported the story indicates how much leeway the media have and how influential they are in determining what citizens learn about a given topic. For example, the *New York Times* ran a front-page story on October 7, 1994, titled "Sex in America: Faithfulness in Marriage Thrives After All." Less-prominent stories appeared in subsequent issues, including one on October 18, 1994, inaccurately titled "Gay Survey Raises a New Question."

Two of the three major newsmagazines featured the sex survey on the covers of their October 17, 1994, issues. The *Time* cover simply read, "Sex in America: Surprising News from the Most Important Survey since the Kinsey Report." The *U.S. News and World Report* cover was more risqué, showing a partially clad man and woman in bed; it read, "Sex in America: A Massive New Survey, the Most Authoritative Ever, Reveals What We Do Behind the Bedroom Door." In contrast, *Newsweek* simply ran a two-page story with the lead, "Not Frenzied, but Fulfilled. Sex: Relax. If you do it—with your mate—around twice a week, according to a major new study, you basically wrote the book of love."

Other magazines and newspapers also reported on the survey in ways geared to their readership. The November issue of *Glamour* featured the survey on its cover with the teaser, "Who's doing it? And how? MAJOR U.S. SEX SURVEY." The story that followed was written by the authors of the book. The cover of the November 15, 1994, issue of *The Advocate* read, "What That Sex Survey Really Means," and the story focused largely on what the survey had to say about the number of gays and lesbians in the population. The lead stated, "10%: Reality or Myth? There's little authoritative information about gays and lesbians in the landmark study *Sex in America*—but what there is will cause big trouble." Finally, the *Chronicle of Higher Education,* a weekly newspaper geared to college and university personnel, in its October 17, 1994, issue headlined its story, "The Sex Lives of Americans. Survey That Had Been Target of Conservative Attacks Produces Few Startling Results."

Both books about the survey contain a vast amount of information and a large number of results and findings. Although most of the media coverage cited above was accurate in reporting the actual survey results, it also was selective in focusing on the more titillating parts of the survey, an unsurprising outcome given the need to satisfy their readerships.

Examining Trends with Polling Data

Researchers often use polling data to describe and analyze trends. To study trends, a researcher must ensure that items relating to the topic under investigation are included in multiple surveys conducted at different times. Ideally, the items should be identically worded. But even when they are, serious problems of comparability can make trend analysis difficult. Identically worded items may not mean the same thing or provide the same stimulus to respondents over time because social and political changes in society have altered the meaning of the questions. For example, consider this question:

> Some say that the civil rights people have been trying to push too fast. Others feel they haven't pushed fast enough. How about you? Do you think that civil rights leaders are trying to push too fast, are going too slowly, or are they moving at about the right speed?

The responses to this item can be greatly influenced by the goals and agenda of the civil rights leadership at the time of the survey. A finding that more Americans think that the civil rights leaders are moving too fast or too slowly may reflect not a change in attitude from past views about civil rights activism but a change in the civil rights agenda itself. In this case, follow-up questions designed to measure specific components of the civil rights agenda are needed to help define the trend.

As another example of the importance of context in assessing the significance of a trend, consider the following question:

How much of the time do you think you can trust government in Washington to do what is right—just about always, most of the time, or only some of the time?

Responses to this question over time had shown a substantial decline in trust from the mid 1960s to 1980, a leveling off in the 1980s, an increase in trust in the 1990s, and a sharp increase in trust after the terrorist attacks of September 2001. But what did this post–9/11 spike in trust really mean? Both Langer (2002) and Bishop (2002) argue that the meaning of the question changed after the terrorist attack, that citizens were now responding to a question that implicitly asked how much they trusted the federal government in matters of defense and national security, whereas in the past they had answered the question in the context of social and domestic programs. Indeed, as the events of 9/11 became more distant and politics in Washington returned to "normal," trust in government once again declined.

In addition to changes in the political environment, there are other obstacles to achieving comparability over time. For example, even if the wording of an item were to remain the same, its placement within the questionnaire could change, and that could alter its meaning (see chapter 3). Likewise, the definition of the sampling frame and the procedures used to achieve completed interviews could change. In short, comparability entails much more than simply wording questions identically. Unfortunately, consumers of poll results seldom receive the information that enables them to judge whether items are truly comparable over time.

Two studies demonstrate the advantages and disadvantages of using identical items over time. Abramson (1990) complained that the biennial National Election Studies conducted by the Survey Research Center at the University of Michigan, Ann Arbor, were losing their longitudinal comparability as new questions were added to the surveys and old ones removed. Baumgartner and Walker (1988), by contrast, complained that the use of the same standard question over time to assess the level of group membership in the United States had systematically underestimated the extent of such activity. They argued that new measures of group membership should be employed, which of course would make comparisons between past and present surveys more problematic. Although both the old and the new measures can be included in a survey, it becomes very costly if the survey must cover many other topics.

Two other studies show how variations in question wording can make the assessment of attitude change over time difficult. Borrelli, Lockerbie, and Niemi (1989) found that polls measuring Americans' political party loyalties in 1980 and in 1984 varied widely in their results. They attributed the differences to three factors: whether the poll sampled voters only; whether the poll emphasized "today," or the present, in inquiring about citizens' partisanship; and whether the poll was conducted close to election day, which would tend to give the advantage to the party ahead in the presidential contest. The implication of this research for assessing changes in party identification over time is evident: to conclude that either of the two polls showed that genuine partisan change had occurred, other possible sources of observed differences, such as modifications in the wording of questions, must be ruled out. In a study of support for aid to the Nicaraguan contras between 1983 and 1986, Lockerbie and Borrelli (1990) argue that much of the observed change in American public opinion was not genuine. Instead, it was attributable to changes in the wording of the questions used to measure support for the contras.

Smith's (1993) critique of three major national studies of anti-Semitism conducted in 1964, 1981, and 1992 is an informative case study of how longitudinal comparisons may be undermined by methodological differences across surveys. The 1981 and 1992 studies were ostensibly designed to build on the 1964 effort, thereby facilitating an analysis of trends in anti-Semitism. But, as Smith notes, longitudinal comparisons among the three studies were problematic because of differences in sample definition and interview mode, changes in question order and question wording, and insufficient information to evaluate the quality of the sample and the design execution. In examining an eleven-item anti-Semitism scale, however, he did find six items highly comparable over time that indicated a decline in anti-Semitic attitudes.

Examining Subsets of Respondents

Although it is natural to want to know the results from an entire sample, often the most interesting information in a poll comes from examining the response patterns of subsets of respondents defined according to certain theoretically or substantively relevant characteristics. For example, a *Washington Post* poll conducted in August 2003 showed that 59 percent of Americans approved of "the way George W. Bush is handling his job as president" and 37 percent disapproved (Balz and Deane 2003). But these overall figures mask some analytically interesting variations. For example, among Democrats, independents, and Republicans, approval of the president went from 28 percent to 55 percent to 86 percent, respectively. A Gallup poll conducted in February 2003 found that 58 percent of all adult Americans approved of the president's performance. But among whites who are Protestants, approval of the president grew to 69 percent.

And among whites who are Protestant and "born-again," approval rose to 75 percent (Newport and Carroll 2003).

There is no necessary reason for public opinion on an issue to be uniform across subgroups. Indeed, on many issues there are reasons to expect just the opposite. That is why a fuller understanding of American public opinion is gained by taking a closer look at the views of relevant subgroups of the sample. In doing so, however, one should note that dividing the sample into subsets increases the sampling error and lowers the reliability of the sample estimates. For example, a sample of 1,600 Americans might be queried about their attitudes on abortion. After the overall pattern is observed, the researcher might wish to break down the sample by religion— yielding 1,150 Protestant, 400 Catholic, and 50 Jewish respondents—to determine whether religious affiliation is associated with specific attitudes toward abortion. The researcher then might observe that Catholics on the whole are the most opposed to abortion. To find out which Catholics are most likely to oppose abortion, she might further divide the 400 Catholics into young and old Catholics, or regular church attendees and nonregular attendees, or into four categories of young Catholic churchgoers, old Catholic churchgoers, young Catholic nonattenders, and old Catholic nonattenders. The more such breakdowns are done, the quicker the sample size in any particular category plummets, perhaps leaving insufficient cases in some categories to draw solid conclusions.

Examples of the advantages of delving more deeply into poll data on subsets of respondents are plentiful. An ABC News/*Washington Post* poll conducted in February 1986 showed major differences in the attitudes of men and women toward pornography; an examination of only the total sample would have missed these important divergences. For example, in response to the question, "Do you think laws against pornography in this country are too strict, not strict enough, or just about right?" 10 percent of the men said the laws were too strict, 41 percent said they were not strict enough, and 47 percent said they were about right. Among women, only 2 percent said the laws were too strict, a sizable 72 percent said they were not strict enough, and 23 percent thought they were about right (Sussman 1986c, 37).

Polls showed dramatic differences by race in opinions about the O. J. Simpson case, with blacks more convinced of Simpson's innocence and more likely to believe that he could not get a fair trial. For example, in a Field poll of Californians (*U.S. News and World Report,* August 1, 1994) only 35 percent of black respondents believed that Simpson could get a fair trial, compared with 55 percent of whites. Also, 62 percent of whites thought Simpson was "very likely or somewhat likely" to be guilty of murder, compared with only 38 percent of blacks. Comparable results were found in a national *Time*/CNN poll (*Time,* August 1, 1994): 66 percent of whites thought Simpson got a fair preliminary hearing, compared with only 31 percent of black respondents, and 77 percent of the white respondents thought the case against Simpson was "very strong" or "fairly strong," compared with 45 percent for blacks. A *Newsweek* poll (August 1, 1994) revealed that 60 percent of blacks believed that Simpson was set up (20 percent attributing the setup to the police); only 23 percent of whites believed in such a conspiracy. When asked whether Simpson had been treated better or worse than the average white murder suspect, whites said better by an overwhelming 52 percent to 5 percent margin, and blacks said worse by a 30 percent to 19 percent margin. These various reactions to the Simpson case startled many Americans, who could not understand how their compatriots of another race could see the situation so differently.

Sometimes the opinions of Americans differ by age. For example, consider the topic of physician-assisted suicide. A *Washington Post* poll conducted in 1996 asked a national sample of Americans, "Should it be legal or illegal for a doctor to help a terminally ill patient commit suicide?" (Rosenbaum 1997). The attitudes of older citizens and younger citizens were markedly different on this question—the older the age group, the greater the opposition to doctor-assisted suicide. For example, 52 percent of respondents between ages eighteen and twenty-nine thought doctor-assisted suicide should be legal; 41 percent said it should be illegal. But for citizens over age seventy, the comparable figures were 35 percent and 58 percent. Even more striking were some of the racial and income differences on this question. Whites thought physician involvement in suicide should be legal by a 55 percent to 35 percent margin; blacks opposed it 70 percent to 20 percent. At the lowest income levels, doctor-assisted suicide was opposed by a 54 percent to 37 percent margin; at the highest income level it was supported by a 58 percent to 30 percent margin.

Another area in which age makes a difference is opinions about whether or not homosexual relations between consenting adults should be legal. A May 2003 Gallup poll showed that among 18-to-29-year-old Americans, 66 percent thought homosexual relations should be legal; 33 percent disagreed. But among Americans 65 years and older, 39 percent believed that homosexual relations should be legal, while 55 percent were opposed (Newport 2003a). There were also age differences in support for going to war with Iraq. According to a *Washington Post*/ABC News poll, only 49 percent of Americans aged 65 or over favored going to war, compared with 60 percent of 18-to-34-year-olds and 67 percent of 35-to-44-year-olds. Indeed, Morin and Deane (2003) note that public opinion polling has often shown older citizens less supportive of going to war.

Two state-level polls on gun ownership and gun rights also demon-strate the importance of examining subsets of respondents. A 1999 Field poll asked Californians, "Which is more important—to protect the right of Americans to own guns, or to impose greater control on gun ownership?" Overall, 64 percent of Californians said it was more important to control gun ownership; 30 percent opted to protect the rights of gun owners. But an examination of responses by the respondent's party affiliation brought sharp differences to light. Democrats cited controlling gun ownership over protecting the right to own guns by a margin of 79 percent to 16 percent. But 49 percent of Republicans thought protecting the right to own guns was more important, with 45 percent opting for greater regulation of gun ownership. Similarly, a 1999 poll conducted for the *Columbus Dispatch* revealed sharp differences by gender in response to the question, "Which one do you think is more important: to protect the right of Americans to own guns or to control gun ownership?"(Rowland 1999). Men divided evenly on this item, but 70 percent of female respondents thought con-trolling gun ownership was more important, compared with only 21 per-cent who gave higher priority to protecting the right to own guns. The *Dispatch* survey also reinforces an earlier point: One cannot assume how respondents stand on particular issues based on their positions on other is-sues. Small-to-sizable majorities of Ohioans supported a variety of gun control and gun safety measures. Ninety percent favored a mandatory waiting period to allow background checks; 70 percent favored registering handguns with the government; 86 percent favored child safety locks; 85 percent favored requiring handgun owners to attend a course on gun safety; and 53 percent favored banning gun shows where guns are bought and sold without much supervision and regulation. But 53 percent would favor legislation (with various safeguards) that would permit adults to carry concealed weapons.

In many instances, the categories used for creating subgroups are al-ready established or self-evident. For example, if one is interested in gen-der or racial differences, the categories of male and female or white and black are straightforward candidates for investigation. Other breakdowns require more thought. For example, what divisions might be used to ex-amine the effects of age? Young, middle-aged, and old? If so, what actual ages correspond to those categories? Is middle age thirty-five to sixty-five, forty to sixty, or what? Or should more than three categories of age be de-fined? In samples selected to study the effects of religion, the typical break-down is Protestant, Catholic, and Jewish. But this simple threefold division might overlook some interesting variations—that is, some Protestants are evangelical, some are fundamentalist, and others are in the so-called main-line denominations. Moreover, because most blacks are Protestants, comparisons of Catholics and Protestants that do not also control for race may be misleading. Also, the threefold division overlooks a growing body of Muslims in the United States.

Creating subsets by ideology is another common approach to analyzing public opinion. The ideological categories used most often are liberal, moderate, and conservative, and typically respondents are assigned to these categories based on their answers to this question: "Generally speaking, do you think of yourself as a liberal, moderate, or conservative?" But do people really assign common meanings to these terms? Do these terms oversimplify reality? Journalist Kevin Phillips (1981) has cited the work of political scientists Stuart A. Lilie and William S. Maddox, who argue that the traditional liberal-moderate-conservative breakdown is inadequate for analytical purposes. Instead, they propose a fourfold classification of liberal, conservative, populist, and libertarian, based on two underlying dimensions: whether one supports or opposes government intervention in the economy and whether one supports or opposes expansion of individual behavioral liberties and sexual equality. They define liberals as those who support both government intervention in the economy and expansion of personal liberties, conservatives as those who oppose both, libertarians as citizens who favor expanding personal liberties but oppose government intervention in the economy, and populists as persons who favor government economic intervention but oppose the expansion of personal liberties. According to one poll, populists make up 24 percent of the electorate, conservatives 18 percent, liberals 16 percent, and libertarians 13 percent. The rest of the electorate is not readily classifiable or is unfamiliar with ideological terminology.

The more elaborate breakdown of ideologies may be helpful to those seeking to better understand public opinion, but the traditional categories still dominate political discourse. Even so, citizens who oppose government programs that affect the marketplace but support pro-choice court decisions on abortion and proposed gay rights statutes cannot be easily labeled liberals or conservatives, because they appear to be conservative on economic issues and liberal on lifestyle issues. Perhaps, then, they are best classified as libertarians.

Another example of the importance of examining subsets of respondents comes from a January 1985 ABC News/*Washington Post* poll that queried Americans about their attitudes on a variety of issues and presented the results not only for the entire sample but also for subsets of respondents defined by their attentiveness to public affairs (Sussman 1985b). Attentiveness to public affairs was measured by whether the respondents were aware of four recent news events: the subway shooting in New York City of four alleged assailants by their intended victim; the switch in jobs by two key Reagan administration officials, Donald Regan and James Baker; a proposal by the Treasury Department to simplify the tax system; and protests against South African apartheid held in the United States. Respondents then were divided into four levels of awareness, with 27 percent in the highest category, 26 percent in the next highest, 25 percent in the next category, and 22 percent falling in the lowest. The next step in the analysis was to compare the policy preferences of the highest-awareness and lowest-awareness subsets.

Some marked differences between the two groups emerged. For example, on the issue of support for the president's military buildup, 59 percent of the lowest-awareness respondents opposed any major cuts in military spending to lessen the budget deficit. By contrast, 57 percent of the highest-awareness group said that military spending should be limited to help reduce the budget deficit. On the issue of tax rates, a majority of both groups agreed with the president that taxes were too high, but the sizes of the majorities differed. Among the lowest-awareness respondents, 72 percent said taxes were too high and 24 percent said they were not; among the highest-awareness respondents, 52 percent said taxes were too high and 45 percent said they were not (Sussman 1985b).

Opinions about the future of Social Security and Medicare also are affected by citizens' knowledge about the two programs (Pianin and Brossard 1997). In one poll, the more people knew about Social Security and Medicare, the more likely they were to believe that the programs were in crisis and that major government action was needed. For example, among highly knowledgeable respondents, 88 percent believed that Social Security either was in crisis or had major problems; only 70 percent of respondents with little knowledge agreed. Likewise, 89 percent of the highly knowledgeable respondents believed Social Security would go bankrupt if Congress did nothing, compared with only 61 percent of the less-informed respondents.

All these findings raise some interesting normative issues about public opinion polls. As mentioned in chapter 1, the methodology of public opinion polls is very democratic. All citizens have a nearly equal chance to be selected for a sample and have their views counted; all respondents are weighted equally (or nearly so) in the typical data analysis. Yet except in the voting booth all citizens do not have equal influence in shaping public policy. The distribution of political resources, whether financial or informational, is not uniform across the population. Polls themselves become a means to influence public policy, as various decision makers cite poll results to legitimize their policies. But should the views of all poll respondents be counted equally? An elitist critic would argue that the most informed segments of the population should be given the greatest weight. Therefore, in the defense spending example above, more attention should be given to the views of the highest-awareness subset (assuming the validity of the levels of awareness), which were more supportive of reducing military spending. An egalitarian argument would assert that all respondents should be counted equally. We will return to the role of the polls in a democratic political system in the last chapter.

Interpreting Poll Results

An August 1986 Gallup poll on education showed that 67 percent of Americans would allow their children to attend class with a child suffering from AIDS; 24 percent would not. What reaction might there be to this finding? Some people might be shocked and depressed to discover that almost one-fourth of Americans could be so mean-spirited toward AIDS victims when the scientific evidence shows that AIDS is not a disease transmitted by casual contact. Others might be reassured and relieved that two-thirds of Americans are sufficiently enlightened or tolerant to allow their children to attend school with children who have AIDS. Some people might feel dismay: How could 67 percent of Americans foolishly allow their children to go to school with a child who has AIDS when there is no absolute guarantee that AIDS cannot be transmitted casually?

Consider this example from a 1983 poll by the National Opinion Research Center: "If your party nominated a black for President, would you vote for him if he were qualified for the job?" Eighty-five percent of the white respondents said yes. How might this response be interpreted? One might feel positive about how much racial attitudes have changed in the United States. A different perspective would decry the fact that in this supposedly tolerant and enlightened era, 15 percent of white survey respondents could not bring themselves to say they would vote for a qualified black candidate.

In neither of the examples just given can a single correct meaning be assigned to the data. Instead, the interpretation favored will be a function of the interpreter's individual values, beliefs, and purposes in analyzing the survey. This observation is demonstrated in an analysis of two national surveys on gun control, one sponsored by the National Rifle Association (NRA) and conducted by Decision/Making/Information, Inc., and the other sponsored by the Center for the Study and Prevention of Handgun Violence and conducted by Cambridge Reports, Inc. (pollster Patrick Caddell's firm). Although the statistical results from both surveys were comparable, the two reports arrived at substantially different conclusions. The NRA's analysis concluded,

Reprinted with special permission of King Features Syndicate.

Majorities of American voters believe that we do *not* need more laws governing the possession and use of firearms and that more firearms laws would *not* result in a decrease in the crime rate. (Wright 1981, 25)

By contrast, the center's report stated:

It is clear that the vast majority of the public (both those who live with handguns and those who do not) want handgun licensing and registration. . . . The American public wants some form of handgun control legislation. (Wright 1981, 25)

Wright carefully analyzed the evidence cited in support of each conclusion and found that "the major difference between the two reports is not in the findings, but in what is said about or concluded about the findings: what aspects of the evidence are emphasized or de-emphasized, what interpretation is given to a finding, and what implications are drawn from the findings about the need, or lack thereof, for stricter weapons controls" (Wright 1981, 38). In essence, it was the interpretation of the data that generated the difference in the recommendations.

Two polls on tax reform provide another example of how poll data can be selectively interpreted and reported (Sussman 1985a). The first, sponsored by the insurance industry, was conducted by pollster Burns Roper. Its main conclusion, announced at a press conference, was that 77 percent of the American public "said that workers should not be taxed on employee benefits" and only 15 percent supported such a tax, a conclusion very reassuring to the insurance industry. However, Roper included other items in the poll that the insurance industry chose not to emphasize. As Sussman points out, the 77 percent opposed to the taxing of fringe benefits were then asked, "Would you still oppose counting the value of employee benefits as taxable income for employees if the additional tax revenues went directly to the reduction of federal budget deficits and not into new spending?" Twenty-six percent were no longer opposed to taxing fringe benefits under this condition, bringing the overall opposition down to 51 percent of the sample.

A second follow-up question asked, "Would you still oppose counting the value of employee benefits as taxable income for employees if the additional tax revenues permitted an overall reduction of tax rates for individuals?" (a feature that was part of the Treasury Department's initial tax proposals). Now only 33 percent of the sample were opposed to taxing fringes, 50 percent supported it, and 17 percent were undecided. Thus, depending on which results are used, anyone reporting this poll could show a majority of citizens supportive of, or opposed to, taxing fringe benefits.

The other poll that Sussman analyzed also tapped people's reactions to the Treasury Department's tax proposal. One poll item read:

> The Treasury Department has proposed changing the tax system. Three tax brackets would be created, but most current deductions from income would be eliminated. Non-federal income taxes and property taxes would not be deductible, and many deductions would be limited. Do you favor or oppose this proposal? (Sussman 1985a)

Not surprisingly, 57 percent opposed the Treasury plan, and only 27 percent supported it. But as Sussman points out, the question was highly selective and leading because it focused on changes in the tax system that hurt the taxpayer. For example, nowhere does it inform the respondent that a key part of the Treasury plan was to reduce existing tax rates, so that 80 percent of Americans would be paying either the same amount in taxes or less than they were paying before. This survey was obviously designed to obtain a set of results compatible with its sponsor's policy objectives.

Morin (1995d) describes a situation in which polling data were misinterpreted and misreported in the *Washington Post* because of faulty communication between a *Post* reporter and the local polling firm that was conducting an omnibus survey in the Washington, D.C., area. Interested in how worried federal employees were about their jobs, given the budget battles going on between the Clinton White House and the Republican Congress in 1995, the reporter commissioned the polling firm to include the following questions in its survey: "Do you think your agency or company will probably be affected by federal budget cutbacks? Do you think your own job will be affected?" The poll discovered that 40 percent of the federal workers interviewed believed their own jobs might be affected. Unfortunately, when the polling outfit prepared a report for its client, the reporter, the report concluded that these federal workers felt their jobs were jeopardized. The reporter's story then stated, "Four out of every 10 federal employees fear losing their jobs because of budget reductions." As Morin points out, this conclusion does not follow from the polling questions asked. The belief that one's job will likely be affected is not equivalent to the fear of losing one's job. Instead, the effects might be lower salary increases, decreased job mobility, increased job responsibilities, and the like. A correction quickly appeared in the *Post* clarifying what the polling data had actually said. One lesson of this example is the responsibility that pollsters have to clients to communicate carefully and accurately what poll results mean. Another lesson is that no one should try to read too much into the responses to any single survey item. In this case, if the reporter wanted to know exactly how federal workers thought their jobs would be affected, a specific question eliciting this information should have been included in the survey.

In August 2003, Zogby International, working with the *American Enterprise* magazine, conducted a survey of Iraqi public opinion that was asserted to be scientific. Within a week after Zogby released the survey on September 10, the National Council on Public Polls' Polling Review Board issued a critique of the poll, claiming that it was not a scientific probability sample but instead simply a convenience sample, in which Iraqis were interviewed in only four cities (excluding Baghdad) in public places such as shopping areas and coffee houses.

Whatever the merits of the sampling procedure, it is the interpretation of this poll that is most noteworthy. At the time of the poll, domestic criticism of President Bush's planning for postwar Iraq was growing in intensity. More and more Americans believed that matters were not going well in Iraq despite the conclusion of the formal war. American soldiers in Iraq were regularly being attacked, and it appeared that many Iraqis were angry at American policies and the American presence. When the results of the poll were made public, supporters of the Bush administration claimed that they demonstrated that American policies in Iraq were going much better than the news media had been reporting. Indeed, Karl Zinsmeister, editor in chief of the *American Enterprise,* concluded his analysis of the poll with the admonition, "We're making headway in a benighted part of the world, America. Hang in there" (Zinsmeister 2003).

Perhaps Zinsmeister is correct. But one would be worried about the accuracy of poll results that did not include respondents from the Baghdad area. More important, some of the interpretations given to the responses may be unduly optimistic. For example, in his article, Zinsmeister wrote, "Iraqis are optimistic. Seven out of ten say they expect both their country and their personal lives will be better five years from now." A skeptic might respond that given the current situation in Iraq, of course Iraqis thought things would be better in five years; they certainly could not get much worse. Another item in the poll asked Iraqis:

If you were asked to name one foreign country you would like Iraq to model its new government on, which one of the following countries would you choose?

Syria	11.9%
Saudi Arabia	17.4%
United States	23.3%
Iran	3.1%
Egypt	7.1%
Other	15.4%
None	21.9%

In reporting these results, Zinsmeister only considered Iraqis who selected one of the five countries specifically listed in the question and wrote that "the most popular model by far was the U.S. The U.S. was preferred as a model by 37 percent (23.3/11.9 + 17.4 + 23.3 + 3.1 + 7.1) of Iraqis. . . ." But another way to look at these figures is to say that 23.3 percent chose the United States, or, even more pessimistically, that when Iraqis were given the opportunity to cite the United States as a model for the new Iraqi government, 76.7 percent of them chose an alternative other than the United States.

Zinsmeister was also optimistic that Iraq would not turn into a fundamentalist Islamic republic. He wrote:

> Perhaps the strongest indication that an Islamic government won't be part of Iraq's future: The nation is thoroughly secularized. We asked how often our respondents had attended the Friday prayer over the previous month. Fully 43 percent said "Never." It's time to scratch Khomeini II from the Iraq critics' list of morbid fears.

Here Zinsmeister has clearly made a huge leap from the results of one survey question to the conclusion that there is no danger of an Islamic republic's being established. Another question asked whether Iraq should have an Islamic government or whether the government should let everyone practice their own religion. About 33 percent preferred an Islamic government, while 60 percent favored letting people practice their own religion. This question shows that one-third of Iraqis want an Islamic government, but it is not at all clear that letting people practice their own religion rules out an Islamic government.

It is obvious that Zinsmeister is using the poll results to encourage Americans to stay the course in Iraq. He makes very clear to the reader that he is writing as an advocate, as well as how he is using and manipulating the polling data. But two other articles about the poll, one in the *Christian Science Monitor* (Hughes 2003) and the other in the *Financial*

Times of England (Dinmore 2003) illustrate how very different spins can be given to the same data. The *Financial Times* story was somewhat negative, with the headline "Opinion Poll Underlines Iraqi Distrust of America." In contrast, the *Christian Science Monitor* story was much more upbeat about Iraqi attitudes toward the United States. At one point Hughes wrote, "Two-thirds of those polled urged that U.S. and British troops should remain for at least another year." This is somewhat misleading since the actual question asked of Iraqis was, "Given a choice, would you like to see the American and British forces leave Iraq in six months, one year, or two years or more?" Thirty-one percent wanted them to leave in six months, and a total of 65.5 percent in a year. Clearly, this is not two-thirds of Iraqis urging that U.S. and British troops stay at least another year, but two-thirds of Iraqis wanting American and British forces to leave within a year.

When Polls Conflict: A Concluding Example

A variety of factors can influence poll results and their subsequent interpretation. Useful vehicles for a review of these factors are the polls that led up to the presidential elections between 1980 and 2000—polls that were often inconsistent. For example, in the 1984 election, polls conducted at comparable times yielded highly dissimilar results. A Harris poll had Reagan leading Mondale by nine percentage points, an ABC News/*Washington Post* poll had Reagan ahead by twelve points, a CBS News/*New York Times* survey had Reagan leading by thirteen points, a *Los Angeles Times* poll gave Reagan a seventeen-point lead, and an NBC News poll had the president ahead by twenty-five points (Oreskes 1984). In September 1988 seven different polls on presidential preference were released within a three-day period with results ranging from Bush ahead by eight points to a Dukakis lead of six points (Morin 1988c). In 1992 ten national polls conducted in the latter part of August showed Clinton with leads over Bush ranging from five to nineteen percentage points (Elving 1992). In 1996 the final preelection polls showed Clinton leading Dole by margins ranging from seven to eighteen percentage points. And in 2000 six polls released on October 26 showed outcomes ranging from a Bush lead of thirteen percentage points to a Gore lead of two percentage points. How can polls on an ostensibly straightforward topic such as presidential vote preference differ so widely? Many reasons can be cited, some obvious and others subtler in their effects.

The method of interviewing and the number of callbacks that a pollster uses to contact respondents who initially were unavailable are among the subtler reasons. Lewis and Schneider (1982, 43) reported that Patrick

Caddell and George Gallup, in their 1980 polls, found that President Reagan received less support from respondents interviewed personally than from those queried over the telephone. Their speculation about this finding was that weak Democrats who were going to desert Carter found it easier to admit this in a telephone interview than in a face-to-face situation.

As for callbacks, Dolnick (1984) reports that one reason a Harris poll was closer than others in predicting Reagan's sizable victory in 1980 was that it made repeated callbacks, which at each stage "turned up increasing numbers of well-paid, well-educated Republican-leaning voters." A similar situation occurred in 1984. Traugott (1987) found that persistence in callbacks resulted in a more Republican sample, speculating that Republicans were less likely to have been at home or available initially.

Among the more obvious factors that help account for differences among compared polls are question wording and placement. Some survey items mention the presidential and vice-presidential candidates; others mention only the presidential candidates. Some pollsters ask follow-up questions of undecided voters to ascertain whether they lean toward one candidate or another; others do not. And as noted in chapter 3, question order can influence responses. Normally, incumbents and better-known candidates do better when the question on vote intention is asked at the beginning of the survey rather than later. If vote intention is measured after a series of issue and problem questions have been asked, respondents may have been reminded of shortcomings in an officeholder's record and therefore be less willing to express support for the incumbent.

Comparable polls also can differ in how the sample is selected and how it is treated for analytical purposes. Some polls sample registered voters; others query adult Americans. There are differences as well in the methods used to identify likely voters, as discussed in chapter 7. As Lipset (1980) points out, the greater the number of respondents who are screened out of the sample because they do not seem to be likely voters, the more probable it is that the remaining respondents will be relatively more Republican in their vote preferences. Finally, some samples are weighted to guarantee demographic representativeness; others are not.

It is also possible that discrepancies among polls do not stem from any of the above mentioned factors but may simply reflect statistical fluctuations. For example, if one poll with a 4 percent sampling error shows Bush ahead of Gore by 52 percent to 43 percent, that result is statistically congruent with other polls that show a very narrow Bush lead of 48 percent to 47 percent and with yet others that show a landslide Bush lead of 56 percent to 39 percent.

Voss, Gelman, and King (1995) summarized and compared many of the methodological differences among polls conducted by eight polling organizations for the 1988 and 1992 presidential elections. Even though all eight organizations were studying the same phenomenon, there were enough differences in their approaches that polls conducted at the same time using identical questions might still obtain somewhat different results for reasons beyond sampling error. One feature Voss et al. examined was the sampling method—that is, how each organization generated a list of telephone numbers from which to sample. Once the sample was selected, polling organizations conducting the telephone interviews still had to make choices about how to handle "busy signals, refusals, and calls answered by electronic devices, how to decide which household members are eligible to be interviewed, and how to select the respondent from among those eligible" (Voss, Gelman, and King 1995). The investigators also examined the various weighting schemes that each survey operation used to ensure a representative sample. Much of this methodological information is not readily available to the consumer of public opinion polls, and if it were, many consumers would be overwhelmed by the volume of methodological detail. Yet these factors can make a difference. For example, the eight polling organizations that these researchers analyzed treated refusals quite differently. Some did not call back after receiving a refusal from a potential respondent; others did. One organization generally tried to call back, but with a different interviewer, but then gave up if a second refusal was obtained.

Thus conflicting poll results on the same topic may be a matter less of genuine, substantive differences than of differing methodological choices. This finding creates a challenge for the consumers of polls who are trying to bring order to divergent results. Because poll consumers are likely unaware of the methodological and design differences among competing surveys, they often find it difficult to decide which poll results are the most compelling and how to reconcile conflicting results. When multiple polls on the same topic yield similar findings, citizens view those results with greater confidence. And when there is only one survey on a topic, citizens must hope that the substantive results obtained are genuine and not simply the product of methodological choices made in the polling process. In short, because at times it is difficult to separate the substantive interpretation of the polling data from the procedures that were used to collect the data in the first place, citizens will find it even more challenging to be informed consumers of polls.

Exercises

1. Review the survey examples in this book. Pick one example and construct two very different interpretations of the same results. That is, write two very different commentaries about the identical set of results.

2. Assume that the job approval rating of President Bush was 54 percent in September 2003. How would you report this result? What commentary might you offer? In thinking about the various issues affecting the context of this result, you may want to consult a national newspaper from that month. How might one judge whether that approval level is high or low? What kinds of comparisons might be helpful in making that judgment?

9 Polling and Democracy

> *It's very clear*
> *The polls are here to stay;*
> *Not for a year,*
> *But ever and a day.*
>
> *The interviews and the questionnaires*
> *And the pollsters that we know*
> *Aren't just passing fancies—*
> *Oh, my goodness, no!*
>
> *The media*
> *Love polls in every way.*
> *It matters not*
> *If polls have scant to say.*
>
> *In time statistics may numb you,*
> *Results may stun you.*
> *Wait for another day,*
> *For—the polls are here to stay.*

—With apologies to George Gershwin

Public opinion polling is a contemporary manifestation of classical democratic theory; it attests to the ability of the rational and wise citizen to make informed judgments on the major issues of the day. Polling makes it possible for political organizations to demonstrate that public opinion is on their side as they promote their ends. News organizations also are enamored of polling, in part because polls seem to elevate the citizen (and thus the media audience) into a more prominent political role; in effect, the polls transform the amorphous citizenry into a unified actor in the political process. Poll results that are not supportive of government actions provide the news media with stories of conflict between the government and the people, just as points of contention between the president and the Congress or between the House and the Senate do.

As the technology of polling has been refined, upgraded, and made more available, many different kinds of groups, for-profit and nonprofit, public and private, have gained the ability to sponsor and conduct polls. Organizations can readily hire pollsters for surveys that will promote their aims, or if they want to be absolutely sure that the poll results will be favorable, they can conduct their own surveys. Such self-serving polls are replete with loaded questions, skewed samples, and faulty interpretations, as, for example, those done by the Tobacco Institute and the Michigan Tobacco and Candy Distributors and Vendors Association to try to head off higher cigarette taxes and antismoking legislation back in the 1980s (Perlstadt and Holmes 1987; Morin 1989a).

The major news organizations have heavily invested in their own polling operations, adding to the proliferation of surveys. When the presidential candidates' debates take place, for example, a news organization that fails to conduct and report a poll on the winner would be accused of providing incomplete news coverage. The unseemly contest among the media to be the first to "call" the outcomes of particular elections illustrates how the pressures of competition and ratings promote the widespread use of polls. The media operate under the assumption that public reactions to major news events are meaningful and that public opinion polls enhance the news value of a story.

How to Evaluate Polls: A Summary

Polls are a significant way for citizens to participate in society and to become informed about the relationship between the decisions of government and the opinions of the citizenry. As more organizations conduct polls and disseminate their results, whether to inform or to sway public opinion, citizens should be wary consumers, sensitive to the factors that can affect poll results. Gaining such sensitivity does not require familiarity with statistics or survey research experience. Consumers need only treat polls with a healthy skepticism and keep in mind the following questions and points as tools to evaluate poll results.

First, poll consumers should ask whether a public opinion survey is measuring genuine opinions or nonattitudes. Are the respondents likely to be informed and have genuine opinions about the topic? Or is the focus so esoteric that their responses reflect the social pressures of the interview situation, pressures that cause respondents to provide answers even when they have no real views on the subject at hand? As Neuman argued, there is often not a clear demarcation between attitudes and nonattitudes. Neuman coined the term *quasi-attitude* to designate something between an attitude and a nonattitude and points out that citizens' responses to survey questions are "a mixture of carefully thought-out, stable opinions, half-hearted opinions, misunderstandings, and purely random responses" (1986, 184).

Another question to consider is, Have the researchers made any effort to screen out respondents who lack genuine attitudes on the topic? Unfortunately, reports frequently omit information about screening questions and their effects—that is, often one cannot tell what proportion of the total sample answered a particular item and what proportion was screened out. To do a better job of reporting this information, news organizations should, at minimum, provide the number of respondents who answered a particular question when they report on a poll. If that number is substantially smaller than the total sample size, they should explain the discrepancy.

When screening information is not presented, citizens are forced to form impressionistic judgments about whether the measurement of nonattitudes has been a problem in the survey. Some issues of public policy that have been hotly contested by political elites, even issues such as tax reform, may not be of much interest to many Americans and thus may be highly susceptible to the measurement of nonattitudes.

Citizens are in a better position to evaluate the potential effects of question wording than the presence of nonattitudes. Because the media usually provide the actual wording of questions, readers (or viewers) can judge whether any words or phrases in the questions are blatantly loaded, whether the alternatives are presented in a fair and balanced fashion, and whether a question accurately reflects the topic under study. If a report of a survey omits question wording, particularly items dealing with controversial issues, the consumer should be wary and ask why.

Question wording is just one reason a complete questionnaire should be made available with a survey report. The questionnaire also is helpful when a survey contains many questions on a topic but reports the results for only one or two. Without the complete questionnaire, a poll consumer is unable to assess whether the selective release of results has created any misleading impressions.

Another reason to examine the entire questionnaire is to assess the potential effects of question order. This is seldom possible because press releases (other than those issued by news organizations) and news stories rarely include the complete survey form. Nevertheless, citizens should be aware that the way earlier questions are asked could affect responses to subsequent ones. This is a subtle phenomenon for which most citizens have little intuitive feel, yet the strategic placement of questions is one of the most effective ways to "doctor" a survey. While each individual question may be balanced and fair, their order could stimulate the specific responses preferred by the sponsor of the survey. One clue that this problem exists is the refusal of an organization, such as a political campaign team, to release the entire poll results.

The next question consumers should address is sampling. Although it is the most mysterious aspect of polling for most poll consumers, sampling is probably the least important to understand in detail. Sampling error is *not* where polls typically go astray. Reputable pollsters pick good samples and typically report sampling error and confidence levels so that citizens can form independent judgments about the significance of results. To make sure that a sample properly reflects the aims of a poll, a poll consumer should pay close attention to how the sample is defined. And certainly the consumer should confirm that the sample is a scientifically selected probability sample rather than a purposive one that an investigator selected for reasons of convenience.

One aspect of sampling that citizens should not overlook is the proportion of the total sample to which a particular finding applies. For a variety of reasons, such as the use of screening questions or the need to study analytically interesting subsets of the original sample, the proportion of respondents on which a result is based may be substantially smaller than the overall sample. Thus one should know not only the sampling error of the total sample but also the sampling error of the subsets.

It is almost impossible for citizens to evaluate the effects of interviewing on poll results because reports usually provide too little information about the interviewing process beyond the method of interviewing (for example, telephone or personal) and the dates of the interviews. The poll consumer normally assumes that an interview was performed competently, undoubtedly a safe assumption with reputable polling firms. But consumers should note that an interviewer bent on generating biased responses has many opportunities to achieve that end while asking questions. The best way for the poll consumer to gain some sense of potential interviewer effects is to be a poll respondent and carefully observe the performance of the interviewer—an opportunity that may or may not come one's way.

The final questions to ask when evaluating a poll relate to the end products, analyses and interpretation. Most citizens do not have access to raw poll data and must rely on the analyses and interpretations of news organizations and other sources. But do these sources of information have a vested interest in a particular poll outcome? If so, consumers should scrutinize poll results even more carefully. For example, a poll sponsored by the insurance industry purporting to demonstrate that the liability insurance crisis is due to the rapacious behavior of trial lawyers should be viewed with greater skepticism than a similar poll sponsored by an organization with a less-direct interest in the outcome. Likewise, election poll results released by a candidate should be viewed more cautiously than those released by a respected news organization.

After evaluating the source of a poll, the consumer then faces the more difficult task of ascertaining whether the pollster's conclusions follow from the data. This task is problematic because often, as noted earlier, only a portion of the relevant evidence is presented in a news story or press release. Or a poll may have included many items on a particular topic, yet the report may present only some of them. Without knowledge of the total questionnaire, one can only hope that the analyst has reported a representative set of results or speculate on how different items on the same topic might have yielded different results. Likewise, reports might include results from the entire sample but not important variations in the responses of subsets of the sample. Without direct access to the data, the citizen is left to ponder how the overall results might differ for subsets of respondents.

Interpretation of a poll is not an objective enterprise; different analysts examining the same polling data may come to different conclusions. Although that may occur for a variety of reasons, an obvious one is that analysts bring different values and perspectives to their task. Often there are no objective standards, for example, for what constitutes a high or low level of support on an issue; it may indeed be partly cloudy or partly sunny depending on one's perspective. Thus poll consumers should ask themselves whether they would necessarily come to the same conclusions on the basis of the data presented. Just because a poll is sponsored by a prestigious organization and conducted by a reputable firm does not mean that consumers have to defer automatically to the substantive conclusions drawn. If a poll is conducted by an organization with an obvious vested interest in the results, that warrants an independent judgment by the consumer.

Polls and Their Effect on the Political System

Do polls promote or hinder citizens' influence in their society? Is the overall effect of polls on the political system positive or negative? These questions continue to be vigorously debated. Writing in 1940, Cherington argued that polls enhanced the public's influence because they provide a way for the voices of a representative cross-section of Americans to be heard; no longer would the views of a tiny segment of the population be the only ones to gain prominence. Meyer (1940) argued further that polls provide information about the preferences of the citizenry that enable political leaders to resist the pressures of narrow groups pushing their own agendas in the name of the broader public.

These arguments are still true today, yet the limitations inherent in polls as a mode of citizen influence must be recognized. First, as discussed in chapter 1, the United States is a representative democracy that comprises, in addition to elected representatives, a wide variety of organized groups trying to promote their own interests. Any assumption that the results of public opinion polls can be translated directly into public policy is naive. It might not be desirable for public opinion polls to be routinely translated into public policy. Polls at times may tap only the most ephemeral and transitory of opinions. Little deliberation and thought may have gone into the responses the public offered. And certainly the rich complexities of issues can never be captured in a public opinion poll as effectively as they are in a legislative debate or a committee hearing.

Second, even if the public's views as reflected in the polls are well formed, polling often demonstrates that there is no majority view on an issue; opinion may be split in many different ways. Moreover, automatically opting for the majority or plurality position would call into question such cherished values as the protection of minority rights. One can envisage situations in which the unqualified use of public opinion polls might threaten rather than enhance representative democracy and related values.

Third, a focus on poll results ignores the processes by which the public's opinions are formed and modified. For example, one factor that shapes popular opinion is the behavior of political elites. When the White House orchestrates a massive public relations campaign, with a nationally televised presidential address, highly publicized presidential travels, and the submission of a legislative package to Congress, it is not surprising to see public opinion shift in the direction the White House intends. Public opinion is not always an independent expression of the public's views; it can be an opinion that has been manipulated, at least in part, by elites.

Sometimes, the president may take the lead on an unpopular issue, as typically occurs during an international crisis. After the president delivers a major address to the nation, public opinion polls usually indicate an upsurge of support for the president's actions, emerging from feelings of patriotism and a desire for national unity in times of crisis. Such was the case with the Persian Gulf crisis that arose in 1990, the terrorist attacks on American soil in 2001, and the war with Iraq in 2003.

Other times, the president may scramble to catch up with and then shape public opinion. That happened in summer and fall 1986 in response to Americans' heightened concern about the drug abuse problem. After the tragic deaths of famous athletes and increased media coverage of the drug crisis, a plurality of Americans cited drugs as the nation's most im-

Jeff Danziger © 2002, Tribune Media Services, Inc. Reprinted with permission.

portant problem in a CBS News/*New York Times* poll conducted in August 1986 (Clymer 1986d). Congress, particularly House Democrats, trying to get out in front on this issue, proposed a major antidrug offensive. The White House responded by taking the initiative from Congress: President Ronald Reagan offered his own proposals, and he and the first lady gave an unprecedented joint address on national television. Major new legislation was passed to address the drug problem. In 1989 President George Bush declared a war on drugs and named a drug "czar" to coordinate federal initiatives. The president announced many antidrug proposals, which, according to the polls, were supported overwhelmingly by Americans even though they felt strongly that Bush's plan did not go far enough.

What do these examples say about citizen influence? Certainly, the drug example suggests the potency of popular opinion on issues that arouse the public. But even there the salience of the issue was very much a function of the behavior of the news media and the political elites who brought it to the fore; the public responded to the issue but did not create it. The adoption of antidrug measures into law suggests that aroused public opinion spurs government policy initiatives. But when the media and political leaders stop talking about an issue, it becomes less salient and recedes from popular consciousness, and citizens may have a misguided feeling that somehow the problem has been resolved.

Sometimes political elites may misinterpret (deliberately or unintentionally) what the polls are actually saying. Unfortunately, political leaders sometimes fail to recognize the limitations and circumstances of poll responses and automatically construe supportive poll results as ringing endorsements of a broad policy agenda. The tendency of Americans to rally around the leadership of the president during an international crisis should not be blindly interpreted as a popular mandate for particular policies.

Ginsberg (1986) has argued that polling weakens the influence of public opinion in a democratic society. He asserts that there are many ways besides participating in a poll for citizens to express their opinions, such as demonstrations and protests, letter-writing campaigns, and interest group activities. But because polling is deemed to be scientific and representative of the broad public, it has dominated the other types of expression.

According to Ginsberg, four fundamental changes in the nature of public opinion are attributable to the increased frequency of polling: First, responding to a public opinion survey is an easier form of expression than writing a letter or participating in a protest—activities usually undertaken by citizens who are intensely committed to their positions. Anyone can respond to a poll question, whether or not the feelings about an issue are strong. Thus in a public opinion poll the intense opinions of a small minority can be submerged by the indifferent views of the sizable majority. Indeed, government leaders may try to dismiss the views of dissidents by citing polls that indicate that most Americans do not support the dissidents' position.

Second, polling changes public opinion from a behavior, such as letter writing or demonstrating, to an *attitude,* as revealed in a verbal response to a poll question. Ginsberg argues that public opinion expressed through polls is less threatening to political elites than are opinions expressed through behavioral mechanisms. Moreover, polls can inform leaders about dissidents' attitudes before they become behaviors. The information on attitudes gives government a kind of early warning as well as an opportunity to change attitudes either by seeking remedies to problems or by relying on public relations techniques to manipulate opinions.

Third, polls convert public opinion from a characteristic of groups to an attribute of individuals. This factor enables public officials to ignore group leaders and instead attend directly to the opinions of citizens. Unfortunately, this attention may effectively weaken individuals' political power because organized activity, not individual activity, is the key to citizen influence in the United States. If government leaders are able to use the polls as an excuse to ignore group preferences, then citizen influence will be lessened.

Finally, polling reduces citizens' opportunities to set the political agenda. The topics of public opinion polls are those selected by the polls' sponsors rather than by the citizenry. Therefore, citizens lose control over the agenda of issues, and the agenda as revealed through the polls may differ in major ways from the issues that really matter to people.

Ginsberg's conclusion is that polling makes public opinion safer and less threatening for government. Opinions expressed through the polls place fewer demands and constraints on decision makers and provide political leaders with an enhanced ability "to anticipate, regulate, and manipulate popular attitudes" (Ginsberg 1986, 85). In short, Ginsberg's thesis is that the advent and growth of public opinion polling have been detrimental to citizen influence.

Ginsberg has raised some important issues about the dangers inherent in the proliferation of public opinion polls, even if one does not agree with all of his conclusions. Clearly, citizens must be on guard against allowing public opinion to become synonymous with the results of public opinion polls. Public opinion manifests itself in many ways, including those Ginsberg mentioned—protests, letter-writing campaigns, direct personal contact with decision makers, and many others. Political elites recognize the potential costs of ignoring these alternative forms of political expression, but it is critical that the media also recognize that polls are not the only legitimate expression of public opinion. Citizens, too, must avoid allowing a passive activity such as responding to a poll to replace more active modes of political participation.

Although there is evidence that direct electoral participation has declined in the United States, other group-based activities are on the rise. And if groups have the resources, they can use polls to promote their agenda when it differs from that of the political elites. Contrary to Ginsberg's assertion, polls need not make public opinion a property of individuals rather than groups. Polls can identify clusters of citizens (often defined by demographic characteristics) who do not share the prevailing views of the citizenry at large. For example, public opinion polls on the ultimate outcome of the 2000 presidential election campaign showed sharp differences between white and black Americans on the perceived legitimacy of the Bush victory and the overall fairness of the legal and election process. Whether Ginsberg's concerns are overstated or not, the polls are playing a growing role in American political life, in campaigns, in governance, and in popular discourse.

Bartels (2003) takes a different view of the role of public opinion polls in democratic governance. He argues that public opinion polls do not and cannot provide political leaders with directions about what policy options to pursue because, while the polls measure citizens' attitudes, they do not measure the public's preferences on issues of public policy. Bartels argues that responses to policy questions in a poll can vary so dramatically, depending on the wording of the questions, the context in which they are placed, and the choices that are offered, that they provide leaders with little real guidance about how they should govern.

Observers have been concerned about the effect of polls not only on citizens' political clout but also on the performance of elected officeholders. More than fifty-five years ago Bernays (1945) warned that polls would dominate the political leadership and that decision makers would slavishly follow the polls to please the people and maintain popularity. The polls might even paralyze political leaders, preventing them from taking unpopular positions and from trying to educate the public on controversial issues. Political observers like Bernays still contemptuously deride politicians who figuratively always keep the polls in their pockets, lacking the courage to act on their own convictions no matter what the polls say.

Some officeholders do blindly follow the polls, but today those who abuse, manipulate, and misinterpret polls are of greater concern. In particular, presidents have increasingly tried to manage public opinion. For example, Altschuler (1986) describes how President Lyndon Johnson tried to take the offensive when his poll ratings began to decline. To convince key elites that he was still strong, Johnson attacked the public polls, selectively leaked private polls, and tried to influence poll results and poll reporting by cultivating the acquaintance of the pollsters. Likewise, the Nixon administration tried to manipulate the Gallup and Harris polling organizations by influencing how they carried out and reported their national polls (Jacobs and Shapiro 1995–1996).

In-house polling was a central part of the skillful public relations efforts of the Reagan presidency (Blumenthal 1981). Writing about the Reagan administration, Beal and Hinckley (1984) argued that polls became more important after the presidential election than before it; indeed, polls were a much more important tool of governing than was commonly recognized. Likewise, polling was central to the operation of the Clinton White House and prominent in the second Bush White House. Jacobs and Shapiro (1995) have shown how the polling operations of the Kennedy, Johnson, and especially the Nixon presidencies served as precursors for the contemporary White House use of polls. Certainly no one would deny the president and other elected officials their pollsters. But the measure of an incumbent's performance should not simply be the degree of success achieved in shaping public opinion in particular ways.

One final effect of polls on the political system merits consideration: their contribution to political discourse. Because they often are cited as evidence in support of particular positions, polls have become a central part of political discussion. But polls have more subtle effects; in particular, Americans' awareness of the attitudes of their fellow citizens, learned through the polls, may alter their opinions and subsequent behaviors. This phenomenon has been explained in terms of the theories of the spiral of silence and pluralistic ignorance.

The spiral of silence thesis, developed by Noelle-Neumann (1974, 1977), argues that individuals desire to be respected and popular. To accomplish this, they become sensitive to prevailing opinions and how they are changing. If, on the one hand, individuals observe that their opinions seem to be in the minority and are losing support, they are less likely to express them publicly. Consequently, such opinions will seem to the individuals who hold them to be weaker than they actually are. On the other hand, if people perceive that their views are popular and on the ascendant, they are more likely to discuss them openly. Such opinions then gain more adherents and seem stronger than they actually are. Thus one opinion becomes established as dominant, while the other recedes to the background. "Pluralistic ignorance" refers to people's misperceptions of what other individuals and groups believe (O'Gorman 1975; O'Gorman and Garry 1976–1977). Those misperceptions affect their own views and their willingness to express them. Lang and Lang (1984) linked the notions of pluralistic ignorance and the spiral of silence in a discussion of American racial attitudes of twenty years ago:

> Typical of pluralistic ignorance has been the unwillingness of many whites to acknowledge their own antiblack prejudice, which they believe to contradict an accepted cultural ideal. As a way of justifying their own behavior, these whites often attribute such prejudice to other whites by saying "I wouldn't mind having a black neighbor except that my neighbors wouldn't stand for it."
>
> But what if such fears about their neighbors' reactions proved unjustified? What if polls showed an expressed readiness for a range of desegregation measures that these whites do not believe others are prepared to accept? Such a finding contrary to prevailing belief would be controversial. Where the real opinion lies may be less important than the change in perception of the climate of opinion. A definitive poll finding can destroy the premise that underlies the justification for behavior clearly at variance with professed ideals. In these circumstances a spiral of silence about the real opinion fosters a climate inhospitable to segregationist sentiment and drives it underground. (141)

PEANUTS reprinted by permission of United Feature Syndicate, Inc.

As this example illustrates, public opinion polls provide citizens with a mechanism for knowing what their fellow citizens think and believe. This is especially important for people who interact mostly with like-minded individuals and may therefore have little sense of the diversity of opinion that may exist on an issue. If the polls can accurately measure the underlying beliefs and values of the citizenry, then people no longer have to be at the mercy of unrepresentative views that they mistakenly believe are those of the majority. The polls can tell people a lot about themselves as part of American society, and that self-knowledge may foster a healthier and more open political debate. That being said, it also is possible that what they learn from polls about the views of their fellow citizens may surprise, shock, offend, and even divide them. Certainly it was shocking to learn from public opinion polls that substantial numbers of Americans believed that weapons of mass destruction had been found in Iraq after the war, when they had not; that weapons of mass destruction had been used against American soldiers during the war with Iraq, when they had not; and that Iraq and Saddam Hussein had worked with al Qaeda on the September 11 terrorist attacks, when no proof of such a link had yet been found. How Americans came to those beliefs is beyond our task in this book. But learning about them from public opinion polls helps us better understand the preferences that Americans did hold regarding various aspects of U.S. policy toward Iraq.

Conclusion

As the *Peanuts* cartoon makes clear, Americans have ambivalent feelings about polls. Citizens resent the polls when surveys become too intrusive and seem to be telling them what they will be doing even before they do it. Yet Americans are also fascinated by what the polls tell them about themselves. They are suspicious because they seldom are respondents in a poll, yet they readily cite the surveys conducted by reputable and even disreputable pollsters. They complain about the pervasiveness of polls, yet they are apt to raise questions that only polls can answer.

Perhaps this ambivalence arises out of people's uncertainty about just what goes into a poll. Polls are called scientific, yet citizens know that the polls are sometimes wrong. Politicians on one day swear by the polls; the next day they swear at them. Americans are in a better position to evaluate polls if they understand the factors that can affect poll results. Thus the aim of this book has been to remove the mystery from public opinion research, so that citizens can master the polls rather than be mastered by them.

Exercise

1. Write an essay about the role of public opinion polls in a democratic political system. How might leaders use public opinion polls? Should leaders follow their own views or the views of the public as expressed in the polls? Are there conditions under which you would argue that leaders should ignore the polls and popular preferences and instead do what they believe to be right? Discuss such conditions. Are there conditions under which leaders should follow the polls even when they disagree with the poll results? Discuss such conditions. Finally, what ways other than public opinion polls might there be to measure and assess public opinion? Do you believe that these other ways of assessing public opinion are better or worse than using polls? Why do you believe this?

Web Sites

Media

www.abcnews.com	ABC
www.cbsnews.com	CBS
www.msnbc.com	NBC
www.foxnews.com/	FOX
www.cnn.com	CNN
www.nytimes.com	*New York Times*
www.washington.post.com	*Washington Post*
www.latimes.com	*Los Angeles Times*
www.usatoday.com	*USA Today*
www.nationaljournal.com	*National Journal*
www.ap.org	Associated Press
www.upi.com/	United Press International

Organizations

www.census.gov	U.S. Census Bureau
www.gallup.com	Gallup Organization
www.harrisinteractive.com	Harris Interactive
www.knowledgenetworks.com	Knowledge Networks, Inc.
www.zogby.com	Zogby International
www.ropercenter.uconn.edu	Roper Center
www.pollingreport.com	The Polling Report
www.aapor.org	American Association for Public Opinion Research
www.ncpp.org	National Council on Public Polls
www.people-press.org	Pew Research Center for the People and the Press

www.umich.edu/~nes	National Election Studies
www.epinet.org/	Economic Policy Institute
www.ama.org	American Marketing Association
www.casro.org	Council of American Survey Research Organizations
survey.rgs.uky.edu/nnsp/	National Network of State Polls
www.cmor.org	Council for Marketing and Opinion Research
www.worldopinion.com	World Opinion
www.amstat.org	American Statistical Association
www.pipa.org/	The Program on International Policy Attitudes (PIPA)

Miscellaneous

www.vanishingvoter.org	The Vanishing Voter Project
www.vote-smart.org	Project Vote Smart

References

Abrams, Floyd. 1985. Press Practices, Polling Restrictions, Public Opinion and First Amendment Guarantees." *Public Opinion Quarterly* 49 (spring): 15–18.

Abramson, Paul R. 1990. "The Decline of Overtime Comparability in the National Election Studies." *Public Opinion Quarterly* 54 (summer): 177–190.

Abramson, Paul R., Brian D. Silver, and Barbara Anderson. 1987. "The Effects of Question Order in Attitude Surveys: The Case of the SRC/CPS Citizen Duty Items." *American Journal of Political Science* 31 (November): 900–908.

Akron Beacon Journal. 1994. "Foreign Pollicy" (editorial), 8 May, A14.

Aldrich, John H., Richard Niemi, George Rabinowitz, and David Rohde. 1982. "The Measurement of Public Opinion about Public Policy: A Report on Some New Issue Question Formats." *American Journal of Political Science* 26 (May): 391–414.

Alpern, David M. 1986. "A *Newsweek* Poll: Sex Laws." *Newsweek,* 14 July, 38.

Altschuler, Bruce E. 1986. "Lyndon Johnson and the Public Polls." *Public Opinion Quarterly* 50 (fall): 285–299.

Alvarez, Lizette. 1998. "After Polling, GOP Offers a Patients' Bill." *New York Times,* 16 July, A1.

Alvarez, R. Michael, and John Brehm. 2002. *Hard Choices, Easy Answers.* Princeton: Princeton University Press.

American Association for Public Opinion Research (AAPOR). 1986. *Code of Professional Ethics and Practices.* www.aapor.org.

———. 1997a. "Major Opinion Research Association Finds Pollster Frank Luntz Violated Ethics Code," press release, April 23.

———. 1997b. *Best Practices for Survey and Public Opinion Research and Survey Practices AAPOR Condemns,* May.

———. 2000. "Standard Definitions: Final Disposition of Case Codes and Outcome Rates for Surveys."

Anderson, Barbara A., Brian D. Silver, and Paul R. Abramson. 1988. "The Effects of the Race of the Interviewer on Race-Related Attitudes of Black Respondents in SRC/CPS National Election Studies." *Public Opinion Quarterly* 52 (fall): 289–324.

Apple, R. W., Jr. 1986. "President Highly Popular in Poll; No Ideological Shift Is Discerned." *New York Times,* 28 January, A1.

Aquilino, William S. 1994. "Interview Mode Effects in Surveys of Drug and Alcohol Use." *Public Opinion Quarterly* 58 (summer): 210–240.

Aquilino, William S., and Leonard A. Losciuto. 1990. "Effects of Interview Mode on Self-Reported Drug Use." *Public Opinion Quarterly* 54 (fall): 362–395.

Asher, Herbert B. 1974a. "The Reliability of the Political Efficacy Items." *Political Methodology* 1 (May): 45–72.

———. 1974b. "Some Consequences of Measurement Error in Survey Data." *American Journal of Political Science* 18 (May): 469–485.

———. 1974c. "Some Problems in the Use of Multiple Indicators." Paper presented at the Conference on Design and Measurement Standards for Research in Political Science, Delevan, Wis., 13–15 May.

———. 1992. *Presidential Elections and American Politics.* 5th ed. Pacific Grove, Calif.: Brooks/Cole.

Associated Press. 2003. "Media Group in Deal to Conduct Exit Polls." February 4.

Baker, Russell. 1988. "Nearing Rope's End." *New York Times,* 9 November, 31.

———. 1990. "Paralyzing Polls." *New York Times,* 4 April, A15.

Balz, Dan. 1989. "About Those Predictions We Made Last Tuesday . . ." *Washington Post* National Weekly Edition, 13–19 November, 38.

Balz, Dan, and Claudia Deane. 2003. "Public Opinion on Bush Stabilizes." *Washington Post,* 13 August, A1.

Barnes, James A. 1993. "Polls Apart." *National Journal* 25 (10 July): 1750–1754.

Bartels, Larry M. 2003. "Is 'Popular Rule' Possible? Polls, Political Psychology, and Democracy." *Brookings Review* 21 (summer): 12–15.

Bauman, Sandra, and Susan Herbst. 1994. "Managing Perceptions of Public Opinion: Candidates' and Journalists' Reactions to the 1992 Polls." *Political Communication* 11: 133–144.

Baumgartner, Frank R., and Jack L. Walker. 1988. "Survey Research and Membership in Voluntary Associations." *American Journal of Political Science* 32 (November): 908–928.

Beal, Richard S., and Ronald H. Hinckley. 1984. "Presidential Decision Making and Opinion Polls." *Annals of the American Academy of Political and Social Science* 472 (March): 72–84.

Belden, Nancy. 2000. "Response Rate by Size of Place." E-mail communication, AAPOR Listserv. 8 May.

Benson, John M. 2001. "Heard Enough: When Is an Opinion Really an Opinion?" *Public Perspective* 12 (September/October): 40–41.

Berke, Richard L. 1996. "As Dole Weighs Tougher Image, Poll Finds He Already Has One." *New York Times,* 16 October, A1, A14.

Berke, Richard L., and Janet Elder. 2000. "Candidates Given High Marks in Poll on Fitness to Lead." *New York Times,* 3 October, A1.

Bernays, Edward L. 1945. "Attitude Polls—Servants or Masters?" *Public Opinion Quarterly* 9 (fall): 264–268b.

Bernick, E. Lee, and David J. Pratto. 1994. "Improving the Quality of Information in Mail Surveys: Use of Special Mailings." *Social Science Quarterly* 75 (March): 212–219.

Bierma, Nathan. 2002. "The Pollsters Are Calling, but Who Is Answering?" *Chicago Tribune* Online Edition, 24 September.

Bishop, George F. 1987. "Experiments with the Middle Response Alternative in Survey Questions." *Public Opinion Quarterly* 51 (summer): 220–232.

———. 1990. "Issue Involvement and Response Effects in Public Opinion Surveys." *Public Opinion Quarterly* 54 (summer): 209–218.

———. 2002. "Illusion of Change: Sometimes It's Not the Same Old Question." *Public Perspective* 13 (May/June): 38–41.

Bishop, George F., Robert W. Oldendick, and Alfred J. Tuchfarber. 1980. "Pseudo-Opinions on Public Affairs." *Public Opinion Quarterly* 44 (summer): 198–209.

———. 1982. "Political Information Processing: Question Order and Context Effects." *Political Behavior* 4: 177–200.

———. 1984. "What Must My Interest in Politics Be if I Just Told You 'I Don't Know'?" *Public Opinion Quarterly* 48 (summer): 510–519.

Black, Joan S. 1991. "Presidential Address: Trashing the Polls." *Public Opinion Quarterly* 55 (fall): 474–481.

Blais, Andre, Neil Nevitte, Elisabeth Gidengil, and Richard Nadeau. 2000. "Do People Have Feelings toward Leaders about Whom They Say They Know Nothing?" *Public Opinion Quarterly* 64 (winter): 452–463.

Blumenthal, Sidney. 1981. "Marketing the President." *New York Times Magazine,* 13 September, 110–118.

Borrelli, Stephen, Brad Lockerbie, and Richard G. Niemi. 1989. "Why the Democrat-Republican Partisan Gap Varies from Poll to Poll." *Public Opinion Quarterly* 51 (spring): 115–119.

Broder, David S. 1984. "The Needless Exit-Polls Battle." *Washington Post* National Weekly Edition, 2 January, 4.

Brodie, Mollyann, Lisa Ferraro Parmelee, April Brackett, and Drew Altman. 2001. "Polling and Democracy." *Public Perspective* 12 (July/August): 10–24.

Broh, C. Anthony. 1980. "Horse-Race Journalism: Reporting the Polls in the 1976 Presidential Election." *Public Opinion Quarterly* 44 (winter): 514–529.

Buchwald, Art. 1987. "The Poll Watcher's Compendium." *Washington Post,* 20 August, C1.

Budiansky, Stephen. 1995. "Consulting the Oracle." *U.S. News and World Report,* 4 December, 52.

Busch, Ronald J., and Joel A. Lieske. 1985. "Does Time of Voting Affect Exit Poll Results?" *Public Opinion Quarterly* 49 (spring): 94–104.

Campbell, Bruce A. 1981. "Race-of-Interviewer Effects Among Southern Adolescents." *Public Opinion Quarterly* 45 (summer): 231–244.

Carroll, Rebecca. 2003. "Millions Getting Rid of Landline Phones." Associated Press, August 4.

Carter, Bill. 1996. "Three Networks Admit Error in Arizona Race Reports." *New York Times,* 29 February, A9.

Cherington, Paul T. 1940. "Opinion Polls as the Voice of Democracy." *Public Opinion Quarterly* 4 (June): 236–238.

Church, Allan H. 1993. "Estimating the Effect of Incentives on Mail Survey Response Rates: A Meta-Analysis." *Public Opinion Quarterly* 57 (spring): 62–79.

Clymer, Adam. 1985. "Pollsters Cite Surveys Indicating Confidence in Their Work." *New York Times,* 20 May, B7.

———. 1986a. "Most Blacks Back Reagan, Poll Finds." *New York Times,* 5 January, 20.

———. 1986b. "One Issue That Seems to Defy a Yes or No." *New York Times,* 23 February, 22-E.

———. 1986c. "A Poll Finds 77% in U.S. Approve Raid on Libya." *New York Times,* 17 April, A23.

———. 1986d. "Public Found Ready to Sacrifice in Drug Fight." *New York Times,* 2 September, D16.

———. 1996. "Phony Polls That Sling Mud Raise Questions over Ethics." *New York Times,* May 20, A1.

Columbus Dispatch. 1994a. "This Is How Dispatch Poll Was Conducted." 11 September, 5B.

———. 1994b. "Random Sampling of Voters Used to Create Gallup Survey." 25 September, 2C.

Converse, Jean M. 1976–1977. "Predicting No Opinion in the Polls." *Public Opinion Quarterly* 40 (winter): 515–530.

Converse, Philip E. 1970. "Attitudes and Nonattitudes: Continuation of a Dialogue." In *The Quantitative Analysis of Social Problems,* edited by Edward Tufte, 168–189. Reading, Mass.: Addison-Wesley.

Coombs, Clyde H., and Lolagene C. Coombs. 1976–1977. "'Don't Know': Item Ambiguity or Respondent Uncertainty?" *Public Opinion Quarterly* 40 (winter): 497–514.

Cotter, Patrick R., Jeffrey Cohen, and Philip B. Coulter. 1982. "Race-of-Interviewer Effects on Telephone Interviews." *Public Opinion Quarterly* 46 (summer): 278–284.

Couper, Mick P. 2000. "Web Surveys: A Review of Issues and Approaches." *Public Opinion Quarterly* 64 (winter): 464–494.

Crespi, Irving. 1980. "Polls as Journalism." *Public Opinion Quarterly* 44 (winter): 462–476.

———. 1988. *Pre-election Polling: Sources of Accuracy and Error.* New York: Russell Sage Foundation.

Crossley, Archibald M., and Helen M. Crossley. 1969. "Polling in 1968." *Public Opinion Quarterly* 33 (spring): 1–16.

Curtin, Michael. 1986a. "Celeste Leading Rhodes 48% to 43%, with Kucinich Trailing." *Columbus Dispatch,* 10 August, 1-A.

———. 1986b. "Here Is How Poll Was Taken." *Columbus Dispatch,* 10 August, 8-E.

Curtin, Richard, Stanley Presser, and Eleanor Singer. 2000. "The Effects of Response Rate Changes on the Index of Consumer Sentiment." *Public Opinion Quarterly* 64 (winter): 413–428.

Davis, Darren W. 1997. "The Direction of Race of Interviewer Effects among African-Americans: Donning the Black Mask." *American Journal of Political Science* 41 (January): 309–322.

Davis, Darren W., and Brian D. Silver. 2003. "Stereotype Threat and Race of Interviewer Effects in a Survey on Political Knowledge." *American Journal of Political Science* 47 (January): 33–45.

Day, Richard, and Kurt M. Becker. 1984. "Preelection Polling in the 1982 Illinois Gubernatorial Contest." *Public Opinion Quarterly* 48 (fall): 606–614.

de Bock, Harold. 1976. "Influence of In-State Election Poll Reports on Candidate Preference in 1972." *Journalism Quarterly* 53 (autumn): 457–462.

Delli Carpini, Michael X. 1984. "Scooping the Voters? The Consequences of the Networks' Early Call of the 1980 Presidential Race." *Journal of Politics* 46 (August): 866–885.

Delli Carpini, Michael X., and Scott Keeter. 1991. "Stability and Change in the U.S. Public's Knowledge of Politics." *Public Opinion Quarterly* 55 (winter): 583–612.

———. 1996. *What Americans Know about Politics and Why It Matters.* New Haven: Yale University Press.

Dinmore, Guy. 2003. "Opinion Poll Underlines Iraqi Distrust of America." *Financial Times,* 11 September, 11.

Dionne, E. J., Jr. 1980. "The Debate Decision Put Polls and Pollsters on the Firing Line." *New York Times,* 14 September, E3.

Dolnick, Edward. 1984. "Pollsters Are Asking: What's Wrong." *Columbus Dispatch,* 19 August, C1.

Dran, Ellen M., and Anne Hildreth. 1995. "What the Public Thinks about How We Know What It Is Thinking." *International Journal of Public Opinion Research* 7 (2): 128–144.

Elving, Ronald D. 1989. "Proliferation of Opinion Data Sparks Debate over Use." *Congressional Quarterly Weekly Report,* 19 August, 2187–2192.

———. 1992. "Polls Confound and Confuse in This Topsy-Turvy Year." *Congressional Quarterly Weekly Report,* 12 September, 2725–2727.

Epstein, Joan Faith, Peggy Ripley Barker, and Larry A. Kroutil. 2001. "Mode Effects in Self-reported Mental Health Data." *Public Opinion Quarterly* 65 (winter): 529–549.

Epstein, Laurily, and Gerald Strom. 1984. "Survey Research and Election Night Projections." *Public Opinion* 7 (February/March): 48–50.

Erikson, Robert S. 1976. "The Relationship between Public Opinion and State Policy: A New Look Based on Some Forgotten Data." *American Journal of Political Science* 20 (February): 25–36.

Eubank, Robert B., and David John Gow. 1983. "The Pro-incumbent Bias in the 1978 and 1980 National Election Studies." *American Journal of Political Science* 27 (February): 122–139.

Faulkenberry, G. David, and Robert Mason. 1978. "Characteristics of Nonopinion and No Opinion Response Groups." *Public Opinion Quarterly* 42 (winter): 533–543.

Felson, Marcus, and Seymour Sudman. 1975. "The Accuracy of Presidential Preference Primary Polls." *Public Opinion Quarterly* 39 (summer): 232–236.

Finkel, Steven E., Thomas M. Guterbock, and Marian J. Borg. 1991. "Race-of-Interviewer Effects in a Preelection Poll: Virginia 1989." *Public Opinion Quarterly* 55 (fall): 313–330.

Fishkin, James. 1992. "A Response to Traugott." *Public Perspective* 3 (May/June): 29–30.

———. 1996. "Bringing Deliberation to Democracy." *Public Perspective* 7 (December/January): 1–4.

Fishkin, James S., Robert C. Luskin, and Henry E. Brady. 2003. "Informed Public Opinion about Foreign Policy: The Uses of Deliberative Polling." *Brookings Review* 21 (summer): 16–19.

Fitzgerald, Michael R., Patra Rule, and Claudia Bryant. 1998. "Polls, Politics and the TV News: A Longitudinal Study of the Uses of Public Opinion Polling on the Evening News Broadcasts." Paper presented at the annual meeting of the American Political Science Association, Boston.

Fowler, Floyd Jackson, Jr. 1992. "How Unclear Terms Affect Survey Data." *Public Opinion Quarterly* 56 (summer): 218–231.

Fox, Richard J., Melvin R. Crask, and Jonghoon Kim. 1988. "Mail Survey Response Rate: A Meta-analysis of Selected Techniques for Inducing Response." *Public Opinion Quarterly* 52 (winter): 467–491.

Frey, James H. 1983. *Survey Research by Telephone.* Beverly Hills, Calif.: Sage Publications.

Gallup, George. 1947. "The Quintamensional Plan of Question Design." *Public Opinion Quarterly* 11 (fall): 385–393.

———. 1965–1966. "Polls and the Political Process—Past, Present, and Future." *Public Opinion Quarterly* 29 (winter): 544–549.

Galtung, Johan. 1969. *Theory and Methods of Social Research.* New York: Columbia University Press.

Gawiser, Sheldon R., and G. Evans Witt. *Twenty Questions a Journalist Should Ask about Poll Results.* 2nd ed. National Council on Public Polls, http://www.ncpp.org/qajsa.htm, 14 October 2003.

Genesys News. 1996. "Unlisted Numbers: What's *Really* Important?" Spring, 1–2.

Genesys Q & A. 1997. "Number Portability." January.

Gilens, Martin. 2001. "Political Ignorance and Collective Policy Preferences." *American Political Science Review* 95 (June): 379–396.

Gilljam, Mikael, and Donald Granberg. 1993. "Should We Take Don't Know for an Answer?" *Public Opinion Quarterly* 57 (fall): 348–357.

Ginsberg, Benjamin. 1986. *The Captive Public: How Mass Opinion Promotes State Power.* New York: Basic Books.

Glanz, James. 2000. "Poll Finds That Support Is Strong for Teaching 2 Origin Theories." *New York Times,* http://www.nytimes.com/library/national/science/031100sci-evolution-poll.html, 13 March 2000.

Goldhaber, Gerald M. 1984. "A Pollster's Sampler." *Public Opinion* 7 (June/July): 47–50, 53.

Goldman, Ari L. 1991. "Portrait of Religion in U.S. Holds Dozens of Surprises." *New York Times,* 10 April, A1.

Goodstein Laurie. 2001. "Support for Religion-Based Plan Is Hedged." *New York Times,* 11 April, A12.

Gow, David John, and Robert B. Eubank. 1984. "The Pro-incumbent Bias in the 1982 National Election Study." *American Journal of Political Science* 27 (February): 224–230.

Goyder, John. 1985. "Face-to-Face Interviews and Mailed Questionnaires: The Net Difference in Response Rate." *Public Opinion Quarterly* 49 (summer): 234–252.

Greenberg, Anna, and Douglas Rivers. 2001. "Pioneer Days, The Promise of Online Polling." *Public Perspective* 12 (March/April): 40–41.

Greenberg, Daniel S. 1980. "The Plague of Polling." *Washington Post,* 16 September, A17.

Grove, Lloyd. 1988a. "New Hampshire Confounded Most Pollsters." *Washington Post,* 18 February, A1.

———. 1988b. "Focus Groups: Politicians' Version of Taste-Testing." *Washington Post,* 6 July, A5.

Harker, Kathryn. 1998. "Asking about Income: A Preliminary Experiment." *National Network of State Polls Newsletter* 33 (summer).

Harmon, Amy. 1998. "Underreporting Found on Male Teen-Ager Sex." *New York Times,* 8 May, A14.

Harris, John F. 2001a. "Presidency by Poll." *Washington Post* National Weekly Edition, 8–14 January, 9.

———. 2001b. "Campaign Promises Aside, It's Politics as Usual." *Washington Post* National Weekly Edition, 2–8 July, 11.

Harwood Group.1993. "Meaningful Chaos: How People Form Relationships with Public Concerns." A report prepared for the Kettering Foundation, Dayton, Ohio.

Harwood, Richard. 1992. "The 'Bumps' and the Reality Are Polls Apart." *Cleveland Plain Dealer,* 29 August, 4C.

Hatchett, S., and H. Schuman. 1975–1976. "White Respondents and Race-of-Interviewer Effects." *Public Opinion Quarterly* 39 (winter): 523–528.

Herbers, John. 1982. "Polls Find Conflict in Views on Aid and Public Welfare." *New York Times,* 14 February, 19.

Hernandez, Debra Gersh. 1995. "Formats Recommended for Presidential Debates." Abridged from *Editor and Publisher,* 18 November.

Herrmann, Robert O., Arthur Sterngold, and Rex H. Warland. 1998. "Comparing Alternative Question Forms for Assessing Consumer Concerns." *Journal of Consumer Affairs* 32 (summer): 1329.

Holbrook, Allyson L., Melanie C. Green, and Jon A. Krosnick. 2003. "Telephone versus Face-to-Face Interviewing of National Probability Samples with Long Questionnaires." *Public Opinion Quarterly* 67 (spring): 79–125.

Howe, Peter J. 2003. "Technology and Innovation: For Many, Caller ID Frustrates: Service Often Doesn't Work as Advertised." *Boston Globe,* 5 May.

Huddy, Leonie, and John Bracciodieta. 1992. "The Effects of Interviewer Gender on the Survey Response." Paper presented at the annual meeting of the American Political Science Association, Chicago.

Hughes, John. 2003. "What Do Iraqis Want? And When Can They Get It?" *Christian Science Monitor,* 17 September, 9.

Hyman, Herbert H., and Paul B. Sheatsley. 1950. "The Current Status of American Public Opinion." In *The Teaching of Contemporary Affairs,* edited by J.C. Payne, 11–34. Twenty-First Yearbook of the National Council of Social Studies. Washington, D.C.: National Council of Social Studies, National Education Association.

Jackson, John. 1983. "Election Night Reporting and Voter Turnout." *American Journal of Political Science* 27 (November): 615–635.

Jackson, John, and William McGee. 1981. "Election Reporting and Voter Turnout." Report of the Center for Political Studies, University of Michigan, Ann Arbor.

Jacobs, Lawrence R., and Robert Y. Shapiro. 1995. "The Rise of Presidential Polling: The Nixon White House in Historical Perspective." *Public Opinion Quarterly* 59 (summer): 163–195.

———. 1995–1996. "Presidential Manipulation of Polls and Public Opinion: The Nixon Administration and the Pollsters." *Political Science Quarterly* 110 (winter): 519–538.

James, Jeannine M., and Richard Bolstein. 1990. "The Effect of Monetary Incentives and Follow-up Mailings on the Response Rate Quality in Mail Surveys." *Public Opinion Quarterly* 54 (fall): 346–361.

Johnson, Timothy P. 1989. "Obtaining Reports of Sensitive Behavior: A Comparison of Substance Use Reports from Telephone and Face-to-Face Interviews." *Social Science Quarterly* 70 (March): 174–183.

Kagay, Michael. 1998. "Stalking the Elusive Likely Voter." *New York Times*, 18 October, 5.

———. 1999. "A Sample of a Sample." *New York Times*, http://www.nytimes.com/library/national/110499poll-watch.html, 9 November.

Kagay, Michael R., with Janet Elder. 1992. "Numbers Are No Problem for Pollsters. Words Are." *New York Times,* 9 August.

Kane, Emily W., and Laura J. Macaulay. 1993. "Interview Gender and Gender Attitudes." *Public Opinion Quarterly* 57 (spring): 1–28.

Keene, Karlyn H., and Victoria A. Sackett. 1981. "An Editors' Report on the Yankelovich, Skelly and White 'Mushiness Index.'" *Public Opinion* 4 (April/May): 50–51.

Keeter, Scott, et al. 2000. "Consequences of Reducing Nonresponse in a National Telephone Survey." *Public Opinion Quarterly* 64 (summer): 125–148.

Kifner, John. 1994. "Pollster Finds Error on Holocaust Doubts." *New York Times,* 20 May, A6.

Kinder, Donald R., and Lynn M. Sanders. 1986. "Survey Questions and Political Culture: The Case of Whites' Response to Affirmative Action for Blacks." Paper presented at the annual meeting of the American Political Science Association, Washington, D.C., 28–31 August.

Knap, Ted. 1980. "League Weighs Anderson's Standing for Debates." *Columbus Citizen Journal,* 9 September, 7.

Koch, Nadine S. 1985. "Perceptions of Public Opinion Polls." PhD diss., Ohio State University.

Kohut, Andrew. 1983. "Illinois Politics Confound the Polls." *Public Opinion* 5 (December/January): 42–43.

———. 1993. "The Vocal Minority in American Politics." *Times Mirror* Center for the People and the Press, Washington, D.C., 16 July.

Kolbert, Elizabeth. 1995. "Public Opinion Polls Swerve with the Turns of a Phrase." *New York Times,* 5 June, A1, C11.

Kostrzewa, John. 1986. "Rhodes Has Solid Edge over Primary Rivals." *Akron Beacon Journal,* 23 March, A5.

Krosnick, Jon A. 1989. "Question Wording and Reports of Survey Results: The Case of Louis Harris and Associates and Aetna Life and Casualty." *Public Opinion Quarterly* 53 (spring): 107–113.

Krosnick, Jon A., and Duane F. Alwin. 1987. "An Evaluation of a Cognitive Theory of Response-Order Effects in Survey Measurement." *Public Opinion Quarterly* 51 (summer): 201–219.

Krosnick, Jon A., and Matthew K. Berent. 1993. "Comparisons of Party Identification and Policy Preferences: The Impact of Survey Question Format." *American Journal of Political Science* 37 (August): 941–964.

Krysan, Maria, Howard Schuman, Lesli Jo Scott, and Paul Beatty. 1994. "Response Rates and Response Content in Mail Surveys versus Face-to-Face Surveys." *Public Opinion Quarterly* 58 (fall): 410–430.

Kurtz, Howard. 2002. "A Slow News Night." *Washington Post* National Weekly Edition, 11-17, November, 34.

Ladd, Everett Carll. 1980. "Polling and the Press: The Clash of Institutional Imperatives." *Public Opinion Quarterly* 44 (winter): 574–584.

———. 1994. "The Holocaust Poll Error: A Modern Cautionary Tale." *Public Perspective* 5 (July/August): 3–5.

———. 1996. "The Election Polls: An American Waterloo." *Chronicle of Higher Education,* 22 November, A52.

Lang, Kurt, and Gladys Engel Lang. 1984. "The Impact of Polls on Public Opinion." *Annals of the American Academy of Political and Social Science* 472 (March): 130–142.

Langer, Gary. 2000. "Under the Hood." *Public Perspective* 11 (September/October): 8–9.

———. 2002. "Touchpoint: Responsible Polling in the Wake of 9/11." *Public Perspective* 13 (March/April): 14–16.

Lardner, George, Jr. 1985. "A Majority of the People Are Against the 'Star Wars' Defense Plan." *Washington Post* National Weekly Edition, 9 September, 37.

Larson, Stephanie Greco. 2003. "Misunderstanding Margin of Error: Network News Coverage of Polls during the 2000 General Election." *Harvard International Journal of Press/Politics* 8 (1): 66–80.

Lau, Richard R. 1994. "An Analysis of the Accuracy of 'Trial Heat' Polls during the 1992 Presidential Election." *Public Opinion Quarterly* 58 (spring): 2–20.

Laumann, Edward O., Robert T. Michael, and John H. Gagnon. 1994. *The Social Organization of Sexuality: Sexual Practices in the United States.* Chicago: University of Chicago Press.

Lavrakas, Paul J. 1986. "Surveying the Survey Differences." *Chicago Tribune,* 17 June, 12.

———. 1987. *Telephone Survey Methods: Sampling, Selection, and Supervision.* Newberry Park, Calif.: Sage Publications.

Lenhart, Amanda, principal author. 2003. *The Ever-Shifting Internet Population.* Washington, D.C.: The Pew Internet and American Life Project. 1–9.

Lever, Janet. 1994. "Sexual Revelations." *The Advocate,* 23 August, 15–24.

Levy, Mark R. 1983. "The Methodology and Performance of Election Day Polls." *Public Opinion Quarterly* 47 (spring): 54–67.

Lewis, I. A., and William Schneider. 1982. "Is the Public Lying to the Pollsters?" *Public Opinion* 5 (April/May): 42–47.

Lipset, Seymour Martin. 1980. "Different Polls, Different Results in 1980 Politics." *Public Opinion* 3 (August/September): 19–20, 60.

Lockerbie, Brad, and Stephen A. Borrelli. 1990. "Question Wording and Public Support for Contra Aid, 1983–1986." *Public Opinion Quarterly* 54 (summer): 195–208.

Margolis, Michael. 1984. "Public Opinion, Polling, and Political Behavior." *Annals of the American Academy of Political and Social Science* 472 (March): 61–71.

Marsh, Catherine. 1984. "Do Polls Affect What People Think?" In *Surveying Subjective Phenomena,* edited by Charles F. Turner and Elizabeth Martin, 565–591. New York: Russell Sage Foundation.

Martin, Elizabeth. 1999. "Who Knows Who Lives Here? Within-Household Disagreements as a Source of Survey Coverage Error." *Public Opinion Quarterly* 63 (summer): 220–236.

Meislin, Richard J. 1987. "Racial Divisions Seen in Poll on Howard Beach Attack." *New York Times,* 8 January, 16.

Merkle, Daniel M. 1996. "The National Issues Convention Deliberative Poll." *Public Opinion Quarterly* 60 (winter): 588–619.

Meyer, Eugene. 1940. "A Newspaper Publisher Looks at the Polls." *Public Opinion Quarterly* 4 (June): 238–240.

Michael, Robert T., John H. Gagnon, Edward O. Laumann, and Gina Kolata. 1994. *Sex in America: A Definitive Survey.* Boston: Little, Brown.

Michaels, Stuart, and Alain Giami. 1999. "The Polls—Review: Sexual Acts and Sexual Relationships: Asking about Sex in Surveys." *Public Opinion Quarterly* 63 (fall): 401–420.

Miller, M. Mark, and Robert Hurd. 1982. "Conformity to AAPOR Standards in Newspaper Reporting of Public Opinion Polls." *Public Opinion Quarterly* 46 (summer): 243–249.

Miller, Tim. 1986. "Statewide Poll Has Rhodes Far Ahead in GOP." *Dayton Daily News,* 23 March, 1.

Mills, Kim I. 1993. "Cheers' Fans Wanted to See Sam Malone Single." *Akron Beacon Journal,* 2 May, A13.

Mitofsky, Warren J. 1992. "What Went Wrong with Exit Polling in New Hampshire." *Public Perspective* 3 (March/April): 17.

———. 1996. "It's Not Deliberative and It's Not a Poll." *Public Perspective* 7 (December/January): 4–6.

———. 1999. "Pollsters.com." *Public Perspective* 10 (June/July): 24–26.

———. 2001. "Fool Me Twice." *Public Perspective* 12 (May/June): 35–38

Moore, David W., and Frank Newport. 1994. "Misreading the Public: The Case of the Holocaust Poll." *Public Perspective* 5 (March/April): 28–29.

Morin, Richard. 1987. "Pay Your Taxes and You, Too, Can Give a Useless Opinion." *Washington Post* National Weekly Edition, 7 December, 38.

———. 1988a. "What Went Wrong?" *Washington Post* National Weekly Edition, 22–28 February, 37.

———. 1988b. "Tracking a Formula for Success." *Washington Post* National Weekly Edition, 25 April–1 May, 37.

———. 1988c. "Behind the Numbers: Confessions of a Pollster." *Washington Post,* 16 October, C1, C4.

———. 1989a. "Where There's a Smoking Poll, There's Smoke." *Washington Post* National Weekly Edition, 30 January–5 February, 37.

———. 1989b. "The Answer May Depend on Who Asked the Question." *Washington Post* National Weekly Edition, 6–21 November, 38.

———. 1990. "Women Asking Women about Men Asking Women About Men." *Washington Post* National Weekly Edition, 15–21 January, 37.

———. 1991. "Two Ways of Reading the Public's Lips on Gulf Policy." *Washington Post,* 14 January, A9.

———. 1992a. "Another Contribution to SLOPpy Journalism." *Washington Post* National Weekly Edition, 10–16 February, 37.

———. 1992b. "This Time in New Hampshire, A Somewhat More Graceful Exit." *Washington Post* National Weekly Edition, 24 February–1 March, 37.

———. 1992c. "Surveying the Surveyors." *Washington Post* National Weekly Edition, 2–8 March, 37.

————. 1992d. "Polling '92: Who's on First." *Washington Post,* 6 June, A1.

————. 1992e. "Putting the Focus on Presidents and Peanut Butter." *Washington Post* National Weekly Edition, 19–25 October, 37.

————. 1993a. "Getting a Handle on the Religious Right." *Washington Post* National Weekly Edition, 5–11 April, 37.

————. 1993b. "Economics: A Puzzle to Many." *Washington Post* National Weekly Edition, 31 May–6 June, 37.

————. 1993c. "Wrong about the Religious Right." *Washington Post* National Weekly Edition, 1–7 November, 37.

————. 1993d. "Ask and You Might Deceive." *Washington Post* National Weekly Edition, 6–12 December, 37.

————. 1994a. "Public Enemy No. 1: Crime." *Washington Post* National Weekly Edition, 24–30 January, 37.

————. 1994b. "Don't Know Much About Health Care Reform." *Washington Post* National Weekly Edition, 14–20 March, 37.

————. 1994c. "The Answer Depends on the Question." *Washington Post* National Weekly Edition, 21–27 March, 37.

————. 1994d. "From Confusing Questions, Confusing Answers." *Washington Post* National Weekly Edition, 18–24 July, 37.

————. 1994e. "When the Data Tell Shockingly Different Stories." *Washington Post* National Weekly Edition, 8–14 August, 37.

————. 1995a. "What Informed Public Opinion?" *Washington Post* National Weekly Edition, 26 June–2 July, 34.

————. 1995b. "How Perceptions of Race Can Affect Poll Results." *Washington Post* National Weekly Edition, 26 June–2 July, 34.

————. 1995c. "Medicare Changes Get a Jaundiced Look." *Washington Post* National Weekly Edition, 10–16 July, 37.

————. 1995d. "Reading between the Numbers." *Washington Post* National Weekly Edition, 4–10 September, 30.

————. 1995e. "How Do People Really Feel about Bosnia?" *Washington Post* National Weekly Edition, 4–10 December, 32.

————. 1996a. "What Nature Never Intended." *Washington Post* National Weekly Edition, 8–14 July, 34.

————. 1996b. "Taking the Pulse on Pulse-Takers," *Washington Post* National Weekly Edition, 23–29 September, 37.

————. 1997a. "Right on the Money." *Washington Post* National Weekly Edition, 3 March, 3.

————. 1997b. "Getting Behind a Bigger NATO." *Washington Post* National Weekly Edition, 24 March, 35.

————. 1997c. "Warts and All." *Washington Post* National Weekly Edition, 13 October, 34.

————. 1997d. "Public Policy Surveys: Lite and Less Filling." *Washington Post* National Weekly Edition, 10 November, 35.

————. 1998a. "The Pollsters' Greatest Enemy: Themselves." *Washington Post* National Weekly Edition, 23 February, 35.

————. 1998b. "Missing the Story on Bosnia." *Washington Post* National Weekly Edition, 27 April, 35.

———. 1999a. "It's All in the Wording." *Washington Post* National Weekly Edition, 18 January, 21.

———. 1999b. "Believe Them, or Not." *Washington Post* National Weekly Edition, 12 July, 34.

———. 2000a. "Flaming the Messenger." *Washington Post* National Weekly Edition, 28 February, 34.

———. 2000b. "Will Traditional Polls Go the Way of the Dinosaur?" *Washington Post* National Weekly Edition, 15 May, 34.

———. 2001a. "Thou Shalt Not Fund..." *Washington Post* National Weekly Edition, 16–22 April, 34.

———. 2001b. "Who Goes to the Polls?" *Washington Post* National Weekly Edition, 4–10 June, 34.

———. 2002. "That Magic Touch." *Washington Post* National Weekly Edition, 18–24 November, 34.

Morin, Richard, and John M. Berry. 1996. "Economic Anxieties." *Washington Post* National Weekly Edition, 4–10 November, 6–7.

Morin, Richard, and Claudia Deane. 2000. "What's Up With Gallup?" *Washington Post* National Weekly Edition, 16 October, 34.

———. 2003. "Reasonable Doubt: Older People Are Less Inclined to Support Invading Iraq." *Washington Post* National Weekly Edition, 10–16 March, 34.

Munro, Ralph, and Curtis B. Gans. 1988. "Let's Say No to Exit Polls." *New York Times,* 4 November, 27.

Murray, Shoon Kathleen, and Peter Howard. 2002. "Variation in White House Polling Operations, Carter to Clinton." *Public Opinion Quarterly* 66 (winter): 527–558.

Nagourney, Adam. 2000. "Sound Bites over Jerusalem." *New York Times Magazine*, 25 April, 42–61,70.

———. 2002. "Cellphones and Caller ID Are Making It Harder for Pollsters to Pick a Winner." *New York Times ,* 5 November, A20.

National Council on Public Polls (NCPP). 2000. "Statement about Internet Polls," 6 August. http://www.ncpp.org/internet.htm.

———. 1995. "A Press Warning from the National Council on Public Polls." Press release, 22 May.

———. 2000. "Errors Associated with 'Instant' and Overnight Polls." Press release issued by NCPP Polling Review Board, 14 August. www.ncpp.org/presspost.htm.

———. 2003. "Poll of Iraq." Polling Review Board. 15 September. www.ncpp.org.

———. n.d. "Principles of Disclosure." www.ncpp.org.

Neuman, W. Russell. 1986. *The Paradox of Mass Politics: Knowledge and Opinion in the American Electorate.* Cambridge: Harvard University Press.

Newport, Frank. 1997. "The Pre-election Polls Performed Well in '96." *Public Perspective* 8 (December/January): 50–51.

———. 2003a. "Six out of Ten Americans Say Homosexual Relations Should Be Recognized as Legal." Gallup Organization, Gallup News Service, 15 May.

———. 2003b. "Six in Ten Americans Agree That Gay Sex Should Be Legal." Gallup Organization, Gallup News Service, 27 June, 1–6.

———. 2003c. "Public Shifts to More Conservative Stance on Gay Rights." Gallup Organization, Gallup News Service, 30 July, 1–6.

———. 2003d. "Americans Maintain Support for U.S. Presence in Iraq." Gallup Organization, Gallup News Service, 28 August, 1–13.

Newport, Frank, and Joseph Carroll. 2003. "Support for Bush Significantly Higher among More Religious Americans." Gallup Organization, Gallup News Service, 6 March, 1–7.

Noelle-Neumann, Elisabeth. 1974. "The Spiral of Silence: A Theory of Public Opinion." *Journal of Communication* 24 (spring): 43–51.

———. 1977. "Turbulence in the Climate of Opinion: Methodological Applications of the Spiral of Silence Theory." *Public Opinion Quarterly* 41 (summer): 143–158.

Norpoth, Helmut, and Milton Lodge. 1985. "The Difference between Attitudes and Nonattitudes in the Mass Public: Just Measurement?" *American Journal of Political Science* 29 (May): 291–307.

O'Gorman, Hubert J. 1975. "Pluralistic Ignorance and White Estimates of White Support for Racial Segregation." *Public Opinion Quarterly* 39 (fall): 313–330.

O'Gorman, Hubert J., and Stephen L. Garry. 1976–1977. "Pluralistic Ignorance—A Replication and Extension." *Public Opinion Quarterly* 40 (winter): 449–458.

O'Neill, Harry W. 1997. "An Honorable Profession, Warts and All." Comments delivered on the occasion of receiving the 1997 Award for Outstanding Achievement, New York Chapter, American Association for Public Opinion Research, June 18, 1997, http://www.mediastudies.org/ho.html, 6 August 2000.

Oreskes, Michael. 1984. "Pollsters Offer Reasons for Disparity in Results." *New York Times,* 20 October, A8.

———. 1990. "Drug War Underlines Fickleness of Public." *New York Times,* 6 September, A22.

Orton, Barry. 1982. "Phony Polls: The Pollster's Nemesis." *Public Opinion* 5 (June/July): 56–60.

Page, Benjamin I., and Robert Y. Shapiro. 1983. "Effects of Public Opinion on Policy." *American Political Science Review* 77 (March): 175–190.

———. 1992. *The Rational Public: Fifty Years of Trends in Americans' Policy Preferences.* Chicago: University of Chicago Press.

Paletz, David L., Jonathan Y. Short, Helen Baker, Barbara Cookman Campbell, Richard J. Cooper, and Rochelle M. Oeslander. 1980. "Polls in the Media: Content, Credibility, and Consequences." *Public Opinion Quarterly* 44 (winter): 495–513.

Payne, Stanley L. 1951. *The Art of Asking Questions.* Princeton: Princeton University Press.

Perlmutter, David D. 2002. "Americans Are Long on Opinions." *Columbus Dispatch,* 1 May, A7.

Perlstadt, Harry, and Russell E. Holmes. 1987. "The Role of Public Opinion Polling in Health Legislation." *American Journal of Public Health* 77 (May): 612–614.

Perry, Paul. 1979. "Certain Problems in Election Survey Methodology." *Public Opinion Quarterly* 43 (fall): 312–325.

Peterson, Robert A. 1984. "Asking the Age Question: A Research Note." *Public Opinion Quarterly* 48 (spring): 379–383.

Pew Research Center for the People and the Press. 1998. "Conservative Opinions Not Underestimated, but Racial Hostility Missed." http://www.people-press.org/resprpt.htm, 14 August 2000.

Phillips, Kevin P. 1976. "Polls Used to Reflect Electability." *Columbus Dispatch,* 19 July, B2.

———. 1981. "Polls Are Too Broad in Analysis Divisions." *Columbus Dispatch,* 8 September, B3.

Pianin, Eric, and Mario Brossard. 1997. "Hands Off Social Security and Medicare." *Washington Post* National Weekly Edition, 7 April, 35.

Piekarski, Linda B. 1989. "Choosing between Directory Listed and Random Digit Dialing in Light of New Demographic Findings." Paper presented at the AAPOR Conference, St. Petersburg, Fla.

Piekarski, Linda, Gwen Kaplan, and Jessica Prestgaard. 1999. "Telephony and Telephone Sampling: The Dynamics of Change." http://www.worldopinion.com/latenews.taf?f=d&news=3966, 26 December 1999.

Plissner, Martin. 2003. "An * for 2002?" *Public Perspective* 14 (January/February): 4–6.

Presser, Stanley, and Howard Schuman. 1980. "The Measurement of a Middle Position in Attitude Surveys." *Public Opinion Quarterly* 44 (spring): 70–85.

Public Opinion Quarterly. 1987. Fiftieth Anniversary Issue. 51, supplement (winter): S1–S191.

Rademacher, Eric W., and Andrew E. Smith. 2001. "Poll Call." *Public Perspective* 12 (March/April): 36–37.

Reese, Stephen D., Wayne A. Danielson, Pamela J. Shoemaker, Tsan-Kuo Chang, and Huei-Ling Hsu. 1986. "Ethnicity-of-Interviewer Effects among Mexican-Americans and Anglos." *Public Opinion Quarterly* 50 (winter): 563–572.

Rivlin, Allan. 1999. "First, Kill All the Pollsters." *National Journal*, 9 November, 2572–2573.

Robinson, Michael J., and Margaret A. Sheehan. 1983. *Over the Wire and on TV: CBS and UPI in Campaign '80.* New York: Russell Sage Foundation.

Romer, Daniel, Kate Kenski, Paul Waldman, Christopher Adasiewicz, and Kathleen Hall. 2004. *Capturing Campaign Dynamics: The National Annenberg Election Survey.* New York: Oxford University Press.

Roper, Burns W. 1985. "Early Election Calls: The Larger Dangers." *Public Opinion Quarterly* 49 (spring): 5–9.

Rosenbaum, David E. 1997. "Americans Want a Right to Die. Or So They Think." *New York Times,* 8 June, E3.

Rothenberg, Stuart, ed. 1983. *Political Report* newsletter. Vol.6, 5 August.

———. 1985. *Political Report. Vol.* 8, 25 October.

Rowland, Darrel. 1998. "Abortion Poll: Government Should Have No Say in Decision." *Columbus Dispatch,* 22 May, 1E–2E.

———. 1999. "Poll Indicates Support for Concealed-Gun Bill." *Columbus Dispatch,* 7 November, 4A.

Rubin, Alissa J. 2000. "Americans Narrowing Support for Abortion." *Los Angeles Times,* 18 June.

Salwen, Michael B. 1985a. "Does Poll Coverage Improve as Presidential Vote Nears?" *Journalism Quarterly* 62 (winter): 887–891.

———. 1985b. "The Reporting of Public Opinion Polls During Presidential Years, 1968–1984." *Journalism Quarterly* 62 (summer): 272–277.

Schneider, William. 1989. "One Poll May Be Worse than None." *National Journal* 2 (December): 2970.

———. 1996. "How to Read a Trial Heat Poll." Transcript, CNN, "Inside Politics Extra," 12 May, http://www.cnn.com.

Schuman, Howard, and Jean M. Converse. 1971. "The Effects of Black and White Interviewers on Black Responses in 1968." *Public Opinion Quarterly* 35 (spring): 44–68.

Schuman, Howard, Graham Kalton, and Jacob Ludwig. 1983. "Context and Contiguity in Survey Questionnaires." *Public Opinion Quarterly* 47 (spring): 112–115.

Schuman, Howard, and Stanley Presser. 1977. "Question Wording as an Independent Variable in Survey Analysis." *Sociological Methods and Research* 6 (November): 151–170.

———. 1981. *Questions and Answers in Attitude Surveys: Experiments on Question Form, Wording, and Context.* New York: Academic Press.

Schuman, Howard, Stanley Presser, and Jacob Ludwig. 1981. "Context Effects on Survey Responses to Questions about Abortion." *Public Opinion Quarterly* 45 (summer): 216–223.

Schwarz, Norbert, and Hans J. Hippler. 1995. "Subsequent Questions May Influence Answers to Preceding Questions in Mail Surveys." *Public Opinion Quarterly* 59 (spring): 93–97.

Sheler, Jeffrey L. 2000. "Hell Hath No Fury." *U.S. News and World Report,* 31 January, 45–50.

Shipler, David K. 1986. "Public Is Confused on Contra Aid Issue, Poll Indicates." *New York Times,* 15 April, 4.

Shlapentokh, Vladimir. 1994. "The 1993 Russian Election Polls." *Public Opinion Quarterly* 58 (winter): 579–602.

Sigel, Roberta S. 1996. *Ambition and Accommodation: How Women View Gender Relations.* Chicago: University of Chicago Press.

Sigelman, Lee. 1981. "Question-Order Effects on Presidential Popularity." *Public Opinion Quarterly* 45 (summer): 199–207.

Smith, Andrew E., and Clark Hubbard. 2000. "First in the Nation: Lessons Learned from New Hampshire." *Public Perspective,* May/June, 46–49.

Smith, Ted. J., III, and J. Michael Hogan. 1987. "Public Opinion and the Panama Canal Treaties of 1977." *Public Opinion Quarterly* 51 (spring): 5–30.

Smith, Ted J., III, and Derek O. Verrall. 1985. "A Critical Analysis of Australian Television Coverage of Election Opinion Polls." *Public Opinion Quarterly* 49 (spring): 58–79.

Smith, Tom W. 1984. "Nonattitudes: A Review and Evaluation." In *Surveying Subjective Phenomena,* vol. 2, edited by Charles F. Turner and Elizabeth Martin, 215–255. New York: Russell Sage Foundation.

———. 1987. "How Comics and Cartoons View Public Opinion Surveys." *Journalism Quarterly* 64: 208–211.

———. 1988. "Speaking Out: Hite vs. Abby in Methodological Messes." *AAPOR News,* spring, 3–4.

———. 1993. "Actual Trends or Measurement Artifacts? A Review of Three Studies of Anti-Semitism." *Public Opinion Quarterly* 57 (fall): 380–393.

———. 2002. "Reporting Survey Nonresponse in Academic Journals." *International Journal of Public Opinion Research* 14 (4): 469–474.

———. 2003. "An Experimental Comparison of Knowledge Networks and the GSS." *International Journal of Public Opinion Research* 15 (2): 167–178.

Sniderman, Paul, Edward Carmines, Philip Tetlock, and Anthony Tyler. 1993. In Richard Morin, "Racism Knows No Party Lines." *Washington Post* National Weekly Edition, 20–26 September, 37.

Solop, Frederic I., and Kristi K. Hagen. 2002. "War or War?" *Public Perspective* 13 (July/August): 36–37.

Specter, Michael. 1996. "Russian Pollsters Are Seldom Right." *New York Times,* 15 May, A1, A4.

Spolar, Christine. 1997. "Not Everyone Is Hot to Trot for NATO." *Washington Post* National Weekly Edition, 30 June, 8–9.

Squire, Peverill. 1988. "Why the 1936 *Literary Digest* Poll Failed." *Public Opinion Quarterly* 52 (spring): 125–133.

Squires, Sally, and Richard Morin. 1987. "What Is This Thing Called Love?" *Washington Post* National Weekly Edition, 16 November, 37.

Stein, Robert M. 1998. "Early Voting." *Public Opinion Quarterly* 62 (spring): 57–69

Stephens, Scott, and John Mangels. 2002. "Poll: Teach More Than Evolution." *Cleveland Plain Dealer,* 9 June, A1.

Stevenson, Richard W. 2000. "Tuesday's Big Test: How Deep in the Heart of Taxes." *New York Times,* 30 January, 3.

Sudman, Seymour. 1986. "Do Exit Polls Influence Voting Behavior?" *Public Opinion Quarterly* 50 (fall): 331–339.

Survey Sampling Inc. 1997. "Sacramento Is Most Unlisted." *The Frame,* March, 1.

Sussman, Barry. 1984a. "Why Both Parties Are Courting 50 Million Opinion-Switchers." *Washington Post* National Weekly Edition, 16 January, 37.

———. 1984b. "Do-It-Yourself Tax Reform: Many Think Cheating Is Okay." *Washington Post* National Weekly Edition, 28 May, 36.

———. 1985a. "To Understand These Polls, You Have to Read the Fine Print." *Washington Post* National Weekly Edition, 4 March, 37.

———. 1985b. "Reagan's Support on Issues Relies Heavily on the Uninformed." *Washington Post* National Weekly Edition, 1 April, 37.

———. 1985c. "Americans Prefer Tax Cheating to Being Paid to Inform the IRS." *Washington Post* National Weekly Edition, 13 May, 37.

———. 1985d. "Social Security and the Young." *Washington Post* National Weekly Edition, 27 May, 37.

———. 1985e. "Pollsters Cheer Up about Public's Opinions of Polls." *Washington Post* National Weekly Edition, 3 June, 37.

———. 1985f. "Do Pre-election Polls Influence People to Switch Their Votes?" *Washington Post* National Weekly Edition, 10 June, 37.

———. 1985g. "These Polls Are Part Public Opinion, Part Public Relations." *Washington Post* National Weekly Edition, 4 November, 37.

———. 1986a. "Do Blacks Approve of Reagan? It Depends on Who's Asking." *Washington Post* National Weekly Edition, 10 February, 37.

———. 1986b. "It's Wrong to Assume that School Busing Is Wildly Unpopular." *Washington Post* National Weekly Edition, 10 March, 37.

———. 1986c. "With Pornography, It All Depends on Who's Doing the Looking." *Washington Post* National Weekly Edition, 24 March, 37.

Swift, Al. 1985. "The Congressional Concern about Early Calls." *Public Opinion Quarterly* 49 (spring): 2–5.

Tanur, Judith M. 1994. "The Trustworthiness of Survey Research." *Chronicle of Higher Education,* 25 May, B1.

Taylor, Humphrey, John Brenner, Cary Overmeyer, Jonathan W. Siegel, and George Terhanian. 2001. "Touchdown! Online Polling Scores Big in November 2000." *Public Perspective,* March/April, 38–39.

Taylor, Humphrey, and George Terhanian. 1999. "Heady Days Are Here Again: Online Polling Is Rapidly Coming of Age." *Public Perspective,* June/July, 20–23.

Taylor, Marylee C. 1983. "The Black-and-White Model of Attitude Stability: A Latent Class Examination of Opinion and Nonopinion in the American Public." *American Journal of Sociology* 89 (September): 373–401.

Teitler, Julien O., Nancy E. Reichman, and Susan Sprachman. 2003. "Costs and Benefits of Improving Response Rates for a Hard-to Reach Population." *Public Opinion Quarterly* 67 (spring): 126–138.

Tenpas, Kathryn Dunn. 2003. "Words vs. Deeds: President George W. Bush and Polling." *Brookings Review,* summer, 32–35.

Torry, Jack. 2002. "Battelle Computer under Fire for Election Flop." *Columbus Dispatch,* 13 November, A4.

Tourangeau, Roger, and Tom W. Smith. 1996. "Asking Sensitive Questions: The Impact of Data Collection Mode, Question Format, and Question Context."" *Public Opinion Quarterly* 60 (summer): 181–227.

Traugott, Michael W. 1987. "The Importance of Persistence in Respondent Selection for Preelection Surveys." *Public Opinion Quarterly* 51 (spring): 48–57.

———. 1992. "A General Good Showing, but Much Work Remains to Be Done." *Public Perspective* 4 (November/December): 14–16.

———. 2001. "Assessing Poll Performance in the 2000 Campaign." *AAPOR News* 28 (winter): 4–5.

Traugott, Michael W., and Vincent Price. 1992. "Exit Polls in the 1989 Virginia Gubernatorial Race: Where Did They Go Wrong?" *Public Opinion Quarterly* 56 (summer): 245–253.

Tucker, Clyde. 2002. "The Current Efficiency of List-Assisted Telephone Sampling Designs." *Public Opinion Quarterly* 66 (fall): 321–338.

Tucker, Clyde, James M. Lepkowski, and Linda Piekarski. 2002. "The Current Efficiency of List-Assisted Telephone Sampling Designs." *Public Opinion Quarterly* 66 (fall): 321–338.

Visser, Penny S., Jon A Krosnick, Jesse Marquette, and Michael Curtin. 1996. "Mail Surveys for Election Forecasting: An Evaluation of the *Columbus Dispatch* Poll." *Public Opinion Quarterly* 59 (spring): 98–132.

Voss, D. Stephen, Andrew Gelman, and Gary King. 1995. "Preelection Survey Methodology: Details from Eight Polling Organizations, 1988 and 1992." *Public Opinion Quarterly* 59 (spring): 98–132.

Wanke, Michaela. 1996. "Comparative Judgments as a Function of the Direction of Comparison versus Word Order." *Public Opinion Quarterly* 60 (fall): 400–409.

Wanke, Michaela, Norbert Schwarz, and Elisabeth Noelle-Neumann. 1995. "Asking Comparative Questions: The Impact of the Direction of the Comparison." *Public Opinion Quarterly* 59 (fall): 347–352.

Washington Post. 1985. "A Grain of Salt Please" (editorial). 17 June.

Weeks, Michael F., and R. Paul Moore. 1981. "Ethnicity-of-Interviewer Effects on Ethnic Respondents." *Public Opinion Quarterly* 45 (summer): 245–249.

Weissberg, Robert. 2001. "Why Policymakers Should Ignore Public Opinion Polls." Cato Policy Analysis No. 402. 1–16. Washington, D.C.: Cato Institute.

Welch, R. L. 2002. "Polls, Polls, and More Polls: An Evaluation of How Public Opinion Polls Are Reported in Newspapers." *Harvard International Journal of Press/Politics* 7 (1): 102–114.

Werner, Jan. 2000. "Misleading Survey Reporting by NY Times." E-mail communication, AAPOR Listserv. 11 March.

Wiese, Cheryl J. 1998. "Refusal Conversion: What Is Gained?" *National Network of State Polls Newsletter* 32 (spring).

Williams, Brian. 2001. "Most Ohioans Back Passenger Trains, OSU Survey Finds." *Columbus Dispatch,* 12 March, C5.

Williams, Dennis A. 1979. "A New Racial Poll." *Newsweek,* 26 February, 48.

Winkler, Karen J. 1996. "Organizer Hails Results of Political-Science Experiment." *Chronicle of Higher Education,* 2 February, A13.

Witt, Evans. 2001. "People Who Count." *Public Perspective* 12 (July/August): 25–28.

Wright, Debra L., William S. Aquilino, and Andrew J. Supple. 1998. "A Comparison of Computer-Assisted and Paper-and-Pencil Self-Administered Questionnaires in a Survey on Smoking, Alcohol, and Drug Use." *Public Opinion Quarterly* 62 (fall): 331–353.

Wright, James D. 1981. "Public Opinion and Gun Control: A Comparison of Results from Two Recent National Surveys." *Annals of the American Academy of Political and Social Science* 455 (May): 24–39.

Yammarino, Francis J., Steven J. Skinner, and Terry L. Childers. 1991. "Understanding Mail Survey Response Behavior: A Meta-analysis." *Public Opinion Quarterly* 55 (winter): 613–639.

Zaller, John, and Stanley Feldman. 1992. "A Simple Theory of the Survey Response: Answering Questions versus Revealing Preferences." *American Journal of Political Science* 36 (August): 579–616.

Zinsmeister, Karl. 2003. "Summary and Analysis of the First Iraq Poll." The American Enterprise Online, 10 September. www.taemag.com/issues/articleID.17697/article_detail.asp.

Index

AAPOR. *See* American Association for Public Opinion Research

ABC News: Carter-Reagan debate poll, 145; pseudopolls, 116–117; *Washington Post* relationship, 3

ABC News/*Washington Post* polls: Iraqi invasion of Kuwait, 163; military strength, 38; 1984 presidential election, 185; pornography, 175; presidential popularity, 62; public affairs attentiveness, 178–179; race-of-interviewer effects, 97; Reagan's health, 4; Strategic Defense Initiative, 81–82; voter choice and polls, 155–156; voter turnout estimation, 152–153

Abortion, 63–64, 96, 112–113, 170–171

Abrams, Floyd, 137

Abramson, Paul R., 65, 97, 173

ACASI (audio computer-assisted self-interviewing), 92–93

Accuracy of polls, 15, 16–17, 84, 101

Action on Smoking and Health, 10

Actual sample size, 80–82

Adasiewicz, Christopher, 129

Advisory Commission on Intergovernmental Relations, 54

Advocate, The, 12, 171–172

Aetna Life and Casualty, 114

Affirmative action, 66, 90

Affluence bias, 76

Afghanistan, 168

African Americans. *See* Blacks

Age differences, 176

Age of respondents, 53

AIDS, 25, 52, 180

Air pollution, 64

Akron Beacon Journal, 24

al Qaeda, 167, 199

Alcohol use, 90, 102

Aldrich, John H., 33

Alexander, Lamar, 18

Altman, Drew, 14, 15, 16

Altschuler, Bruce E., 198

Alvarez, Lizette, 24

Alvarez, R. Michael, 44

Alwin, Duane F., 39–40

Ambiguous questions, 54

America on the Line, 10

American Association for Public Opinion Research (AAPOR): best practices, 19–20; disclosure standards, 19–20, 105–108, 115; fund-raising and polling, 6; Luntz case, 20; push polls, 139; response rates, 83, 84

American Association of Political Consultants, 140

American Enterprise, 183–185

American Farmland Trust, 9

American Foundation for AIDS Research, 52

American Jewish Committee, 54–55

American National Election Studies, 32–37, 95

American Viewpoint Inc., 118–119

Analyzing polls, 159–187; choosing items to analyze, 160–172; conflicting polls, 185–187; interpreting results,

180–185; subsets of respondents, 174–180; trend analysis, 172–174
Anderson, Barbara, 65, 97
Anderson, John, 146
Answering machines, 82
Anti-Semitism, 174
Antisodomy law, 4, 66–67
AOL, 13
Apartheid, 179
Aquilino, William S., 90, 92, 102
Argumentative questions, 52, 55
Art of Asking Questions, The (Payne), 52
Asher, Herbert B., 53, 60, 61, 118, 125
Asians, 22–23
Assault weapons ban, 9
Associated Press, 136
Atlanta Constitution, 108
Attentiveness to public affairs, 178–179
Attitude change, 30, 44, 45, 133, 173–174
Attitude stability, 59–60
Attitudes, 28n. See also Nonattitudes
Atwater, Lee, 131
Audio computer-assisted self-interviewing (ACASI), 92–93
Ayres, Whit, 82

Baker, Helen, 109
Baker, James, 179
Balanced budget, 38, 58–59
Balz, Dan, 151, 174
Bandwagon effect, 155, 156
Barker, Peggy Ripley, 92
Barnes, James A., 24
Bartels, Larry M., 197–198
Bauman, Sandra, 141
Baumgartner, Frank R., 173
Beal, Richard S., 198
Beatty, Paul, 90
Becker, Kurt M., 154
Behavior, versus verbal responses, 23
Benchmark surveys, 126
Benson, John M., 36–37
Berent, Matthew K., 59–60
Berke, Richard L., 123
Bernays, Edward L., 198
Bernick, E. Lee, 91
Berry, John M., 169
Best practices, 19–20

Bias, 159–160; affluence bias, 76; class bias, 74; nonresponse bias, 83; selection bias, 12, 70–71; weighting and, 85
Bierma, Nathan, 82
Bigotry, 22–23
Bishop, George F., 29, 32, 38–40, 63, 173
Black, Joan S., 19
Blacks: first black governor and mayor, 151; interviewer effects, 97–98; presidential candidate question, 180; Simpson case, 175–176; views of other minority groups, 22–23
Blais, Andre, 45
Blumenthal, Sidney, 198
Bolstein, Richard, 91
Borg, Marian J., 97–98
Borrelli, Stephen, 173–174
Bosnia, 115
Bracciodieta, John, 96
Brackett, April, 14, 15, 16
Brady, Henry E., 134
Brady law, 21
Branching, 33, 59–60, 92
Breast size pseudopoll, 117
Brehm, John, 44
Brenner, John, 100, 101
Broder, David S., 138
Brodie, Mollyann, 14, 15, 16
Broh, C. Anthony, 118
Brossard, Mario, 179
Brown, Kathleen, 128
Brown, William, 55
Bryant, Claudia, 117, 118
Buchanan, Pat, 34–37, 130, 135, 147
Buddhist temples, 163
Budget, balanced, 38, 58–59
Budget cuts, 38, 54, 58, 168, 182–183
Budget deficit, 59, 179, 181–182
Budget surplus, 25, 57–58, 167–168
Budiansky, Stephen, 58
Busch, Ronald J., 137
Bush, George H. W.: exit polls, 135; focus groups, 131; Iraqi invasion of Kuwait, 164–165; 1988 election, 118, 149–150, 185; 1992 election, 119, 169, 185; polling by, 25; pseudopolls and, 10; war on drugs, 195
Bush, George W.: attitudes toward, 56; cross-sectional survey, 129–130; debate,

145–146; exit polls, 18, 136; Iraq, 165–166, 183; New Hampshire primary, 149; performance of, 62, 174–175; polling by, 24–25, 198; push polls, 140; ratings of, 34–37; responses to negative poll results, 141; tax cuts, 167–168; tracking polls, 129; trial heat surveys, 127, 128; 2000 election, 18, 24–25, 101, 110, 119, 128, 148–149, 185; 2002 midterm elections, 155; 2004 election, 127

Caddell, Patrick, 143, 180, 185–186
California: collection of race data, 53; gubernatorial election, 128; gun ownership, 177; Simpson trial, 175–176
Call-in polls, 10–11, 70–71
Callbacks, 83, 108, 185–186
Caller ID, 82
Cambridge Reports, Inc., 180–181
Campaign contributions, 18, 141, 143
Campaign strategy, 128–129
Campbell, Barbara Cookman, 109
Campbell, Bruce A., 97
Canada, 45, 138
Candidates: electoral strength of, 168–169; packaging, 18; polls sponsored by, 125; uses of polls, 141–142
Carmines, Edward, 23
Carroll, Joseph, 175
Carroll, Rebecca, 77
Carter, Jimmy, 186; debate, 145; double vote question, 62; exit polls, 135–136; inaccurate predictions, 148; job rating, 169; polling by, 25; presidential primary, 144; trial heat question, 169; turnout estimation, 152
CASI (computer-assisted self-interviewing), 89, 92
CASRO (Council of American Survey Research Organizations), 105, 106–107
Catholic churches, 163
CATI (computer-assisted telephone interviewing), 93
Caucuses, 143–145
CBS News, 19; disclosure standards, 106, 109; *New York Times* relationship, 3
CBS News/*New York Times* polls, 106; budget cuts, 38; drug abuse, 195; 1984 election, 185; opinions of Clinton and

Bush, 56; 2000 election, 129–130; voter turnout estimation, 152
CBS News polls: New Hampshire primary, 150; Panama Canal, 114; tax cuts, 167–168
CBS News/*Washington Post* poll, 164–165
Celeste, Richard, 55, 85–86
Cell phones, 77
Census (2000), 53, 74
Center for Political Studies, 32
Center for the People and the Press, 4
Center for the Study and Prevention of Handgun Violence, 180–181
Chang, Tsan-Kuo, 98
Charter schools, 36–37
Cheers poll, 4
Cherington, Paul T., 193
Chicago Tribune, 108
Childers, Terry L., 91
Children, number in household, 53
Christian Science Monitor, 184–185
Chronicle of Higher Education, 172
Church, Allan H., 91
Cigarette taxes, 190
Citizen duty, 65
Citizen influence, 193–196
Citizen views of polls, 15–20, 69
Citizens, as consumers of polls, 2, 14–15
Civil justice system, 114
Civil rights, 90, 172
Civil unions, 66–67, 162
Clark, Wesley, 127
Class bias, 74
Classical democratic theory, 189–190
Cleveland Plain Dealer, 115–116
Clinton, Bill: approval ratings, 56; attitudes toward, 56; budget, 58, 182; government gridlock, 56; impeachment, 59; 1992 election, 119, 148, 169, 185; 1994 midterm elections, 154; 1996 election, 148, 185; polling by, 1, 24–25, 198; primaries, 144
Cluster sampling, 73–74
Clymer, Adam, 112–113, 139, 195
CNN, 3, 13, 21–22, 56, 119, 129, 176
CNN/*USA Today* polls, 129, 170
Code of Professional Ethics and Practices, 20
Cohen, Jeffrey, 97

Coleman, Marshall, 98
Columbus Dispatch: abortion, 170–171; accuracy of vote predictions, 83; disclosure and, 110–112; gubernatorial elections, 85–86; gun ownership, 177; 1994 elections, 110–112; voter turnout estimation, 153
Commission on Presidential Debates, 146–147
Commissioned polls, 5–14
Committee Against Government Waste, 9
Committee for the Study of the American Electorate, 137
Communist newspaper reporters, 63, 65
Comparable polls, 185–187
Comparative questions, 64
Compound questions, 52
Computer-assisted self-interviewing (CASI), 89, 92
Computer-assisted telephone interviewing (CATI), 93
Computerized mailings, 6, 9, 141
Computerized self-administered questionnaire (CSAQ), 89
Confidence levels, 69, 79
Conflicting polls, 185–187
Congress: Brady law, 21; budget cuts and, 38; exit polls, 137; House of Representatives, 71, 137, 148; questionnaires as pseudopolls, 11–12; war on drugs, 195
Conservatives, 23, 178
Contact rates, 83
Context: framework and, 66; Internet surveys and, 65; question order and context, 61–67; in self-administered surveys, 65; societal context, 66–67
Contract with America, 20
Contras, 174
Controversial behavior, 90, 92
Converse, Jean M., 39, 97
Converse, Philip E., 29
Converted refusals, 84
Coombs, Clyde H., 39
Coombs, Lolagene C., 39
Cooper, Richard J., 109
Cooperation rates, 83
Cosmopolitan, 12
Cotter, Patrick R., 97
Coulter, Philip B., 97

Council of American Survey Research Organizations (CASRO), 105, 106–107
Couper, Mick P., 99–100
Crask, Melvin R., 91
Creationism, 115–116
Crespi, Irving, 120–121, 149, 150
Cross-sectional surveys, 129–130
Crossley, Archibald M., 145
Crossley, Helen M., 145
CSAQ (computerized self-administered questionnaire), 89
Curtin, Michael, 85–86, 153
Curtin, Richard, 84

Daily News/Eyewitness News polls, 4
D'Amato, Alphonse, 141
Danielson, Wayne A., 98
Data collection, 90–94; Internet polling, 98–102; personal interviews, 93–94; self-administered questionnaires, 90–93; telephone interviews, 74–77, 82–83, 93
Davis, Darren W., 97, 98
Day, Richard, 154
de Bock, Harold, 155
Dean, Howard, 127
Deane, Claudia, 129, 174, 176
"Dear Abby," 12
Death penalty, 131
Deats, Jim, 139–140
Debates, 145–147
Decision/Making/Information, Inc., 180–181
Defense Department, 9
Deliberative polls, 132–134
Delli Carpini, Michael X., 29, 44, 136
Democracy: direct democracy, 21; evaluating polls, 190–193; nonattitudes and, 44–47; polling and, 15–16, 20–26, 189–201; polling effects on political system, 193–200; representative democracy, 21, 194
Democratic Congressional Campaign Committee, 6, 8
Democratic Party, 1, 55, 127
Department of Defense, 9
Department of the Treasury, 179, 182
Dewey, Thomas, 147
Dinkins, David, 151
Dinmore, Guy, 185

Direct democracy, 21
Direct mail, 6, 9
"Direction of the country" question, 62
Disclosure standards, 19–20, 105–106, 115, 195; effectiveness of, 106–108; observing, 108–112
DiVall, Linda, 118–119
Dole, Robert, 119, 185
Dolnick, Edward, 186
Domestic policy, 42, 115
"Don't ask, don't tell" policy, 170
"Don't know" responses, 39
Double negative questions, 54–55
"Double vote" question, 61–62
Dran, Ellen M., 17
Drug abuse, 48, 90, 92, 102, 194–195
Dukakis, Michael, 118, 131, 136, 185

Eagleton Institute, 4–5, 96
Economic climate, 154–155
Economics knowledge, 29, 169
Economy polls, 29, 133, 169
Education level of respondents, 35–36, 39, 92
Efficacy, political, 60, 95
Elder, Janet, 56, 123
Election polls, 18, 118–119, 125–158, 185–187; benchmark surveys, 126; candidate use of, 141–142; caucus and primary season, 143–145; citizen views of, 18; cross-sectional versus panel surveys, 129–130; debates, 145–147; deliberative polls, 132–134; disclosure and, 109; exit polls, 134-138; focus groups, 130–132; incorrect predictions, 147–155; media treatment of, 118; 1948 elections, 147; 1968 primaries, 144–145; 1976 elections, 144, 152; 1980 elections, 135–136, 146, 148, 185–186; 1982 elections, 154; 1984 elections, 69, 155–156, 185, 186; 1988 elections, 131, 149–150, 152–153, 185; 1989 elections, 151; 1992 elections, 119, 135, 148, 150, 185; 1994 midterm elections, 20, 154; 1996 elections, 119, 133, 139–140, 146–147, 148, 185; packaging candidates, 18; political and economic climate, 154–155; presidential selection process, 142–147; push polls, 139–140; spon-
sors of, 125–126; timing of, 149–150; tracking polls, 128–129; trial heat surveys, 127–128; 2002 elections, 136, 154–155; 2004 elections, 13, 127; undecided votes, 150–151; voter choices and, 155–156; voter turnout estimation, 151–153. *See also* 2000 elections
Election predictions, 83, 147–155
Electoral strength of presidential candidates, 168–169
Elving, Ronald D., 118–119, 185
Employee benefits, taxing, 181–182
Entitlement programs, 115
Epstein, Joan Faith, 92
Epstein, Laurily, 136
Equivalence, 95
Erikson, Robert S., 21
Ethnicity of interviewer, 97–98
Evaluating polls, 190–193
Evangelical Christians, 21
Evans, John, 141
Evolution, 115–116
Exit polls, 18, 134–138
External validity, 131
Extramarital affairs, 12
Eyewitness News, 4

Fairness in Media, 9
Faith-based initiatives, 162–163
Family issues, 133
Farmland, 9
Faulkenberry, G. David, 39
Federal "bailouts," 50
Federal employees, 182–183
Feldman, Stanley, 41–42
Felson, Marcus, 149
Females, overrepresented in polls, 86–87
Feminist responses, 96
Ferraro, Geraldine, 141
Field polls, 175–176, 177
Financial Times, 185
Finkel, Steven E., 97–98
First Amendment, 138
Fishkin, James, 132, 133, 134
Fitzgerald, Michael R., 117, 118
Florida, 136
Florio, Jim, 128
Focus groups, 24–25, 130–132
Ford, Gerald, 144, 145, 152
Foreign aid, 50, 134

Foreign policy, 24, 42, 43, 133, 134
Fowler, Floyd Jackson, Jr., 53–54
Fox, Richard J., 91
FOX News/Opinion Dynamics poll,
    166–167
Framework, and context, 66
Frankovic, Kathy, 19
Frey, James H., 93
FRUGing, 6, 9
Fund-raising, 6, 9, 90, 143
Fundamentalist Christians, 21

Gagnon, John H., 171
Gallup, George, 26, 43–44, 186
Gallup Organization: accuracy of polls, 15,
    17; AIDS in children, 180; attitudes to-
    wards Clinton and Bush, 56; citizen views
    of polls, 15; Columbus Dispatch polls,
    110, 111, 153; gay rights, 161–162;
    gays in the military, 170; Holocaust, 55;
    homosexual relations, 66–67, 176; Iraq
    war, 165–166; Iraqi invasion of Kuwait,
    163; New Hampshire primary, 150;
    1992 elections, 148; Nixon and, 198;
    secret ballot technique, 150; 2000 elec-
    tions, 129; voter turnout estimation, 152
Galtung, Johan, 23
Gans, Curtis B., 18
Garry, Stephen L., 199
Gawiser, Sheldon R., 121–122
Gay marriage, 66–67, 162
Gay rights, 4, 66–67, 161–162, 176
Gays in the military, 170
Gelman, Andrew, 186–187
Gender, and weighted samples, 86–87
Gender differences, 175, 177
Gender of interviewer, 96
Gender relations, 132
General political knowledge, 45
Genesys News, 75
Genesys Q & A, 76
Gephardt, Dick, 127
Gershwin, George, 189
Giami, Alain, 66
Gilens, Martin, 45
Gilljam, Mikael, 39
Ginsberg, Benjamin, 3, 196–197
Glamour magazine, 171
Glenn, John, 144
Global polling, 1

Goeas, Ed, 119
Goldhaber, Gerald M., 152
Goodstein, Laurie, 162
Gore, Al: cross-sectional survey, 129–130;
    debate, 145–146; exit polls, 18, 136; In-
    ternet polling, 101; poll performance,
    148–149, 185; ratings of, 34–37; sam-
    pling error, 110; tracking polls, 129; trial
    heat survey, 128; 2004 election, 13;
    volatility of poll results, 119
Government: citizen effectiveness and, 60;
    intervention in economy, 178; response
    to polling, 21, 24; trust in, 173
Government gridlock, 56
Government services, 33–34, 168
Government waste, 9
Governmental power, 32–33
Goyder, John, 91
Granberg, Donald, 39
Green, Melanie C., 94
Greenberg, Anna, 101
Greenberg, Daniel, 18–19
Greenberg, Stanley, 1, 24, 143
Group membership, 173
Grove, Lloyd, 131, 150
Gubernatorial elections: California, 128; Illi-
    nois, 154; New Jersey, 128; Ohio, 55,
    85–86, 142, 151; Virginia, 97–98,
    135, 151
Gun control, 9, 21–22, 177, 180–181
Gun ownership, 177
Gun rights, 177
Guterbock, Thomas M., 97–98

Hall, Kathleen, 129
Handgun Control, 9
Harker, Kathryn, 53
Harmon, Amy, 92
Harris, John F., 24–25
Harris/Excite daily poll, 100
Harris Interactive, 3, 100–101
Harris polls, 22–23, 61, 114, 185, 186,
    198
Hart, Gary, 144
Hart, Peter, 152
Harwood, Richard, 119
Harwood Group, 131
Hatchett, S., 97
Health care, 24
Health surveys, 53–54

Hell poll, 4
Henry J. Kaiser Family Foundation, 15–16
Herbers, John, 54
Herbst, Susan, 141
Hernandez, Debra Gersh, 146
Hildreth, Anne, 17
Hinckley, Ronald H., 198
Hippler, Hans J., 65
Hispanic interviewers, 98
Hite, Shere, 12
Hogan, J. Michael, 114–115
Holbrook, Allyson L., 94
Holmes, Russell E., 190
Holocaust, 54–55
Homosexual relations, 176
Homosexuality, 4, 66–67, 161–162, 170
Horton, Willie, 131
House of Representatives, 71, 148
House Task Force on Elections, 137
Household members, 53
Howard, Peter, 25
Howe, Peter J., 82
Hsu, Huei-Ling, 98
Hubbard, Clark, 149
Huddy, Leonie, 96
Huffington, Arianna, 19
Hughes, John, 185
Humphrey, Hubert, 143, 145
Hurd, Robert, 108–109
Hussein, Saddam, 199
Hutchison, Bill, 46–47
Hyman, Herbert H., 63

I-PAPI (interviewer-administered, paper-and-pencil), 92–93
Idaho elections, 141
Ideological categories, 178
Illegal behavior, 90, 92
Illinois gubernatorial election, 154
Impeachment, 59
Imports, 42–43
Income level, 53, 176
Incumbency, 168–169, 186
Independents, 149
Index of Consumer Sentiment, 84
Indexes, 60–61
Industry, and air pollution, 64
Instability of responses, 30, 41–44
Instant polls, 146
Insurance industry, 181–182

Intelligent design, 115–116
Intercept polls, 100
Interest groups, 90
Interest level, 35–36, 37
Internal Revenue Service (IRS), 5–6
Internationalization of polling, 1
Internet access, 98–99, 101
Internet polling, 13, 14, 89, 98–102; accuracy of, 101; media and, 102; order and context effects, 65; sampling and, 99–100; self-selected, 99–100; typology of, 99–100
Interpreting poll results, 159–160, 180–185; substantive interpretation, 112–117
Interviewer-administered, paper-and-pencil (I-PAPI), 92–93
Interviewer effects, 89, 94–98; gender and status, 96–97; interviewer skills and demeanor, 95–96; race and ethnicity, 97–98
Interviewer skills and demeanor, 95–96
Interviewing method, 185–186
Interviews: personal interviews, 93–94; secret ballot technique, 150; telephone interviews, 74–77, 82–83, 93
Iowa precinct caucus, 144
Iraq: invasion of Kuwait, 163–165; Islamic government in, 184; public opinion in, 183–185
Iraq war: choice of analysis items, 163, 165–166, 168; context and, 67; deliberative polls, 134; international polls on, 1; interpreting poll results, 183–185; political system and polls, 194, 199; response alternatives, 58; sampling error, 79–80; subgroups and, 176
IRS (Internal Revenue Service), 5–6
Israeli elections, 1
Issues, importance of, 44

Jackson, John, 136
Jacobs, Lawrence R., 115, 198
James, Jeannine M., 91
Jewish synagogues, 163
Job approval ratings, 169
Job security, 182–183
Johnson, Lyndon, 198
Johnson, Timothy P., 102
Journals, 83–84

Kagay, Michael, 56, 83, 152
Kagen, Kristi K., 58
Kaiser Family Foundation, 168
Kalton, Graham, 63
Kane, Emily W., 96
Kaplan, Gwen, 76–77, 82
Keene, Karlyn H., 42–43
Keeter, Scott, 29, 44, 84
Kennedy, Edward, 62
Kennedy, John F., 198
Kennedy School of Government, 168
Kenski, Kate, 129
Kerry, John, 127
Kettering Foundation, 131–132
Kifner, John, 54
Kim, Jonghoon, 91
Kinder, Donald R., 66
King, Gary, 186–187
Knowledge base, 29, 43, 45, 169
Knowledge level, 45
Knowledge Networks, 100, 101
Koch, Nadine S., 16
Kohut, Andrew, 11, 154
Kolata, Gina, 171
Kolbert, Elizabeth, 59
Krosnick, Jon A., 39–40, 59–60, 94,
    113–114, 153
Kroutil, Larry A., 92
Krysan, Maria, 90
Kucinich, Dennis, 85–86
Kurfess, Charles, 151
Kurtz, Howard, 136
Kuwait, 163–165

Labeling, 59–60
Labor unions, 9, 69
Ladd, Everett Carll, 54, 55, 120, 148
Lake Sosin Snell and Associates, 3
Land use survey, 31–32
Landon, Alf, 78
Lang, Gladys Engel, 19, 199
Lang, Kurt, 19, 199
Langer, Gary, 110, 173
Lardner, George, Jr., 82
Larson, Stephanie Greco, 110
Latinos, 22–23
Lau, Richard R., 150
Laughlin, Greg, 139–140
Laumann, Edward O., 171
Lavrakas, Paul J., 75

Lawrence v. Texas, 4
Leadership, 24–25, 198
Leading questions, 55
League of Women Voters, 137, 146
Leaking information, 142
Lenhart, Amanda, 98, 99
Lepkowski, James M., 76
Level of confidence, 69, 70
Lever, Janet, 12
Levy, Mark R., 134
Lewis, Bud, 119
Lewis, I. A., 185–186
Liberals, 23, 178
Libertarians, 178
Lieberman, Joe, 127
Lieske, Joel A., 137
Lilie, Stuart A., 178
Lipset, Seymour Martin, 186
List-based surveys, 100
Literary Digest poll, 78, 147
Loaded words, 52
Local government, 132
Lockerbie, Brad, 173–174
Lodge, Milton, 29
Longitudinal comparisons, 172–174
Los Angeles Times, 108, 119, 170, 185
Losciuto, Leonard A., 102
Louis Harris and Associates, 22–23, 114
Ludwig, Jacob, 63–64
Luntz, Frank, 20
Luskin, Robert C., 134

Macaulay, Laura J., 96
Maddox, William S., 178
Magazine surveys, 12–13, 14
Mail surveys, 14, 83, 90–92, 153
Males, underrepresented in polls, 86–87
Mangels, John, 115–116
Margolis, Michael, 23
Marijuana penalties, 38
Marital relations polls, 12
Marquette, Jesse, 153
Marsh, Catherine, 155
Martin, Elizabeth, 53
Mason, Robert, 39
McCain, John, 140, 144, 149
McCarthy, Eugene, 152
McGee, William, 136
"Meaningful Chaos: How People Form
    Relationships with Public Concerns,"
    131–132

Measurement error, 60
Media, 104–121, 189–190; drug war and, 48; election polls and, 18, 118, 125–126; exit polls, 18, 134–138; federal budget and, 58; focus groups and, 131; Internet polling and, 102; news reporting emphasis, 117–121; pseudopolls and, 116–117; selecting items to analyze, 171–172; as sponsor of election polls, 125–126; standards for reporting results, 105–112; statistical analysis and, 117; substantive interpretation of polls, 112–117
Medicare, 58–59, 179
Meislin, Richard J., 97
Mental health, 92–93
Merkle, Daniel M., 133
Methodological differences, 186–187
Meyer, Eugene, 193–194
Michael, Robert T., 171
Michaels, Stuart, 66
Michigan Tobacco and Candy Distributors and Vendors Association, 190
Middle category, 33–34, 37–41
Military spending, 179
Military strength, 38
Miller, M. Mark, 108–109
Mills, Kim I., 4
Minority groups, 22–23
Missile defense, 81–82
Mitofsky, Warren J., 100, 133, 135, 136
Mixed-mode surveys, 100
Moderates, 178
Mondale, Walter, 69, 136, 155, 169, 185
Moore, David W., 54
Moore, R. Paul, 97
Morin, Richard, 10, 11–12, 15, 19, 21, 29, 43, 54, 56, 58, 59, 62, 96, 97, 115, 117, 119, 129, 131, 135, 148, 150, 152, 162, 169, 176, 182–183, 185, 190
Mormon churches, 163
Mortgage refinancing, 13
MSNBC, 128
Multiple items, 60–61
Multistage sampling, 73–74
Munro, Ralph, 18
Murray, Shoon Kathleen, 25
Mushiness index, 42–44
Muslim mosques, 163

Nader, Ralph, 34–37, 130, 147
Nagourney, Adam, 1, 82
Name recognition, 128
National Annenberg Election Survey, 128–129
National Council on Public Polls (NCPP): disclosure standards, 105, 106–108; instant polls, 146; Internet polling, 102; pamphlet for journalists, 121–122; Polling Review Board, 183; Principles of Disclosure, 195; push polls, 139
National Election Studies, 173
National Elections Pool, 136
National Issues Convention, 133
National Opinion Research Center, 171, 180
National Rifle Association (NRA), 9, 180–181
National Right to Work Committee, 9
NATO expansion, 43
NBC News, 3, 109, 114, 185
NBC News/*Wall Street Journal* polls, 164
NCPP. See National Council on Public Polls
Needle exchange program, 25
Neuman, W. Russell, 190–191
New Hampshire primary, 135, 144, 149–150
New information, introducing, 42
New Jersey, 4–5, 128
New York City, 4, 151
New York Times, 106, 109, 122–123; abortion attitudes, 112–113; CBS News relationship, 3; Medicare cuts, 58; Panama Canal, 114–115; sexual behavior, 171; tort reform, 113–114
New York Times/CBS News polls, 59, 122–123
New York Times/WCBS-TV poll, 4, 128
Newark Star-Ledger, 4–5
Newport, Frank, 54, 66–67, 148, 161, 165, 175, 176
Newsmagazines, 3, 113, 171
Newspaper reporters, in communist countries, 63, 65
Newspapers, 3, 106–107, 108–109, 113, 138
Newsweek, 3; Medicare cuts, 58; Panama Canal, 114–115; Reagan's health, 4; sexual behavior, 171; Simpson trial, 176; trial heat surveys, 127

Newsworthiness, 117, 120
Nicaraguan contras, 174
Niemi, Richard, 33, 173–174
Nixon, Richard, 144–145, 198
Noelle-Neumann, Elisabeth, 64, 199
Nonattitudes, 28–48, 55; example,
    31–32; implications for democracy and
    public policy, 44–47; middle position
    and, 37–41; response instability and,
    41–44; screening questions, 32–37
Nonprobability sampling, 70–71, 99–100
Nonresponse, 82
Nonresponse bias, 83
Normative issues, 179–180
Norpoth, Helmut, 29
NPR/Kaiser Family Foundation/Kennedy
    School of Government poll, 168
NRA (National Rifle Association), 9,
    180–181

Oeslander, Rochelle M., 109
O'Gorman, Hubert J., 199
Ohio: abortion, 170–171; gubernatorial
    elections, 55, 85–86, 142, 151; gun
    ownership, 177; passenger rail service,
    46–47; science education, 115–116
Ohio AFL-CIO, 69
Ohio Association of Railroad Passengers,
    46
Oldendick, Robert W., 29, 32, 38, 63
Omnibus surveys, 42, 160-161, 182–183
O'Neill, Harry, 19
Opinions, defined, 28n
Order of questions, 30, 51, 61–67, 92,
    186
Order of response alternatives, 39–40
Oreskes, Michael, 48, 185
Orton, Barry, 10
Overmeyer, Cary, 100, 101
Overnight polls, 82–83, 146

Page, Benjamin I., 21
Paletz, David L., 109
Panama Canal, 114–115
Panel surveys, 129–130
Parents survey, 84
Parmelee, Lisa Ferraro, 14, 15, 16
"Partnership for a Poll-Free America," 19
Party affiliation, 85–86, 128, 177
Party identification, 60

Party loyalty, 60, 173–174
Party nominations, 143, 144
Passenger train service, 46–47
Paul, Ron, 139–140
Payne, Stanley L., 52
Percentage distributions, 117
Periodicity, 71–72
Perlmutter, David D., 45
Perlstadt, Harry, 190
Perot, Ross, 119, 146
Perry, Paul, 150, 152
Persian Gulf crisis, 163–165, 194
Personal characteristics of interviewers,
    96–97
Personal interviews, 93–94
Personal liberties expansion, 178
Peterson, Robert A., 53
Pew Forum on Religion and Public Life,
    162
Pew Research Center for People and the
    Press, 162
Phillips, Kevin, 144, 178
Physical attraction, 117
Physician-assisted suicide, 176
Pianin, Eric, 179
Piekarski, Linda, 75, 76–77, 82
Playboy, 12
Pledge of Allegiance, 131
Plissner, Martin, 136
Pluralistic ignorance, 199
Policy-specific information, 45
Political advertising, 128–129
Political cartoonists, 19
Political climate, 154–155
Political discourse, 199
Political efficacy, 60, 95
Political elites, 194, 195, 196
Political figures, rating, 34–37
Political groups, 6, 9
Political interest level, 63
Political knowledge, 45
Political leadership, 198
Political party affiliation, 85–86, 128, 177
Political party identification, 60
Political party loyalty, 60, 173–174
Political party nominations, 143, 144
Political system: knowledge of, 29; poll ef-
    fects on, 193–200
Politicians' use of polls, 16, 20
Politics, impact of polls on, 18–19

Poll-based reporting, 117–121
Polls: impact on leadership, 24–25; importance of, 2–3; pervasiveness of, 3–5
Pollsters: credibility of, 15; prominence of, 143
Pollution, 64
Populists, 178
Pornography, 175
Pratto, David J., 91
Prayer in schools, 161
Pre-recruited panels, 100–101
Predetermined results, 6–10, 11
Predictions, 83, 147–155
Preelection polls, and voter choice, 155–156
Prejudice, 22–23
Presidential candidates, electoral strength of, 168–169
Presidential debates, 145–147
Presidential nominations, 143, 144
Presidential primaries, 14, 61–62, 143–145
Presidential selection process, 18, 19, 142–147
Presidents: approval ratings, 56, 62, 169; budget cuts and, 38; controlling polls, 198; impact on public opinion, 43, 48, 194–195; performance, 62; popularity of, 62, 118; reliance on polls, 24–25
Presser, Stanley, 38, 44, 62–63, 64, 84
Prestgaard, Jessica, 76–77, 82
Pretesting questions, 53–54
Price, Vincent, 135
Primaries, 14, 61–62, 143–145
Princeton Survey Research Associates, 3, 127
Principles of Disclosure (NCPP), 195
Privacy rights, 4, 66–67
Probability sampling, 69, 70–71, 99–100
Probability theory, 78
Protestant churches, 163
Pseudopolls, 3, 10–14, 116–117
Public affairs, attentiveness to, 178–179
"Public Affairs Act" survey, 29–30, 32
Public funding, 143, 147
Public lands, 9
Public opinion, versus poll results, 23, 197
Public Opinion Quarterly, 5, 15
Public Perspective, 5, 15
Public policy, 21, 23–24, 44–47

Push polls, 20, 55, 139–140

Quasi-attitudes, 191
Question order and context, 30, 51, 61–67, 186
Question wording, 30, 47, 50, 51, 52–61, 186; argumentative, leading questions, 55; branching and labeling effects, 59–60; double negative questions, 54–55; impact of response alternatives, 56–58; multiple items and indexes, 60–61; small wording changes, 58–59; straightforward, factual questions, 52–54
Questionnaires: as pseudopolls, 11–12; self-administered, 90–93
Questions: ambiguous questions, 54; argumentative questions, 52, 55; comparative questions, 64; compound questions, 52; double negative questions, 54–55; leading questions, 55; middle category, 33–34, 37–41; pretesting, 53–54; screening questions, 31, 32–37, 41; subjective questions, 54; thermometer questions, 34–36
Quota sampling method, 147

Rabinowitz, George, 33
Race categories, 53
Race effects, 80, 151, 175–176
Race polls, 22–23
Race relations in New York City, 4
Racial attitudes, 199
Racial differences, 176, 197
Racial integration, 90
Rademacher, Eric W., 149
Radio call-in surveys, 70–71
Radio talk shows, 10–11
Rail system, 46–47
Random-digit dialing, 75–77, 84, 93
Random measurement error, 60
Random sampling, 71–72
Reagan, Ronald: debates, 145; exit polls, 135–136; health of, 4; in-house polling, 25, 198; job rating, 169; 1976 election, 144; 1980 election, 135–136, 148, 169, 186; 1984 election, 69, 155, 169, 185; straight-ticket voting and, 154; Strategic Defense Initiative, 81–82; war on drugs, 195
Reagan Democrats, 131

Redbook magazine, 12
Reese, Stephen D., 98
Referenda, 23
Reform Party, 147
Refusals, 53, 82, 83, 84
Regan, Donald, 179
Reichman, Nancy E., 84
Reliability, 94–95
Religion issues, 162–163
Religious right, 21
Representative democracy, 21, 194
Republican Congressional Committee, 139
Republican National Committee, 6, 7
Republican Party, 20, 141, 154–155
Respondent needs, 19
Response alternatives, 38–40, 60
Response instability, 30, 41–44
Response rates, 70, 82–85; accuracy and, 84; mail surveys and, 90–91
Reuters/MSNBC/Zogby poll, 128
Reverse discrimination, 66
Rhodes, James, 85–86, 151
Rivers, Douglas, 101
Rivlin, Allan, 18
Robinson, Michael J., 118
Rockefeller, Nelson, 144–145
Rohde, David, 33
Rolling samples, 128–129
Romer, Daniel, 129
Roosevelt, Franklin D., 78
Roper, Burns W., 137, 181
Roper organization, 17, 19, 54–55
Rosenbaum, David E., 176
Rothenberg, Stuart, 141, 154
Rove, Karl, 25
Rowland, Darrel, 170, 177
Royko, Mike, 18, 137
Rubin, Alissa J., 170
Rule, Patra, 117, 118
Russia, 43, 125, 157
Rutgers University, 4–5

Sackett, Victoria A., 42–43
Salwen, Michael B., 109
Sample size, 69–70, 77–80; citizen views of, 16–18; pseudopolls, 12; total versus actual, 80–82
Sampling, 5, 69–70; cluster and multistage sampling, 73–74; conflicting results and, 186, 187; Internet polling and, 99–100;

quota method, 147; response rates, 82–85; rolling samples, 128–129; sample size and sampling error, 77–80; sampling designs, 70–77; simple random and systematic sampling, 71–72; stratified sampling, 72; for telephone interviewing, 74–77; total versus actual sample size, 80–82; weighting techniques, 85–87, 129
Sampling design, 70–77
Sampling error, 69, 70, 72, 78–80; disclosure and, 109110; subgroups and, 175
Sanders, Lynn M., 66
Schneider, William, 138, 168–169, 185–186
School prayer, 161
School vouchers, 36–37
Schuman, H., 97
Schuman, Howard, 38, 44, 62, 63, 64, 90, 97
Schwarz, Norbert, 64, 65
Science education, 115–116
Scientific polls, 69–70
Scott, Lesli Jo, 90
Screening questions, 31, 32–37, 41
SDI (Strategic Defense Initiative), 81–82
Secret ballot technique, 150
Selection bias, 12, 70–71
Self-administered questionnaires, 90–93
Self magazine, 117
Self-selected Internet polling, 99–100
Self-selection, 12–13, 14, 20
Separation of church and state, 163
Sex in America: A Definitive Survey, 171–172
Sex surveys, 12–13
Sexual behavior, 66, 92, 171–172
Shapiro, Robert Y., 21, 115, 198
Sheatsley, Paul B., 63
Sheehan, Margaret A., 118
Shlapentokh, Vladimir, 157
Shoemaker, Pamela J., 98
Short, Jonathan Y., 109
Siegel, Jonathan W., 100, 101
Sierra Club, 9
Sigel, Roberta, 132
Silver, Brian D., 65, 97, 98
Simple random sampling, 71–72
Simpson, O. J., 175–176
Singer, Eleanor, 84

Skinner, Steven J., 91
Smith, Andrew E., 149
Smith, Ted J., III, 114–115
Smith, Tom W., 12, 19, 39, 83–84, 90, 101, 174
Smoking, 190
Sniderman, Paul, 23
Social Organization of Sexuality, The: Sexual Practices in the United States, 171
Social science journals, 83–84
Social Security, 25, 58, 179
Social services, 162–163
Social status of interviewer, 96–97
Societal context, 66–67
Solop, Frederic I., 58
South Carolina primary, 140
Soviet Union, 38
Specter, Michael, 157
Spiral of silence thesis, 199
Sprachman, Susan, 84
Springer, Jerry, 55
Squire, Peverill, 78
Squires, Sally, 12
Stability of attitudes, 59–60
Standards for disclosure, 19–20, 105–106, 115, 195; effectiveness of, 106–108; observing, 108–112
"Star Wars" poll, 81–82
State and local polls, 4–5, 46–47, 137, 177
"State of the Nation Public Opinion Research Survey," 6, 7
State of the Union address, 10
Statistical analysis, 117
Statistical theory, 69, 70, 78
Stein, Robert M., 135
Stephens, Scott, 115–116
Stereotypes, 21–23
Stevenson, Adlai, III, 154
Stevenson, Richard W., 57
Straight-ticket voting, 154
Strategic Defense Initiative (SDI), 81–82
Stratified sampling, 72
Straw polls, 10
Strom, Gerald, 136
Subgroups, 23, 44, 174–180; categories for creating, 177–178; disclosure and, 110; sampling error and, 79–80
Subjective questions, 54

Subjectivity, 159
Substantive interpretation of polls, 112–117
Sudman, Seymour, 136, 149
Suicide, physician-assisted, 176
Supple, Andrew J., 92
Supreme Court, 4, 66–67
Survey Research Center, 73, 173
Survey Sampling Inc., 74, 75, 76
Sussman, Barry, 5, 6, 11, 17, 62, 155–156, 178, 179, 181–182
Swift, Al, 137
Symms, Steve, 141
Systematic sampling, 71–72

Taft, Seth, 142
Tanur, Judith M., 19
Tarrance & Associates, 119
Tarrance Group, 3
Tax cheating, 5–6
Tax cuts, 25, 57–58, 167–168
Tax rates, 179, 182
Tax reform, 181–182
Tax system, 179, 182
Taxing employee benefits, 181–182
Taylor, Humphrey, 100, 101
Taylor, Marylee C., 29
Teitler, Julien O., 84
Telemarketing, 82, 139
Telephone directories, 74–76
Telephone interviews, 82–83, 93; response rates, 82; sampling techniques for, 74–77
Telephone numbers: portability of, 76; volume of, 77
Telephones in U.S. households, 74, 77
Television, 3, 109–110, 138
Tenpas, Kathryn Dunn, 25
Terhanian, George, 100, 101
Terrorism, 58, 166–167, 173, 194, 199
Tetlock, Philip, 23
Texas antisodomy law, 4, 66–67
Texas primary, 139–140
Thermometer questions, 34–36
Thompson, James, 154
Time, 3, 4, 114–115, 171
Time/CNN polls, 56, 119, 176
Times Mirror polls, 4, 10–11
Tobacco, 10, 190
Tobacco Institute, 190

Topics, 28–29
Torry, Jack, 136
Tort reform, 114
Total sample size, 80–82
Tourangeau, Roger, 90
Town hall meetings, 16
Tracking polls, 128–129, 148, 150
Traffic, and air pollution, 64
Traugott, Michael W., 135, 148, 149, 186
Treasury Department, 179, 182
Trend analysis, 172–174
Trial heat surveys, 118, 127–128, 142
Truman, Harry, 147
Trust in government, 173
Tuchfarber, Alfred J., 29, 32, 38, 63
Tucker, Clyde, 76
20/20, 117
2000 American National Election Study, 32–37
2000 elections: conflicting polls, 185; cross-sectional survey, 129–130; debates, 147; democracy and polling, 24–25; disclosure standards and, 109–110; exit polls, 18, 136; incorrect predictions, 148–149; Internet polling, 101; legitimacy of, 197; media and, 109–110, 119; primaries, 140; tracking polls, 128–129; trial heat surveys, 128
"2003 Democratic Leadership Survey," 6, 8
Tyler, Anthony, 23

Undecided voters, 150–151
Underdog effect, 155, 156
Unemployment, 154, 169
Unions, 9, 69
U.S. News and World Report, 3, 4, 171, 175
University of Akron, 153
University of Cincinnati, 153
University of Michigan, 32, 73, 173
Unlabeled response options, 60
Unlisted telephone numbers, 74–75
USA Today, 129, 170
USA Today/CNN/Gallup polls, 21–22, 129

Validity, 95, 131
Van Buren, Abigail, 12
Verbal responses, versus behavior, 23
Vice-presidential debates, 145

Virginia gubernatorial election, 97–98, 135, 151
Visser, Penny S., 153
Voice mail, 82
Volatility of public opinion, 43
Volunteer opt-in panels, 100–101
Voss, D. Stephen, 186–187
Voter choice, poll effects on, 45, 155–156
Voter News Service, 136, 138
Voter turnout, 148, 151–153

Waldman, Paul, 129
Walker, Jack L., 173
Wall Street Journal, 3, 164
Wanke, Michaela, 64
Washington Post, 3, 122–123, 182–183
Washington Post/ABC News polls, 59, 168, 176
Washington Post polls, 29–30, 174–175, 176. See also ABC News/Washington Post polls
Washington state exit polls, 137
Weapons of mass destruction, 199
Weeks, Michael F., 97
Weighting poll respondents, 179–180
Weighting samples, 85–87, 129
Weissberg, Robert, 23–24
Welch, Robert L., 108
Welfare, 54
Whitman, Christine Todd, 128
Wiese, Cheryl J., 84
Wilder, Douglas, 97, 135, 151
Williams, Brian, 46–47
Wilson, Pete, 128
Winkler, Karen J., 133
Wirthlin, Richard, 143
Witt, G. Evans, 15, 121–122
Wording, and trend analysis, 172–174
Wording of questions. See Question wording
Wright, Debra L., 92
Wright, James D., 181

Yammarino, Francis J., 91
Yankelovich, Skelly, and White, 42, 44
Yankelovich Partners Inc., 3

Zaller, John, 41–42
Zinsmeister, Karl, 183–184
Zogby International, 128, 183–185